Mad Technology

Mad Technology

How East Asian Companies are Defending Their Technological Advantages

Ingyu Oh

Hun-Joon Park

Shigemi Yoneyama

Hyuk-Rae Kim

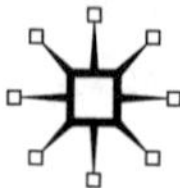

First published 2005 by
PALGRAVE MACMILLAN
Houndmills, Basingstoke, Hampshire RG21 6XS and
175 Fifth Avenue, New York, N.Y. 10010
Companies and representatives throughout the world

PALGRAVE MACMILLAN is the global academic imprint of the Palgrave Macmillan division of St. Martin's Press, LLC and of Palgrave Macmillan Ltd. Macmillan® is a registered trademark in the United States, United Kingdom and other countries. Palgrave is a registered trademark in the European Union and other countries.

ISBN 1–4039–4507–1 hardback

This book is printed on paper suitable for recycling and made from fully managed and sustained forest sources.

A catalogue record for this book is available from the British Library.

Library of Congress Cataloging-in-Publication Data
Mad technology : how East Asian companies are defending their technological advantages / Ingyu Oh . . . [et al.].
p. cm.
Includes bibliographical references and index.
ISBN 1–4039–4507–1
1. Technological innovations—Economic aspects—East Asia.
2. Technological innovations—East Asia—Management. 3. Information technology—Moral and ethical aspects—East Asia. 4. Business intelligence—Moral and ethical aspects—East Asia. I. Oh, Ingyu.

HC460.5.Z9T447 2004
338′.064′095—dc22

2004053523

10 9 8 7 6 5 4 3 2 1
14 13 12 11 10 09 08 07 06 05

Printed and bound in Great Britain by
Antony Rowe Ltd, Chippenham and Eastbourne

Contents

List of Figures

List of Tables

Preface

It has been more than twenty years since the publication of Charles Perrow's *Normal Accidents*. Nuclear, nano-, and bio-technologies, which Perrow considered to be responsible for major cataclysms of our industrial and post-industrial world, which occurred so often that he even called them 'normal,' continue to be sources of uncertainty in the twenty-first century. For example, semiconductor plants consume megatons of water everyday, although the toxic level of its hydraulic wastes is not as high as traditional heavy industries such as steel. More important than environmental hazards, however, is the potential of these technologies to cause an economic meltdown in the form of a market crash, like that of the so-called "dot.com" or IT venture stocks. Like a computer virus that travels fast throughout the global internet networks, international hedge funds and "angel" investments infiltrate into various stock markets and manipulate the prices of dot.com and other IT or biotech stocks.

We began this study as dot.com stocks suddenly surged overnight in the Nasdaq, Kosdaq, Jasdaq, and GTSM (Taiwanese market) in the late 1990s. Just as we feared, the price also plummeted overnight, resulting in many corporate bankruptcies and individual traders being financially ruined, and some even committing suicide. The obvious gambling nature of the market, however, has rarely been a subject of close scrutiny by scholars and professionals in the field. In fact, when we presented some of the chapters of this book to our colleagues in the field, most of them could not understand why gambling in the dot.com stock markets was undesirable in the first place, not to mention their feelings about the addition of the word "mad" that we placed in front of "technology." On top of the economic instability that mad technologies can create, current computer and internet-based political, economic, and social activities have reached a level where they are capable of triggering major industrial and military disasters, as witnessed by the Y2K warning, CIH virus, WORM virus, and US Defense Department hacking incidents.

Unregulated technological knowledge has been of constant concern throughout human history. As Shattuck (1996) carefully documented, human societies have always wanted to regulate knowledge, especially when it was potentially disruptive to the dominant social order. Examples include fire making, love making, pornography, bomb making, the Human Genome Project, and even addictive marketing strategies. Dawson (2003), for instance, was appalled at how modern American marketing strategies had been systematically kept secret from the public, who mass consume the products these American mammoth corporations produce and deliver. To most human societies, whether religious control of forbidden knowledge had to be annulled by Enlightenment and Darwinism was not important, since the fear of subsuming all of human civilization, which was based on knowledge, to knowledge itself appeared more imminent than the perfection of science.

In our modern industrial and postindustrial societies it is corporations, rather than religious authorities, who want to regulate knowledge, mad technology, and unregulated industrial and postindustrial scientific and technological knowledge, which poses a threat to these corporations and the governments that provide R&D funds for basic, developmental, and applied research projects for national and corporate purposes. Since our capitalist societies are so hung up on this system of developing new technologies, which many call the national innovation system (NIS), external shocks to the NIS of liberating mad technology and introducing it to local and regional economies turned out to be too scary or risky to be attempted. It was for this particular reason that we devoted the other half of this book to an analysis of how firms and governments defend their normal technology from the invasion of mad technology and its newly established industries.

We fundamentally agree with Darwin in the sense that knowledge has to be contested, and new knowledge must be revealed to the public for the betterment of our human condition. However, we also concur with Kant, who contended that "a public can only slowly arrive at enlightenment," especially when we have no clue as to whether new knowledge is after all beneficial or harmful to human beings. The progress of the internet age must be welcomed as long as more people can participate in exchanging ideas and information. However, when unregulated corporate or venture interests dominate the internet, problems arise.

Throughout the book, we tried to present cases of successful mitigation of mad technologies in East Asia, especially in Japan, Korea, and Taiwan. Although we cannot safely argue that these countries will succeed in reshaping their economies after neutralizing and regulating mad technologies, this book presents some evidence regarding why they have the potential of doing so. After all, people must decide their own economic fate. We decided to write this book, because we had some hope for the peoples of these three countries to regulate and reform their economic institutions.

This book is the result of six years of toil by the four authors. But it would not have been possible without help provided by numerous colleagues, research assistants, research funding, and those who voluntarily provided information from the field. Mr Soon Bong Yoon, Mr Eonho Lee, Mr Yamada Hajime, Dr Aoyama Shûji, Mr Koji Tawara, Professor Yun Han Chu, Professor Jung Ku-Hyun, Dr Hu Cheng Da, Dr Chang Shan Chong, Mr Liu Ying-hui and the anonymous interviewees at the Ministry of International Trade and Industry (Japan), the ITRI, the ERSO, the National Council of Science and Technology (Taiwan), and LG R&D Institute (Korea) provided us with crucial information. Research assistants Seungyi Han, Hyoyoung Yoon, Tyler McPeek, Princess de Leon, Ji Yeun Nam, Chang Wook Lee, Richard Chou, Vaughan Allison, Sung-Hoon Park, and Sang Jun Kim made this manuscript possible through their proof-reading, editing, indexing, and referencing. Our thanks are due also to the Royal Society of New Zealand (00-BRAP-26-OHI), the Korea Research Foundation (KRF-2001-042-C00134), the Japan Society for the Promotion of Science for Grant-in-Aid for Scientific Research (15330082 and 11730068), the Seki Memorial Foundation for Promoting Science and Technology for Research and Publication Grant, the University of Waikato, Yonsei University, and Ritsumeikan Asia Pacific University for their generous research support. Dr Walter Kim at Keosan, Co., Ltd. also provided us with a generous fund that we used to polish the final manuscript. Finally, we thank our editor Jacky Kippenberger at Palgrave Macmillan for her decision to publish our manuscript and her wonderful editing efforts. Nick Brock did a fine job of looking after the copy-editing and proofing stages. We devote this book to the individuals and peoples everywhere who have suffered as a result of the proliferation of mad technologies, and to those researchers and government and corporate leaders who are devoted to the responsible regulation and containment of mad technology.

Ingyu Oh, Jumonjibaru and Auckland
Hun-Joon Park, Seoul
Shigemi Yoneyama, Tokyo and Paris
Hyuk-Rae Kim, Seoul

1
Introduction

> The most urgent problems of the technology of today are no longer the satisfactions of primary needs, but the reparation of the damages wrought by the technology of yesterday. (Dennis Gabor (1900–1979), the 1971 Nobel physics prize winner)

In secluded seminar rooms with dim lights and curtained windows at both NTT Docomo in Tokyo and the LG Research and Development (R&D) Institute in Seoul, we met with chief technology officers from each company to learn about how the large Korean and Japanese corporations were coping with globalization and changes in the national innovation system (NIS) after the rise of what we have termed "mad" technology. Our meetings took place in late fall 1999, when "dot.com" companies dominated the headlines in most economic newspapers and magazines. As we will show in Chapter 2, when we discuss what mad technology is and what is "mad" about mad technology, recent changes in the NIS and the global technology markets have been so revolutionary and alarming to us at the time that we felt it was imperative to meet and talk with these people in their corporate headquarters.

In our opinion, the overall conclusion that these corporate experts of technology offered regarding our concern over whether mad technology would destroy the traditional NIS and ultimately their business stronghold (i.e., high-technology industries) was shocking. They contended that both NTT Docomo and LG Electronics had no need to worry about globalization or mad technologies, because they had already achieved strong technological foundations, advanced knowledge, and monetary resources with which they could either fight against or tranquilize the effects of mad technologies through a policy of mergers and acquisitions (M&A). LG Electronics went further by stating that dot.com businesses were bound to fail, because the chaebols' business plans were so perfect that no new business using mad technologies would be able to find a niche market that could yield huge profits in Korea.

This level of apparent complacency, shared by both the chaebols and the large Japanese corporations, surprised us, because at this time the information technology (IT) sector and the so-called dot.com companies were generating huge amounts of money through the initial public offering (IPO) system on the Nasdaq, Jasdaq, and Kosdaq exchanges (see Table 1.1). In colleges, offices, dark internet cafés, and average households, students, office workers, the unemployed and retired, and housewives were busy discussing IPOs and dot.com stocks. The volume of internet-based stock trading was also astonishing, as millions of stocks were being traded daily on these global dot.com stock markets (Cassidy, 2002; Chang, 2003) (see Figures 1.1, 1.2).

Facing two contradictory phenomena – the wave of investment in dot.com stocks and IPOs on the one hand and the unusual optimism

Table 1.1 Comparison of IPO frequencies

Year	*Number of IPOs*		
	NASDAQ	*KOSDAQ*	*JASDAQ*
1992	442	—	—
1993	520	—	—
1994	444	—	—
1995	476	—	—
1996	680	—	—
1997	494	109	—
1998	273	3	—
1999	485	69	73
2000	397	182	97
2001	63	166	98
2002	35 (to Sept.)	122	70
2003	—	70	63

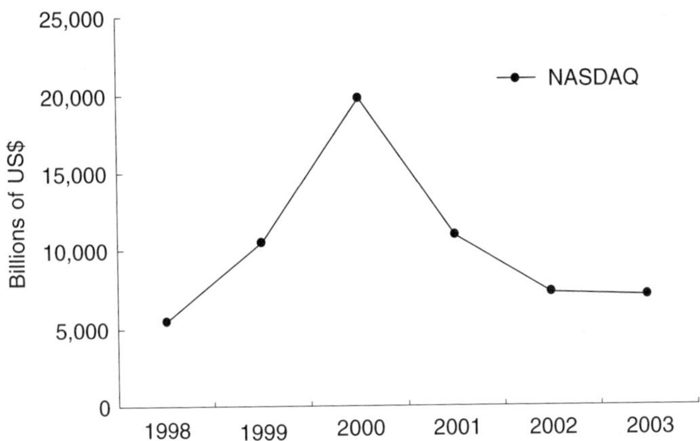

Figure 1.1 Trading total

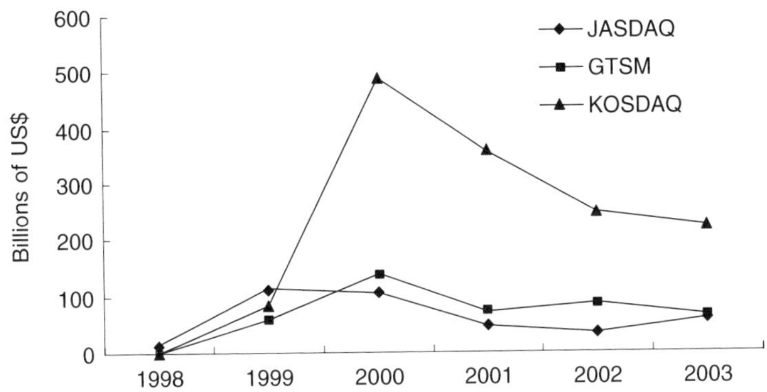

Figure 1.2 Trading total
Sources: JASDAQ (2004); KOSDAQ (2004); NASDAQ (2004)

among chaebol and keiretsu managers about their future business fortunes on the other – we decided to pursue a new study to examine how mad technology came into being in the first place, how it progressed to its current state of madness, and how the NIS and big corporations defended their markets in East Asia, especially Japan, Korea, and Taiwan, where dot.com venture firms were most heavily concentrated in Asia.

Briefly stated, in the course of our research two different sets of understanding regarding this mad phenomenon surrounding dot.com companies and their internet-based technologies emerged. One, which was often associated with neoclassical economics and was favored by most day traders, was that a new form of economy centred around an infrastructure of fiber optic cables, the internet, digital routers, and computers was replacing traditional industries with old machines that produce big, heavy, chemical commodities (Bell, 1999; Castells, 1991; Friedman and Friedman, 2002; Norberg et al., 2003). The other view, often linked to various global NGO/NPO groups that were opposed to the idea of globalization, was that the new internet technology, although undoubtedly useful to many, was destroying local and regional industrial structures; delimiting the supply of intellectual properties through global patent rights or TRIPS; and further subjugating local and regional economies to the global markets dominated by North America, the EU, and Japan (Bello, 1990, 1994; Cohen, 1998; Kaneko, 1999; Mander and Goldsmith, 1996).

The first of these views, supported by neoliberalism, failed to address the dynamics of how traditional industrial establishments tried to defend themselves, and how some succeeded in strengthening their presence in the market despite the presence of thriving dot.com venture firms. For instance, the neoliberal view fails to explain why traditional companies like IBM could maintain the largest number of IT patents in the United States, even though Microsoft and its allied personal computer (PC) cloning companies have come close to destroying IBM through the exploitation of the globally patented Windows operating system and cloned PCs. In a similar vein, the second view, albeit resembling that adopted by LG and Docomo managers, could not capture the dynamics of the invention, spread, and incorporation of mad technologies, not to mention the defense mechanism devised and employed by the traditional business corporations. Although some indigenous and local big firms can survive globalization, the spread of mad technology is certainly detrimental to many small and medium-sized local and indigenous industries, as our case studies from Japan, Korea, and Taiwan will illustrate. Furthermore, neither could the surviving large firms immunize themselves from the effects of the stock market crash engineered by the dot.com companies.

While reading and teaching some of the precursors' books on globalization and technological changes, we noticed that internet-based technologies work in the same manner as the "mad" money identified by Susan Strange (1998) (see also Chapter 2). However, whereas Strange noticed that internet-based technologies are the foundational technology for mad money, we find that these technologies have lives of their own, being first invented, but then immediately equipping themselves with the power of semi-automatic dissemination and reproduction in a mad fashion, through the global fiber optic networks of the internet and satellites. Although mad technologies may not enjoy the kind of omnipotent power that Strange explores in her book, in terms of its dissemination and reproduction, it certainly assists the rise of mad money and creates markets for mad money through internet-based dissemination and reproduction. They also provide opportunities for making overnight fortunes (or mad money) through IPOs and day trading.

Since we were sure that mad technologies existed and were the cause of global dot.com madness, we wanted to uncover the difference between mad technologies and normal technologies. This, then, is the first research question addressed by this book. By the term "mad technology" we refer to the phenomenon of technologies being invented, disseminated, reproduced, and commercialized in the global market with little or no control or regulation on the part of domestic or international supervisory authorities.

Our definition of mad technology is followed by a consideration of how the national innovation system has changed in the years that have followed its rise. This was an important issue in Korea, Japan, and Taiwan, where the impact of mad technologies on normal technologies was so evident and far-reaching that the entire economy in that region seemed to be completely transformed in a matter of three or four years, a process driven by the dictates of the new global economic regime, guided and protected by the World Trade Organization (WTO), the International Monetary Fund (IMF), and the World Bank. We find that during this period the NIS in this region became increasingly similar to one another, in order to cope with or neutralize the effects of mad technologies. In so doing, the entire economy in that region unnecessarily faced volatile environmental uncertainties and suffered from a long list of new types of economic irregularities and corruption emanating from the dot.com IPO scandals and deceptive practices of stock trading.

Our final research question concerns how regional NIS structures and corporations deal with the threat from mad technologies. Although managers in both LG and Docomo showed considerable pride in establishing IT industries that displayed no fear of mad technologies, we wanted to know why. By using case studies of both success and failure, we noticed that information sharing, the reorganization of corporate knowledge depositories, and managing corporate culture and memories were crucial in defending and strengthening old corporate market shares in the face of the illusionary new economy.

In our attempts to answer these three central questions, we utilized small and manageable subquestions in each chapter. These include the evolution of the NIS in Japan, Korea, and Taiwan, models of the flow and stock of Korean NIS decision making, analyses of the innovation strategies of the Korean chaebols, the evolution of international innovation networks in the Taiwanese semiconductor industry, the corporate perceptions of commercialization in Japan, the issue of transactional governance structures in Korea, and the reform of the economic governance structure in East Asia.

Thesis

Our operating theses share one underlying assumption – that mad technology is a virus in our global economic system and needs either to be curtailed or to be incorporated into normal technology before it can create disastrous effects similar to the atomic bombs dropped in Hiroshima and Nagasaki. Therefore, we adopted the following working ideas for this book:

Q1: What is mad technology? How does it distinguish itself from normal technology?

T1: Mad technology is a release of "forbidden" or regulated knowledge to the global internet community for free dissemination and utilization. Mad technology is an uncontrolled nuclear fusion, whereas normal technology is a cold fusion.

Q2: What are the main factors in the rise of mad technologies?

T2: The privatization and commercialization of military technologies of satellites, the internet, electronic messaging, and computers provided a breeding ground for mad technology. However, it was the institutionalization of the global economy through the World Trade Organization (WTO), the Trade Related Aspects of Intellectual Property Rights (TRIPS), and regional and local compliance with the requirements of WTO membership that enabled mad technologies to penetrate the global market. However, the free flow of mad money in the global market using electronic means must precede mad technologies for the latter to flourish.

Q3: How are governments and firms in East Asia (Japan, Korea, and Taiwan) defending their traditional national innovation system (NIS) networks or technology markets from mad technology?

T3: NIS in these three countries are now getting similar to each other by adopting structures that are universally appropriate for new global environmental constraints. Incorporation of private R&D infrastructures (see Chapter 3) into the NIS and the governmental targeting of private IT industries (see Chapter 4) enhance the flexibility of the government-run research and development (R&D) programs, while they also neutralize the harmful potential of mad technologies. Corporations in these countries are also using various strategies for incorporating and neutralizing mad technologies through the enculturation of mad technology, knowledge management and information sharing within and between corporations, and strengthening transactional governance structures (see Chapters 5, 6, 7, and 8).

Q4: What can be done to stop mad technologies altogether or to enhance the flexibility of the NIS and traditional high tech firms, so that they can fend off the influence of mad technologies from the market?

T4: Japan's strength in curtailing the disastrous effect of mad technology lies in continuous commitment to funding R&D projects for foundational technologies. Korea and Taiwan can certainly learn this principle, although short-term profits from nurturing add-on and application technologies may shrink (see Chapter 4). It is also argued in this book that economic governance in these countries has to be reformed in order to give transparency to the process of making decisions in prioritizing economic policies, including NIS management.

Each question and thesis will be explained and justified in later chapters. At this point, we will address only possible ambiguities. The definitional issue of mad technology should not invite any confusion, with the exception of the functional adjective "mad." We borrowed the term from the work of Susan Strange (1998), as we understood that the basic logic of movement within the mad money regime can be applied to the types of technology that has appeared in the global market after the Cold War.

We have employed an analogy with nuclear fusion, because the effect of hot (or uncontrolled) fusion, as has been witnessed in some of the most devastating nuclear explosions or meltdowns, was deemed to be similar to that observed in the spread of mad technologies. In the end, unregulated dissemination of nuclear bombs – or of the knowledge of how to create nuclear bombs – without any national or international supervision offers a clear case of mad technology. What is more interesting to us, however, is a linkage between mad technology (i.e., unregulated use of scientific knowledge that can produce devastating effects on human beings) and the image of "forbidden" knowledge. We borrowed this qualifier from Shattuck (1996), who envisaged that the bombing of Hiroshima and Nagasaki was also a mad act of using "forbidden" knowledge. By expanding the notion of madness through the use of the imagery of forbidden knowledge, we wanted to emphasize the fact that mad technologies have existed throughout human history (see Chapter 2). The only demarcation for the current upsurge in mad technology is the ever-increasing potential for global annihilation.

Many factors have contributed to the rise of mad technology. In this book, we do not intend to construct a causal model that will explain the rise of mad technology. Nor do we plan to make functional arguments that emphasize the evolution of the global system from the birth of human civilization – a gargantuan mental exercise undertaken by world system theorists (see Arrighi, 1994, 1999; Braudel, 1992, 1993; Wallerstein, 1979). Instead, we simply want to underline the fact that the rise of mad technology was an outcome of intentional conditions manufactured by the new post-Cold War global regime that is trying to universalize economic conditions across the world. Of course, there were accidental factors intervening in this process, such as the coincidental invention of the internet, satellite systems, and computers, and the similarly accidental combination of these separate sets of knowledge. However, the institutionalization, dissemination, and commercialization of these accidental discoveries were outcomes of intentional forces, such as the policies of the WTO.

The disastrous consequences of "mad" technology have been documented throughout human history. Notably infamous cases have to do with nuclear meltdowns and other environmental disasters (Chernousenko, 1991; Fortun, 2001; Foster, 1999, 2000; Marples, 1988; Shrivastava, 1987). The current wave of mad technology, however, has produced economic disasters in the form of stock market crashes, sudden asset deflation, and similarly strenuous bubble inflations, along with computer malfunctions, hacking, and biochemical disasters (Perrow, 1984; Thomas, 2003; Thomas and Loader, 2000). Cases such as these provide cogent reasons for making a case for devising and implementing strategies for defending regulated domestic, regional, and global technological innovations.

Although regulated innovations initiated by the NIS and corporate R&D programs did indeed produce the Chernobyl and Bhopal catastrophes, these were unintended consequences that led to calls for structural scrutiny and the introduction of further regulation. However, unregulated technological innovation, the dissemination of knowledge, and commercialization only increase the dangers our global village is already facing, such as nuclear annihilation and environmental destruction. On top of this moral situation, which creates the need for the regulation of mad technologies, we analyze how governments and corporations in Korea, Japan, and Taiwan have launched different strategic programs to fight or incorporate mad technologies into a regulated scientific body of knowledge. The overall goal of these programs is to reduce the gap between the intended and unintended consequences of mad technologies. Indeed, the internet and e-mail are generally considered to be beneficial for human social activities, although their unintended consequences, for instance, might include the destruction of a nuclear power plant by criminal or terrorist hacking.

The final question of what can be done requires us to adopt a philosophical stance. We need to devise and offer alternatives to mad technologies. This is a strategic response to mad technology, reinforcing the benefit of the NIS and publicly assisted private R&D programs. However, what we really intend to do at this point is to improve the extant institutions of innovation in order to promote the common good of our global society. Economic governance is the term we use to introduce debates about the new economic challenges that East Asia is facing in the twenty-first century. The creation of an alternative economic governance structure in this region is a prerequisite for a democratic conversion from one economic system to another. A first step to a new economic governance structure for East Asia, we believe, lies in a rigorous analysis of its past institutions, while we carefully trace new changes concomitantly.

Cases and methods

Japan, Korea, and Taiwan occupy a unique position in the economic and technological history of the world. They are the only non-European or non-North American states that currently participate in global high-tech trade. They export value-added products across the world, while importing raw materials from the Middle East, Africa, Asia, and America. In the course of the last five decades, the so-called export-driven economic development strategy gave these countries the highest rates of economic growth, allowing them to catch up with the West in a short period of time in the areas of finance and technological knowledge (Haggard, 1989, 1990; Koo, 1993; Lie, 1998). These countries also received a heavy dose of mad technology during the 1990s, as Table 1.1 and Figures 1.1 and 1.2 indicate. More importantly, it was these three countries, too, that suffered from the global financial meltdown that, according to some economists, started in the UK in the late 1970s and ended in Asia in the late 1990s.

In short, these cases provide similarities that allowed us to compare their economic outcomes in the face of mad technology, although we also clarified differences between them. In addition to comparison and contrast, we utilized corporate-specific case studies, of Taiwan Semiconductor Corporation and Samsung Electronics, to highlight how a corporate-level actor can mobilize its resources to fight and/or neutralize the effects of mad technology. We chose these two companies because they had achieved considerable success in defending their R&D bases in the face of mad technologies. In company-specific case studies, we designed in-depth interviews and carried out participation observations. In addition, a survey method involving 59 Japanese companies was used to try and uncover factors leading to success in knowledge management and the commercial development of new technology. Finally, we used simulation modeling methods to explain the decision-making structure within the Korean NIS.

Together, the combination of case-driven macro comparisons, in-depth interviews, survey studies, and simulation modeling contribute to the achievement of reliable and consistent data and findings.

Plan of the book

Chapter 2 deals with definitional and theoretical issues surrounding mad technology. The factors involved in the rise of mad technology after the Cold War are presented alongside the theoretical discussion. This is followed by a short analysis of the strategies for defending traditional NIS and corporate R&D institutions. Next, Chapter 3 outlines the similarities and differences between traditional NIS institutions in Korea, Japan, and Taiwan. The chapter finds that NIS in these countries underwent significant changes in recent years with the intention either to neutralize or to incorporate mad technology into a normal body of scientific knowledge.

Two theoretical chapters are then followed by four other chapters that address the Korean, Taiwanese, and Japanese structures of innovation. The two chapters on Korea deal with a simulation modeling of the Korean NIS funding decision mechanisms, drawing the conclusion that the Korean NIS needs to spend more money on foundational R&D projects in order to neutralize mad technologies, while encouraging private sector investment in developing corporate knowledge management programs that emphasize the benefits of a creative and innovative corporate culture. The chapter on Taiwan analyzes how a small semiconductor company, in alliance with NIS institutions, created domestic and international networks of technological innovation on the one hand to fight mad technology and on the other to enhance NIS programs that can accommodate the new knowledge economy. The chapter on Japan addresses the issue of why the country is lagging behind in terms of knowledge application. We find that its huge depository of knowledge created a bottleneck problem because it did not know how to manage existing repertoires of patented technologies. Statistical analyses find that a successful organizational innovation for information sharing and knowledge management can neutralize mad technology and its potential domination in Japanese technology markets.

Chapters 8 and 9 consider theoretical propositions related to why corporate and economic governance are important in innovation and how governance structures in East Asia can be improved. The success of Korean innovation at Samsung Electronics led us to a theoretical proposition that corporate "transactional" governance was key to cultivating innovative corporate culture, although it also blocked attempts to reform corporate governance. Chapter 9 presents a vision of corporations and governments in East Asia working together to create a more transparent economic governance regime that can neutralize and incorporate mad technologies into a regulated body of scientific knowledge. The final chapter provides a synopsis of the theoretical and empirical findings in the book.

2
Globalization and "Mad" Technology

Globalization and mad technologies have coexisted throughout human history (Braudel, 1992, 1993; Gerschenkron, 2000; Heilbroner, 1989; Mumford, 1963, 1964; Schumpeter, 1947, 1961; Shattuck, 1996; Wallerstein, 1979). The discovery of crude oil and the invention of gunpowder by the Mongolian army enabled them to conquer most of the Eurasian continent in the course of the twelfth century (Curtin and Roosevelt, 2003). In a similar vein, the invention of pistols and other firearms by Western European armies enabled them to successfully undertake long distance wars in Asia, America, and Africa (Ellis and Ezell, 1986; Fuller, 1998; Smith, 2003). In both cases, states and their armies profited from technological innovations. With regard to these innovations in weaponry, we label them "mad," because it was simply impossible for any civilians to stop these deadly military machines from killing human beings and engaging in long distance wars. What was worse, over a long period of time, states and their armies could no longer control the unchecked proliferation of firearms throughout the world.

Historically, however, other commercially successful technological innovations – such as casinos, pachinko parlors, pornographic movies and videos, alcohol and other patented drugs, prostitution and similar entertainment organizations, and televisions – have yielded profits for both state and private organizations (Dawson, 2003; Gambetta, 1988, 1993; Lie, 1997; Oh and Varcin, 2002; Strange, 1998). In addition, these were spread widely throughout the world, as if state or global regulations on these mad technologies had not existed. Even in the presence of strong domestic controls on these products, black markets sprang up in all major cities, ruled by private mafia groups who, in many cases, had connections to state bureaucrats. Nevertheless, no one termed these entertainment establishments "mad" technologies, because, as we conjecture, these technological innovations found it very difficult to cross international boundaries because of strong state regulations on the one hand and the presence of organized mobs in every country on the other.

We are now living in an era characterized by new types of technological innovations that defy both (inter)national regulations and organized mobs. It is this type of new technology that we term "mad" in this book. It has witnessed the invention of the WTO, free-market or any other market essential ideologies, and three technological essentials that Susan Strange (1997, 1998) sees to have been pivotal in bringing about mad money – computers, chips, and satellites. For mad technologies, however, we want to add that computers, chips, and satellites were but a few fundamental mad technologies that constitute the whole of what we now call information technology (IT) and other risky venture industries.

The purpose of this chapter is to clarify what we mean by "mad" technologies, to explain why they appeared at this time of globalization, and to consider how states and firms are defending their traditional technology bases from mad technologies in order to prevent another technological and financial meltdown such as one that which occurred throughout Asia in 1997. In other words, as we clarified in our research question in the previous chapter, we strongly believe that mad technology, along with mad money in casino capitalism, has a clear correlation with global financial instabilities and drastic financial meltdowns, including those that occurred in the United Kingdom in the 1970s, the United States in the 1980s, and in East Asia (including Japan) in the 1990s.

"Mad" technology

To reiterate, mad technologies emerged only when the three essentials of electronic globalization occurred simultaneously – that is, computers, chips, and satellites. This means that electronic globalization was possible only after the invention of digitized money, as early as the 1960s following the invention of plastic money or credit cards.

In 1968, the Chief Executive of Visa Card, Dee Hock, proclaimed that "money had become nothing but guaranteed alphanumeric data recorded in valueless paper and metal. It would eventually become guaranteed data in the form of arranged electrons and photons which would move around the world at the speed of light" (quoted in Strange, 1998).

The invention of mad (or digitized) money that can travel around the world instantly allowed the private sector to enter into business contracts with no intervention by either the state or organized mobs (Castells, 1991, 1996; Cohen, 1998; Kobrin, 1997; Kogut, 2003). For instance, in the past, a Filipina working illegally in Tokyo had to rely on an underground banking network, run by the mafia both within her community in Japan and its counterpart in her home country, to send her savings to family members back home. Today, with the existence of electronic transactions between the two countries, she can now send money without any fear of getting caught by Japanese immigration officers or being molested by gang members who run such an underground banking network.

Similarly, in an era of digitized money, an entrepreneur in Russia, who has made millions in illegal prostitution and women trafficking, can purchase a software package from the United States which will run his new computer network designed to sell Russian pornography throughout the world. In return, he simply collects digitized money submitted to his network computer from across the world. This constitutes a new type of globalization without parallel in our human history, and its seeds were sown with the previous global system, one based on controlled technological innovations, mainly for military weapons and other commercial purposes.

In an age of digitized money and electronic globalization, we need to analyze the process of conversion from formerly military technologies to mad technologies. Yet, before we do that we need to give a brief definition of mad technology for conceptual purposes. For our purposes, mad technology is defined as a set of knowledge that defies national boundaries, trade regulations, tariffs, and traditional systems of intellectual property rights protection. New knowledge travels around the world either on real trade routes or through the fiber optical network of the internet, which offers virtual trade markets 24 hours a day and 365 days a year. The way in which electronic transactions are agreed upon and completed is a matter to which no nation of this world can easily apply legal scrutiny. It is not uncommon, therefore, to witness various crimes being committed on the internet, using many different types of mad technologies (Cassidy, 2002; Jewkes, 2002; Shattuck 1996; Taylor and Quayle, 2003; Wall, 2001).

New knowledge takes different contents and forms. For instance, when existing knowledge is simply digitized and can travel freely around the world, we term it "digitally coded" knowledge (DCK), for it is valuable only with digital encoders and decoders such as computers, chips, and satellites. Digitized Beatles music from an old analog album can be seen as DCK, as can all e-books and digital visual images sold in internet book stores and other shops.

When new knowledge is valued by digitizing physical space and turning it into virtual space, it is called "digital rent seeking" (DRS). In other words, DRS occupies virtual space and is rented out to DCK owners and operators. As virtual landlords, DRS can either rent out a portion of their original website or provide a whole web domain to DCK owners and operators (Kogut, 2003; Verzola, 2002). Yahoo!, for instance, is an example of the first kind, whereas domainname.com is an example of the second.

When new knowledge becomes valuable by providing infrastructures to DCK and DRS, it is termed "digitized construction firms" (DCF). This category includes the internet itself, computer and chip manufacturers, satellite launchers and maintainers, cellular phone networks, and major software developers. If DRS owners are to be seen as virtual landlords, DCF owners are the virtual pontifical authority that provides power and legitimacy to the rest of the mad technology community through churches (networks) and bibles (software). Although it is very difficult to establish DCF companies due to the existing framework of national and international regulations, once established, they promote business transactions between DCK/DRS owners and all other participating consumers in a borderless, nation-less, state-less, and global fashion.

Finally, new knowledge can take the form of virtual terrorism and crime by spreading computer viruses across global cyber-networks. Much network hacking constitutes a form of digitized crime motivated by fanaticism and a mob mentality, constructing a virtual underground community within the internet. On the other hand, new knowledge becomes valuable when it can protect the network from hackers and their destructive knowledge. We shall term the first "digitized criminal activity" (DCA) and the second "digital police department" (DPD).

Mad technology or digitized knowledge became available to end-users even before the rise of the WTO regime, although the regime did install a global system of regulation for protecting the property rights of digitized knowledge of all kinds (the Trade Related Intellectual Properties agreement). Thus, WTO is a virtual Vatican for the whole global operation of mad technologies and digitized money. This new regime destroyed the traditional R&D sector that relied on piracy, licensing, and government protection for profits (Kogut, 2003).

As Figure 2.1 shows, since 1990 the global trend of NIS spending on traditional technologies has slowed down dramatically, whereas governmental support or private investment in IT, nano-tech, and biotech industries has snowballed. Although some can interpret these figures as signs of converting traditional industrial structures to the new economy or postindustrial economy (Schumpeter 1947, 1961; Piore and Sabel, 1984; Castells, 1991, 1996; Kogut, 2003), others view

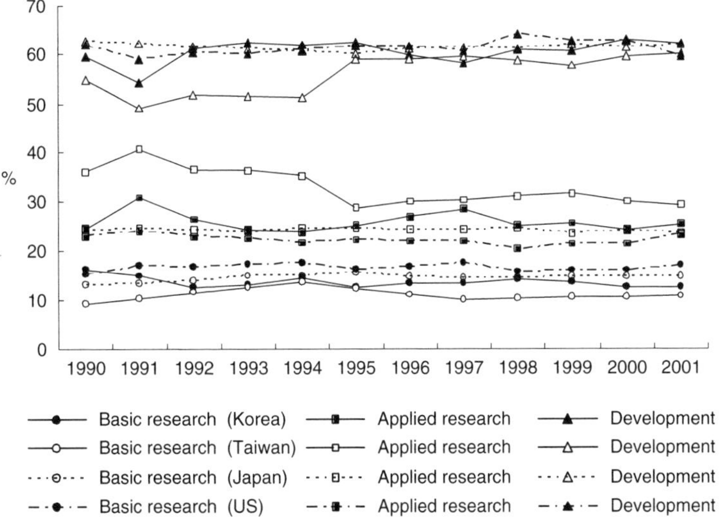

Figure 2.1 R&D spending in Korea, Taiwan, Japan* and the United States
Sources: Korea National Statistical Office (2004); Executive Yuan (2004); METI (2004); National Science Foundation (2004).
* For Japan, Natural Science only.

them as signs of the increasing dominance of the global market by mad technologies (Strange, 1997, 1998; Henwood, 2003; Pollin, 2003; Verzola, 2002). It also indicates a structural displacement of NIS-related industries and other traditional economic agents by the rise of newly formed capital and the mad technologies workforce.

Therefore, mad technology creates a state of chaos in new technology development, dissemination, and commercialization on a global scale, however short that interim period might be, until a new regulatory regime succeeds in restoring an equilibrium to the market. Under the mad technology regime, a typical R&D venture scenario has the following features: borderless cooperation and competition in technology development, knowledge dissemination, and commercialization; no national centers of R&D and technology spin-offs; borderless capital lending institutions that move around the world for new R&D investments; international movements of scientists and engineers who defy national boundaries; stock brokerage firms that promote the initial stock offerings (IPO) of new venture firms in the global stock markets; daily sales and purchases of new venture firms on a global scale; and sales and purchases of new patented technologies on a global technology market.

Although we will analyze changes in the traditional national innovation system (NIS) in Chapter 3, the new features of mad technologies listed above pose a formidable threat to the NIS currently operating in our sample East Asian countries. The following is a brief synopsis of what has happened to the NIS after the emergence of mad technologies in recent years. First, mad technologies cannot be claimed under national ownership of new technological invention, in contrast to the old technologies that were under the protection of the NIS and its nation-state. For example, when Japanese firms first invented transistor radios, the technology belonged to the Japanese NIS. However, these days a Toyota car, with all those newly invented electronic fancies and digital technologies, cannot be claimed by a single nationality, because its knowledge is drawn from several different countries. Nowadays, technological innovation occurs through exchanges of knowledge in international alliances. A clear example of this is the entire IT industry, where Silicon Valley itself is a mixture of different nationalities working toward new innovation through international alliances. Knowledge exchange is also carried out through electronic means, enhancing the flexibility of "virtual" alliance networks (Child and Faulkner, 1998). The breeding ground of mad technology is no longer provided by the protected national R&D market, but by the free-flowing nature of the international technological exchange that occurs either online or offline.

Secondly, mad technologies do not require the same level of protection under the NIS as much as old technologies used to, because their commercial values are protected by the WTO. Sharing new knowledge with others and/or selling it on the global market increases the value of mad technology. For instance, shareware software has provided more people with more diverse ways of communicating with more people in the world (through, Internet Explorer, Netscape, Hotmail, Yahoo!, and so on). These technologies do not come cost-free, yet their commercial value is created when more and more people use it for free. Free dissemination of internet software and/or technologies allows more people to participate in the internet market, which by definition increases the value of the market itself. Software piracy is thus meaningless, and even the piracy of non-shareware has lost much of its commercial value, because, to use the words of Bill Gates himself, producers can always upgrade their products, making inferior or old versions obsolete very quickly (Gates, 1999). The use of free or pirated software basically makes more people addicted to the software, so much so that it eventually forces them to buy the license under the TRIPS agreement (as can be seen, for example, in the instances of MS Windows and MS Office).

Thirdly, mad technology defies the level of infrastructure investments in each country, because it can be disseminated to any point in the world that has access to a computer server, chips, phone lines, and satellite hook-ups. Under the old NIS regime, it was clear that the level of the infrastructure development – especially the availability of monetary stocks – was very important in inducing technological development (see also Chapter 4). However, mad technology can be spread into poor countries without mature monetary or infrastructure bases – i.e., mad technology operates in a virtual space run by imperialist rent seekers and construction firms. Anyone who has access to the internet and credit cards can participate in software transactions. This means that individual internet users are not only users but also learners of new technologies themselves, who eventually become disseminators of these new technological breakthroughs, as can be seen in the emergence of India and Ireland as forerunners in the internet industries. Moreover, many underdeveloped countries – and even least developed countries, such as Vietnam – run internet servers and networks, not because these countries have enough technological know-how or infrastructure bases, but because they have easy access to internet technologies that foreign firms can provide relatively cheaply. In other words, DCF owners profit from their inventions, not through the service of providing internet infrastructures in just one poor country, but from a combination of local and global net users who pay rent to DCK and DRS owners. In this way, the cost of digital infrastructure's and DCF's construction and provision can also be lowered.

In the past, the state could target particular sectors and push selected elite students to learn new technologies (e.g., atomic bomb development, atomic energy development, etc.). Mad technology does not necessitate state intervention. Individual internet users can easily turn into learners and creators of new technological know-how, creating their own networks of internet communities (i.e., virtual networks). We do not underestimate the governments' efforts to support these online industries in India and Ireland, but the level of such support is minor when compared to the development of nuclear bombs and other NIS-funded projects.

Fourthly, mad technology destroys the conventional network of industrial and technological hierarchies among companies. This does not mean that offline technologies are no longer effective in shaping and maintaining interfirm networks. What we emphasize here is that new online technologies, an exemplar of mad technology, intend to replace old interfirm networks with new online-based networks. An upshot of the inauguration of business-to-business (B2B) networks is closely webbed business communities with the free exchange of information and frequent participation in partners' decisions, especially in matters of supply and procurement (e.g., B2B Just-In-Time Systems). Digitized buyers thus demand traditional suppliers to comply with the system and software requirements of this new online technology in order to form a new virtual corporation with revolutionary supplier–finisher networks. Global B2B networks that are being crafted by major market players require a new understanding of their purpose. The bottom line is that this is not an effort to replace old networking technologies with new ones, but to overhaul the traditional networks. That is, networking itself becomes a new market for mad technology, while those who fail to comply with new technological requirements perish from the market.

Finally, mad technology encourages the development and spread of so-called "casino capitalism." This concept is germane to an explanation of the changing financial systems in each developed country, threatening tenacious resistance from the old financial establishments. Global stock portfolios and international currency trading were attributed to the birth of mad money and casino capitalism (Strange, 1997, 1998). Bankers are no longer conservative calculators of interest rates and investment options. They are now the millions of chain-smoking casino game players worldwide, sitting in front of computer monitors that are connected to internet servers (Cohen, 1998; Strange, 1997, 1998). Their game partners come from all around the world, and they can play for 24 hours a day. Mad technology encourages – even if it does not directly lead to – casino capitalism. Investment decisions in new R&D projects or internet-based ventures are no longer subject to the Prisoner's dilemma game. Venture capital firms and individual "angel" investors are now only calculating the timing of pulling their money out from the share markets, rather than fretting about whether they should invest their money in the first place (Cassidy, 2002). We also notice that governments are increasingly opting for this angel's position in East Asian NIS decisions (see Chapter 4). The whole series of investing and divesting works like a global casino game. It occurs over a short period of time, as if successful R&D were not the investors' immediate priority. Added to this madness of R&D investment is the growing phenomenon of individual day traders, popping up everywhere in local internet cafés or office cells. We can summarize our discussion about mad technology regarding its origins and characteristics in Table 2.1.

Mad technology, thus, poses a threatening question to the NIS – can the NIS fight the mad technology regime? Before we answer this question, let us first consider the issue of conversion – why mad technology appeared at the end of the Cold War.

The rise of mad technology

As stated earlier, mad technologies have been with us throughout human history. However, what distinguishes post-Cold War mad technologies from earlier manifestations is their magnitude and the

Table 2.1 Factors and characteristics of mad technology

Factors	— End of the Cold War; a need to add new value to ex-military technologies — Deregulation of financial and R&D resources — Deregulation of international markets for technology transfers — Increased market value of new technologies — TRIPS (Trade Related Aspects of Intellectual Property Rights) — Birth of New International Technology Regime (NITR) — Destruction of traditional industries
Characteristics	— Ownership not defined by nationality — Protection by NIS not desired — Powerful dissemination capability — Tendency to replace old physical networks with virtual ones — Encouraging "casino capitalism"

speed of proliferation, as we explained above. For one thing, the rise of mad technology was possible due to the establishment of a new international technology regime (NITR). The birth of the WTO, along with its infamous TRIPS agreement, has created NITR, which protects the entire system of inventing and spreading mad technologies throughout the world. Although NITR's official purpose was to boost the economic and social conditions of innovation by providing property rights to new knowledge, as a way of providing incentives to those interested in creating such knowledge, various scholars immediately began debates regarding its real impact on developing economies (Gadbaw and Richards, 1988; Sell, 1998; Sherwood, 1990).

In our study of Japan, South Korea, and Taiwan, however, we affirm that both governments and corporations in all three countries welcomed the TRIPS, indicating the maturity of economic development in these countries. For instance, in the case of Hangul and Computer, a South Korean software company, scholars attributed its miraculous escape from bankruptcy or a merger with Microsoft to the TRIPS and the government's crack-down on software piracy (Kwon and Song, 1998).

The mechanism of this new world order under WTO leadership was to fill the vacuum left by the Soviet Union. The Cold War ideology and its organizational principles of world capitalist order were replaced by free-trade ideals that protected global profiteering with no systemic interference by government and other authorities. What could be sold in the global market was now sold until its relative utility was exhausted. In the former Soviet Union and its satellite countries, old military weaponry was sold in tandem with their impoverished scientists. The number of Eastern European scientists working for global corporations in the West and East Asia is considerable, not to mention the stockpiles of old submarines, aircraft carriers, and fighter planes which these countries imported for commercial use. In many of our interviews with Korean IT firms, we noticed that Russian scientists were favored for R&D projects developing software for internet security and message encrypting technologies for internet business transactions. In our eyes, if the Irish connection to Silicon Valley was an interesting discovery (O'Riain, 1999), the Russian connection to Korean IT industries was equally exhilarating.

Simultaneously, the United States and Japan made every effort to apply old military technologies to IT industries. The internet, e-mail, cellular phones, video conferencing, and global positioning systems (automobile navigation systems, etc.) are just a few examples of such technologies. Furthermore, the process of conversion has been much quicker since the end of the Cold War than it was during the peak of confrontation between the East and the West.

When Toshiba transferred sensitive technologies to the Soviet Union in the 1980s, US congressmen and women smashed a Toshiba TV set in front of Capitol Hill to make a point – that commercially motivated technology transfers would only lead to corporate disasters (Haruna, 1993; Irie, 2001; Judis, 2001). The WTO, NITR, and the TRIPS agreement destroyed this political barrier to technology transfers. It is not unreasonable to assume that Osama Bin Laden and his Al-Qaeda group exploited sophisticated IT technologies to fight US troops in Afghanistan – goods and services that they can easily obtain from virtual mad technology markets.

Finally, we have seen a wave of deindustrialization involving the destruction of traditional industrial sectors, including the financial sector. This began in the G-7 countries in the late 1970s and ended with the Asian financial crisis in the 1990s. The apparent trend of post-industrialization and the inauguration of the digital and IT era led to massive unemployment in traditional heavy and chemical industries, which moved their manufacturing facilities to developing countries. Although the new IT sector created jobs, slow job retraining and mad IT technologies, that ruined the hope of building a sound and sturdy industrial basis for the IT sector, removed any possibility of reducing high unemployment rates, at least in Japan and Korea. Nonetheless, it was these unemployed ex-industrial blue- and white-collar workers who actively participated in mad technology industries, setting up or working for small venture firms, working day and night in front of a small computer screen, and trading IT and other venture firm stocks electronically.

The rise of this new wave of mad technology in the world is the result of a complex web of historical factors (see Table 2.1). This process of converting old technologies to mad ones, however, may not last long, if nations and corporations use various tactics to fight back.

Strategies for defending the NIS

There has been little scholarly analysis of how governments and firms are fighting back against mad technologies, although a sizable number of scholars appreciate the problems posed by globalization and acknowledge the significance of mad technology. As this book demonstrates, both governments and firms in Japan, Korea, and Taiwan have been active in neutralizing environmental uncertainties surrounding mad technologies.

As Chapter 3 will show, in recent years the NIS in Korea, Japan, and Taiwan, despite the huge differences that existed in the past has become noticeably similar. The NIS programs and funding decisions in these countries now seem to favor mad technologies or venture firms that pursue short-term R&D for quick profits. However, this change was in fact part of a longer process of incorporating mad technologies into national institutions of innovation and technological development. We have used the success of Samsung Electronics as a case study to illustrate how the use of the incorporation process as a systemic way of neutralizing the damaging effects of mad technologies generated unexpected economic growth and profit return, not only for one company, but for the whole of the Korean economy.

We then went on to study the innovation structures at Samsung in order to support our assertion that corporations can devise strategies for fighting mad technologies by cultivating cultural and educational programs that will allow radical technological innovations without seeking assistance from mad technologies and their borderless markets (see Chapter 5). We found that the Korean NIS worked as an effective facilitator for fighting mad technologies by providing enormous funds to R&D projects that can incorporate DCK, DRS, and DCF knowledge into the NIS infrastructure.

Although the Japanese and the Taiwanese NIS proved to be far-sighted in their emphasis on foundational scientific and technological knowledge rather than myopic knowledge, in contrast to the strategy of the Korean NIS (see Chapter 4), the Korean way of fighting mad technologies in a quick fashion also helped the country to recover from the financial crisis that mad technologies had created in the late 1990s. Nevertheless, we found that the Taiwanese road to technological independence – involving the incorporation of international mad technologies into its NIS system through various international and domestic networks – also proved successful in securing specialized knowledge by defusing some of the dangerous elements of mad technologies.

In a similar vein, Japan succeeded in defending its NIS bases by focusing on foundational science and add-on technologies. The quantity and quality of patented knowledge possessed by Japanese corporations is unparalleled. This is why Japan was able to conquer global IT markets before the rise of mad technologies. However, it is apparent that Japanese NIS and corporations seem to have problems inducing innovations that use short-term application knowledge. However, the pursuit of conservative NIS policies prevented disastrous effects from investment in mad technologies, such as the dot.com stock crash experienced by Korea in 1999–2000. In our survey of Japanese corporations, we found that information sharing through both technological and institutional complementarity boosted innovation using application knowledge (see Chapter 7). Overall, we can conclude that Korea and Taiwan utilized massive spending in R&D for application knowledge, whereas Japan focused on foundational research to fight the adverse effects of mad technologies. The rest of the book presents empirical case studies to substantiate our theoretical underpinning.

3
Changes of NIS in Japan, Korea, and Taiwan

As shown in the preceding chapter, the developing states in East Asia controlled uncertainties of technological developments, including decisions over issues such as investment, commercialization, the dissemination of knowledge, and the protection of intellectual property rights. The emerging global technology market and the unregulated encroachment of mad technology in the form of the internet and other interactive media mechanisms created a new political economic force that is destroying traditional NIS in many developing and developed countries. In this chapter we will analyze what has changed in the Japanese, Korean, and Taiwanese NIS since the inauguration of the TRIPS agreement.

Significance of the issues

The dynamic nature of the global market has provided a fertile breeding ground for international cooperation in relation to technological innovation and commercialization. The internet, for instance, is one such industrial playground, where several multinational media and technology gurus got together to cooperate in bringing about a global Information Technology (IT) revolution. Not only the internet itself, which provides a virtual marketplace for global business transactions, but also all other IT-related businesses, including digital communication device manufacturing, were part of this new international cooperation.

The new international technology regime (NITR), which we refer to as the "global technology markets," under the supervision of the Trade Related Aspects of Intellectual Property Rights (TRIPS) agreement, might have reduced the level of uncertainties surrounding new technology development. The TRIPS regulations, which replaced the old regional and domestic provisions of intellectual property rights protection, might have been the institutional backbone of increased international cooperation in the creation of the global IT markets. However, it is our contention that the NITR, as a new global governance structure of innovation, is not fulfilling its proposed task, at least so far as the cases of Japan, South Korea, and Taiwan are concerned.

As we sketched out in the first two chapters, two opposing hypotheses can be obtained from the development of the NITR:

H1: NITR's main effect is to encourage technological innovation and commercialization by reducing market entrance barriers and increasing property rights protection.

H2: NITR's main effect is to encourage unregulated technological innovation and commercialization by destroying national and regional innovation facilities and subjecting all new knowledge creating activities to the laws of profit maximization and free market.

In order to analyze the effects of NITR on the East Asian technology markets, we designed a longitudinal study that compares and contrasts before/after changes of the TRIPS. In other words, we first assess the characteristics of the NIS in Japan, South Korea, and Taiwan before the birth of the NITR, and, secondly, we consider what has changed, or, more precisely, what went wrong, in these three countries following the emergence of the NITR. The first question gives us a chance to review our understanding of the NIS in that region, allowing us to take a more critical look at the NIS, that was once dubbed as "developmental" and viewed as being successful or miraculous. The apparent failure of the NIS in this region during the financial crisis of the 1990s and the early 2000s supports the contention that the traditional NIS was not always beneficial to the nation. Pace the developmentalist view that everything that Japan, Korea, and Taiwan championed in the formation of the developmental states is good for the nation and the region, we posit that the NIS in Japan was very different from that which existed in South Korea and Taiwan.

The second question relates to changes in the global economic system that are occurring, especially in the wake of the Asian financial crisis and the Japanese deflationary recession. Although the export powerhouses of Japan, South Korea and Taiwan had very different NIS in the past, these are now coming to resemble one another. This similarity, which may have been a result of their responses to the NITR, has a characteristic akin to gambling, whereas national and private R&D investment decisions are made by chain-smoking young men and women who sit in front of computer monitors 24 hours a day, in an attempt to make the right move at the right time for overnight profits. As R&D investments are now more privatized and flexible than ever before, long-term plans for innovating upon existing technologies are rapidly overtaken by short-term plans for immediate economic gain.

To substantiate the central theme of this chapter, we start by clarifying the core concepts that are employed widely throughout this chapter – namely, the NIS and the NITR. We then highlight new changes in firms' innovation strategies since the inception of the NITR.

The national innovation system in mature industries

The most widely accepted definition of the NIS is to be found in Lundvall (1992), who explains its success in terms of: (a) internal organizations of firms and interfirm alliance patterns; (b) the institutional structure of the financial sector; (c) the role of the public sector; and (d) R&D intensity and R&D organizations. Correspondingly, Nelson and Rosenberg (1993) have defended the importance of the NIS by arguing that it is a germane source of national economic power and an indicator of future economic development. Lundvall's contribution to the study of innovation lies in his expansion of the scope of innovation from a single-firm level to a nation-wide dimension that includes policy networks (i.e., the role of the public sector), external institutional networks of interfirm relations, and R&D organizations.

During pre-NITR times, national innovation programs included firm-level organizational innovations that allowed firms to enjoy the benefits of reducing uncertainties of innovation by encouraging state intervention through NIS programs (Kam, 1995; Kim, 1993, 1997; Soh, 1997). For example, the role of the policy network in innovation was to expedite the R&D process and to direct national resources toward successful R&D organizations and interfirm alliances. In fact, Japan, South Korea, and Taiwan were exemplars of successful NISs, propelled by a strong policy network and hierarchical governance of interfirm alliances. All of these observations confirm the utility of Lundvall's NIS model.

However, the domestic factors behind the NIS, albeit necessary to induce innovation, fail to explain innovations that are either preempted or accelerated by international factors. Failures of innovation, especially in developing or less developed countries, could be attributed to international factors, although the lack of a domestic NIS organization is also a significant factor. Even the mature industries of Japan, Korea, and Taiwan, all of which had overcome the international environmental irregularities through strong domestic alliances and policy networks, faced the problems of innovation governance, especially during and after the financial crisis of 1997 (Makino, 1998). The international factors of the crisis were all but visible.

The maturity of the industrial bases in each of these countries indicates that they had overcome the initial hurdle of establishing efficient organizational forms, financial institutions (either private or public), policy networks, and R&D organizations. In return, mature economies reduced uncertainties regarding R&D investments and product developments. Therefore, other factors being equal, the impact of domestic and international factors on NIS is more easily traceable in mature economies than it is in developing countries, where the complicated economic conditions often mislead researchers into highlighting only the domestic causes of failure.

To investigate how East Asian NIS systems have changed over the years, we narrow down Lundvall's NIS factors to government policies (i.e., the role of the public sector), NIS infrastructure (i.e., the institutional structure of R&D personnel and the financial sector of both domestic and international origins), and private innovation systems (i.e., the internal organizations of firms, interfirm relationships, and R&D organizations). We first discuss how Lundvall's endogenous factors were successful in the past, and how they are changing as a result of exogenous factors. These three factors all have two contradictory

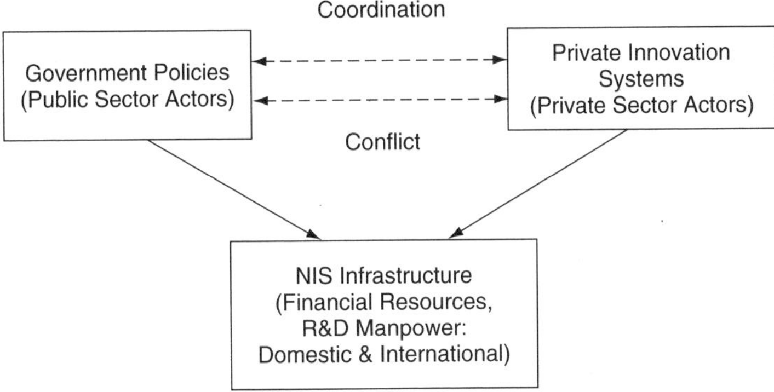

Figure 3.1 Dynamic view of organization of NIS programs

agents of innovation – the public (government policies) and the private sector of innovation (private innovation systems) – that vie continuously for domination of the NIS infrastructure (see Figure 3.1). This means adopting a more dynamic view of explaining the NIS process than that proposed by Lundvall, and emphasizing a continuous conflict between public and private sectors of innovation as a possible reason for the success or failure of a particular organization of NIS programs. In other words, whereas Lundvall's explanatory model is geared toward NIS success in a cohesive and harmonious network of innovation agents, our model seeks a possible disarray and division within the network of innovation agents, especially when international factors are not favorable to NIS programs.

Governmental policies

Policy networks either encourage or suppress the private systems of innovation. Private systems of innovation, like their public counterparts, are constantly seeking access to NIS infrastructures. As we have briefly mentioned, NIS infrastructures originate from both domestic and international sources. Suppressing the private systems of innovation can either promote or discourage international alliances between private firms, depending on the degree of governmental suppression involved.

In our sample, for instance, the Taiwanese government suppressed private systems of innovation, which consequently led to increased international cooperation and alliance between private sector firms for the advancement of technological innovation (Chang, 1999). In the case of Korean firms, international cooperation was less frequent than in the case of Taiwanese family firms, because the government encouraged private systems of innovation through technology licensing. By contrast, the Japanese policy network emphasized the full utilization of private systems of innovation, which in turn encouraged both international and domestic alliances of firms for innovation (Nonaka and Takeuchi, 1995). We want to analyze these differences first, by considering three patterns of state–business relations in this region regarding NIS strategies: the private trust of private R&D in Japan, the public trust of private R&D in Korea, and the public trust of public R&D in Taiwan.

The state–business relations in Japan occurred through the organization of what many people call the *keiretsu*. The keiretsu, a loose yet dense network of firms, was possible because members of each keiretsu group voluntarily organized their group interests under the roof of state protection – policy networks (Oh, 1999, 2004). The policy network between keiretsu and governmental actors provided shelters (*yamagoya*) in times of economic downturn and weeded out enterprise redundancy (*mugi fumi*) in times of strong economic growth (Tsuru, 1993: 97–8). The unity of state and private interests toward innovation was in large part a result of the aftermath of defeat in the Second World War, which brought about a consensus regarding the roles that public and private sectors should play in the organization of innovation (Oh, 1999). Therefore, as long as the private firms in a keiretsu group did not fight each other for the sake of self-interest, the state did not bother to intervene in the private sector (a situation we can term private trust). The trust achieved between state and private actors in a policy network completed the process leading to the private domination of the NIS infrastructure.

Government subsidies for private R&D efforts through tax breaks were thus minimal compared to the total level of private investment in new technology development. On average, the Japanese government had provided roughly 20 percent tax breaks for each dollar spent on R&D by private firms. This amount has now been reduced as a result of the recent reforms (MITI, 1999). The lack of public commitment to NIS, however, has not worked as an incentive for corporate defection from the NIS programs. As we will discuss below, the private systems of R&D were strictly defended by the public sector (i.e., establishment of a domestic governance structure for intellectual property protection). The governance structure that was under the purview of the overall policy network was based on trust.

Consequently, the system of the keiretsu, a private protection of private interests, readily secured two important resources of the NIS infrastructure – money and human resources for innovation. The system of keiretsu main banks was pivotal in providing the bulk of R&D investments, that were roughly twice the amount of the cash-based assets of each keiretsu (i..e., private trust of private R&D) (Ishizawa-Grbic, 2000; Tsuru, 1993). In addition, elite scientists and innovation managers from leading universities rushed to keiretsu firms for lifetime employment (Oh, 2004).

The picture in South Korea was exactly the opposite. The private protection of private interests had never existed in the country, as firms of all kinds sought state protection – a disintegrated policy network. In order to control disintegration within the policy network, the state protection went beyond sheltering and weeding out – it called for targeting and favoritism (Kim, 1997; Lie, 1998; Oh, 1999). Not one single pair of firms trusted each other to form an alliance or consortium in a Japanese fashion. The state had no choice but to use its powers to eliminate firms that were not favored either by political leaders' personal preferences or by macroeconomic priorities. Those selected and protected by the state formed conglomerates, which we often refer to as the *chaebol* (i.e., public trust of private interests). The chaebol was a system of extreme inter-chaebol competition through which a winner could secure public trust in the policy network – a hegemonic domination of the policy network by a winning chaebol. Therefore, competition of this nature necessitated innovation through overspending in R&D and facilities investment, as long as the state would underwrite such extravagances (Kim, 1997; Oh, 1999).

Facilities investment was particularly important in the case of the chaebol, because it could quickly upgrade the chaebol's technological capacity through the transfer of technologies from international sources, in particular from Japan and the United States (usually through new technology licensing). Frequent transfers of foreign technologies restricted most R&D activities to learning and exploiting new knowledge (Hong, 1993; Koo and Kim, 1992; Lee, 1994; Soh, 1997). In addition to underwriting loans to the chaebol groups, the state also had to subsidize and endorse chaebol's R&D and facilities investments, because of its strong alliance with the "chosen" chaebol groups (i.e., public trust of private R&D). Over the decades, the state provided, on average, more than twice the total cash-based assets for a single chaebol (Koo and Kim, 1992; Wade, 1990). This meant that the NIS infrastructure in Korea was dominated by the state, which simply allowed the chaebol to have oligopolistic access to it.

Taiwan is characterized by a different pattern of state–business relations. Medium-sized firm networks (*guanxiqiye*) and small-sized family firms have tried to distance themselves from state funding (Cheng, 1986; Fields, 1995). Instead, family or private networks (e.g., money clubs), as their financial resources, played a major role in the formation of the guanxiqiye in Taiwan. Distrust between the state (run by the recently immigrated Chinese from mainland China) and the guanxiqiye (run by the long-established Taiwanese, who had lived in Taiwan for many generations) prevented any close cooperation between the two (Cheng, 1993; Cheng and Haggard, 1987; Fields, 1995). Despite this distrust, the necessity of developing the Taiwanese economy in the face of the Chinese threat called for some sort of macroeconomic policies directed toward the development of these Taiwanese-owned firms. However, until the ascendance of Taiwanese politicians in the nationalist KMT (Kuomintang), the state had focused on spending exorbitant amounts of money on building public corporations which were owned and controlled by the mainlanders – i.e., public trust of public interests (Cheng, 1993). However, this particular policy network, that delimited the access of Taiwanese to the public NIS infrastructure, in no way blocked the attempts of the guanxiqiye and family firms to obtain international alliances for innovation.

In the absence of a public NIS infrastructure available to the private sector firms, the international business network of the guanxiqiye and family firms developed as a viable alternative for innovation and survival of these firms in the domestic and international markets. The birth of the Taiwanese semiconductor industry was based entirely on the policy network that initiated the importation of international technology through strategic alliances with foreign firms and with overseas Chinese engineers and scholars. From the late 1970s, the government began to provide finances to the guanxiqiye. Also, more importantly, it started selling technologies to these firms in the form of technology spin-offs and joint ventures (Chang, 1999). This change was in large part due to the innovative work carried out by private sector managers, who succeeded in building international alliance networks (see Chapter 6).

Over the years, changes in the policy network in Taiwan stepped up competition among family firms in obtaining public sector technology spin-offs, in addition to other NIS infrastructures. The growth of the integrated circuit (IC) chips and computer parts industries is a case in point, since this was a result of the competitive transfer of new technologies. The rapid growth of high-tech industries in Taiwan, therefore, was still contingent upon state guidance and direction, as the banking sector was either owned or controlled by the government, a fundamental institutional norm shared by the Korean government.

Government R&D policies in all three countries grew out of the interaction between state and business actors. Trust between them was a key factor in shaping the NIS in each country. The Japanese NIS policy proved very effective in developing value-added technologies, that could sometimes surpass the level achieved by their American or Western counterparts (e.g., in the areas of automobiles and electronics). The South Korean NIS policy proved very effective in concentrating resources into the hands of chaebol groups and in rapidly expanding the depository of new technology. The Taiwanese NIS policy proved successful in concentrating R&D resources in the hands of state officials and encouraging competition among family firms in their bid to gain access either to joint ventures with foreign providers of NIS infrastructures or to state-developed technologies.

NIS infrastructures

R&D infrastructures are important boosters for policy success. Resources in the public and private sectors provide critical materials and human capital for R&D institutions, in either the public or the private realm. NIS infrastructures are also said to enhance the application of new technologies to actual end-users (Carlson, 1997; Nishiguchi, 1994; North, 1990). As was discussed above, both public and private sector innovators vie for NIS infrastructures for the above reasons. Through the policy network, government policies can either promote or suppress the private domination of NIS infrastructures. We also argue that the role international NIS infrastructures play in national innovation can be significant, as long as domestic policy networks do not prohibit international innovation alliances.

Domestic or international, the central elements of the NIS infrastructure are monetary institutions, high-quality education and manpower placement systems, and widely respected laws relating to intellectual property protection. As we argued in the preceding chapter, securing these elements is subject to the usual expected outcomes of participation and defection games (i.e., the Prisoner's dilemma), calling for governmental intervention. In our sample countries, the public sector policies, through the policy network, had an enormous impact on the formation of the NIS infrastructure, although outcomes differed from one country to another.

Japanese NIS policies guaranteed the private protection of private interests. In order for this to happen, monetary resources must be in the hands of the keiretsu main banks, which was in fact the case. As we indicated earlier, these banks underwrote the bulk of R&D expenditures. This also means that the flow of monetary resources between member firms within each keiretsu group was much smoother and more flexible than inter-keiretsu lending (Gerlach, 1992; Mukai, 1997; Tsuru, 1993). The evidence of flexible intra-keiretsu lending is the traditional practice of overborrowing and overlending that enabled banks to be bullish in their long-term R&D investments. In addition, low interest rates, which did not exceed 6 percent (although real borrowing interest rates remained around 10 percent), have eased member firms' access to the bank. Low interest rates are still the norm in Japan, in stark contrast to the situation in both South Korea and Taiwan. The Japanese financial infrastructure for R&D efforts continued to be effective in ushering in innovation until the end of the Heisei boom in the early 1990s.

If the policy network in Japan led to the cooperation of public and private sectors in the over-utilization of R&D through the flexible organization of the private banking sector, then this type of trust between public and private sectors was conducive to a well-functioning system of intellectual property protection. Domestic intellectual property rights protection was relatively reliable in Japan, not because of its institutional commitment to protection, but because of the trust-based state action to fend off foreign competitors in the domestic R&D and technology markets (Itami et al., 1998). For instance, the government patent office deliberately prolonged the patent pending periods of any foreign application (often to more than 12 years) so that their Japanese competitors could learn or copy such new technologies (Johnson, 1995). Therefore, the banking sector and the patent rights protection intended to protect domestic innovation and technology transfer markets, not to encourage international alliances.

However, many critics of Japan agreed that her educational system is incompetent and enforces group uniformity rather than individual creativity (Beauchamp, 1989; Ishida, 1993; Makino, 1998). The system of selection and advancement in the Japanese corporate society favored graduates of prestigious universities on the basis of merit. Yet, merit in the Japanese context meant excellence based upon standardized national college entrance tests, that checked students' knowledge levels and reasoning capabilities, that they could obtain only through regimented rote education in cram schools. The nationalized system of evaluating educational achievements resulted in the unbalanced distribution of talents across different sectors of the economy, because corporations could easily classify job applicants in terms of test scores, the rankings of universities they attended, and GPAs. For instance, major keiretsu firms received the majority of graduates from the leading universities, while small and medium-sized firms could not. Small and medium-sized firms, instead, had to rely on a rather peculiar system of attracting retired bureaucrats to their firms for post-career high ranked positions through the system of *amakudari*, or "descending from heaven" (Calder, 1989). All in all, in contrast to the banking sector, the Japanese policy network preferred the state domination of education, a striking factor of innovation in all three countries included in our sample.

The system of public protection of private interests in South Korea required the placing of monetary resources in the hands of state bureaucrats, and it was these public sector actors who had a centralized and hierarchical control over the selection of loan recipients. Consequently, monetary resources for R&D were concentrated in a few big enterprise groups, resulting in a very static and bureaucratic banking sector that was not designed to make independent loan decisions. Historically, the entire Korean economy had suffered from "irregular" and often "corrupt" loan decisions (Cole and Park, 1984; Kang et al., 1991; Krugman, 1999; Oh, 1999; Paik, 1994). Chaebol owners often found it necessary to talk to important state decision makers before they met with bank officials to request large loan packages. Those who couldn't participate in the behind-the-curtain state–business networks or exert influence over key government decision makers were forced to leave the market. Many corporations were forced to accept high interest loans from non-bank financial institutions (along with overborrowing, the real interest rates were more than 21 percent) and from the curb market (where interest rates were between 30 and 40 percent) (Kim, 1997). On one occasion, the state nullified corporate loans after a series of cries for help from the chaebol. However, the fundamental problems of banking sector corruption remained a time bomb, even after the partial privatization of both urban and regional banks in the 1980s.

Neither domestic nor international intellectual property rights protection had been satisfactorily institutionalized in South Korea. Due to flagrant practices of illegal copying and piracy, serious international court disputes have flared up around the world, especially after South Korea started the export drive in the early 1970s (Han, 1994; Kwon and Song, 1998). Domestically, a chaebol's new invention was a target for another's illegal copying, unless the state intervened on behalf of the chaebol. Despite the underdeveloped nature of intellectual property rights protection, chaebols spent large sums of money on R&D and technology transfers at the behest of the state, because corporate "size" was given the greatest prominence the high growth period (for a discussion of the reasons why size mattered, see Oh, 1999).

The South Korean educational system resembled that of the Japanese, but differed most visibly in the area of educating the most intelligent students. Secondary schools did not have selective entrance exams – a factor which obviously lowered educational standards and the quality of university education. Thus, the South Korean elite often sought further degrees from the United States and other advanced countries, a phenomenon that did not exist in Japan. The retention and utilization of the best brains were more or less deadlocked, as US-educated PhDs found employment outside of Korea. Even when a few returned from the United States, they mostly remained on university campuses, rather than seeking positions in the chaebol or the government (Kim, 1998; Lee, 1996; Soh, 1997; Sung, 1994).

On the other hand, domestic university graduates could not function in the global corporate world without undertaking a long period of on-the-job training. Given the prestige of the state sector in the economy and society, many high-caliber domestic students sought employment within the government bureaucracies. The rest of the elite university graduates – that is, those who had neither the opportunity of overseas study nor government employment – worked for the chaebol firms. As was the case in Japan, the South Korean small and medium-sized firms had to rely on mediocre college graduates. Although the Korean version successfully led the country toward high GNP growth and sustained development until the outbreak of the 1997 Asian financial crisis, the public trust of private R&D resulted in an inferior structure of innovation similar to that found in Japan.

The system of public trust of public R&D in Taiwan required the government to control both financial and R&D resources (e.g., intensity and organization) of the country. The KMT nationalist government of the island of Taiwan maintained a firm grip on its banking system (Lin, 1991). Most urban and regional banks remained in public hands until the recent round of privatization (Cheng, 1993). In contrast to South Korea, however, these banks did not invest heavily in private firms, safeguarding it against possible loan defaults and consequently high BIS (Bank for International Settlements) rates – a nightmare that became a reality in Japan and South Korea. Private firms instead borrowed money from family members and relatives, naturally reinforcing a low ceiling on the size of those corporations (Chang, 1999).

The government's utilization of its public R&D facilities boosted innovation within public corporations (top one-hundred guanxiqiye account for only 34 percent of total GNP, compared to 90 percent+ in South Korea). Although some private firms bought innovation generated by the government, most guanxiqiye had no other option but to sign OEM (original equipment manufacturing) or ODM (original design manufacturing) contracts with Japanese corporations for limited technology transfers and licensing, that were done mostly in the form of foreign direct investment (FDI) and joint ventures. Contrary to the nationalistic standpoint of the KMT, the Taiwanese flow of monetary and R&D resources had originated from Japan until the 1980s boom in semiconductor and computer parts industries (Chiang and Mason, 1988; Chou and Shy, 1991; Chu, 1994). The benefit of the Japanese NIS infrastructures in Taiwan was to allow family firms to have limited access to innovation that the Taiwanese government had intentionally avoided offering. However, Japanese NIS infrastructures deterred technological innovation, because Japanese partner firms did not allow technology transfers that went beyond "adaptive engineering, circuit design, or software redesign" (Hatch and Yamamura, 1996: 110).

Intellectual property rights protection was non-existent in Taiwan. Public R&D and its breakthroughs, if there were any, were for large public corporations only. Most private firms remained untouchables. This began changing only when Taiwan joined the PC revolution as some innovative guanxiqiye firms (for example, Acer, UMC, TSMC) produced semiconductor chips either through incorporating R&D infrastructures from the Chinese-American establishments in Silicon Valley or through technology spin-offs from government laboratories (e.g., ITRI and ERSO). These new developments in Taiwan changed the system of public trust of public R&D to the system of "private trust of public R&D." Private trust of public R&D was most visible in the areas of memory chips and flat panel industries (ITRI, 1998; MOEA, 1999).

The Taiwanese educational system had suffered from a severe "brain drain," mostly to the United States. Many of the best university graduates went to the United States to obtain higher degrees and even when they returned, they remained on college campuses. Mediocre college graduates sought employment within family businesses, whereas the government and public corporations could recruit high caliber candidates from national universities. The public R&D infrastructure turned out to be more developed in Taiwan than was the case in South Korea, due partially to the close ties that existed with Japanese multinational corporations. However, its apparent weakness was not being able to develop cutting-edge technologies for high-tech industries. The small nature of private industries restricted the potential to develop a wide range of new technologies that required large production facilities. This tendency, however, changed dramatically after the successful establishment of the semiconductor industry, which gave incentives for US-educated engineers and scientists to return back home and join the technology spin-offs (see Chapter 6).

Depending upon the nature of the state–business relations in each country, the pattern of sharing NIS infrastructures between public and private sectors changed between countries. The cooperative policy network in Japan allowed the private domination of the NIS infrastructure, except in education. The competitive policy network in South Korea placed limits upon the private ownership of monetary resources for innovation, although innovative breakthroughs occurred due to the calculated transfer of state-owned NIS infrastructures to selected chaebol firms. In Taiwan, NIS infrastructures were off-limits to many family firms, although the state did not care to block guanxiqiyes' access to Japanese and American NIS infrastructures. Breakthroughs in the semiconductor sector of the country were made possible by the gradual opening of the NIS infrastructures to private firms, with the help of Silicon Valley-based Taiwanese engineers and scientists.

Despite innovative successes in all three countries, the Japanese policy network proved to be the most effective in bringing about long-term innovation. This, we believe, was the result of the sophisticated organization of the private innovation system, which secured an oligopolistic access to NIS infrastructures of the nation.

The private innovation system

If the Japanese private innovation system (PIS) secured trust from the state in order to dominate the NIS infrastructure in the areas of banking and R&D organizations, we need now to consider the internal mechanism of the Japanese PIS that enabled such a success to be achieved. First and foremost, the Japanese PIS had an advantage in controlling R&D monetary resources as well as retaining a steady inflow of talents in the R&D sector. In order to further encourage the PIS, the NIS also discouraged foreign licensing and patenting. We mentioned earlier that the reason why the Japanese PIS could secure the ownership and control of the banks was that it had succeeded in establishing a trust-based policy network between the public and private sectors. However, the real catalyst for the privatization of the banks and the fusion between main banks and keiretsu member firms was the failure of American efforts to reform the post-war Japanese economy to ensure the separation of banks from corporations (Johnson, 1982). After the ending of the American occupation of Japan in 1952, the government and the private sector leaders found it to be more in their interests to place firms under private bank control than to complete the separation process of banks and corporations.

Secondly, with the full support of the main banks, the keiretsu focused considerable resources on R&D in order to catch up with the level of technological innovation in the United States and Europe (Itami et al., 1998; Kakurai, 1998; Makino, 1998). The goal of catching up pushed the keiretsu firms away from buying licenses or patents from the foreign PIS, although outright copying or learning through international alliances did occur occasionally. The pool of investment capital went directly into central keiretsu R&D institutes or keiretsu members' laboratories, with the result that both types of laboratories achieved great success. Channeling R&D monetary resources to these R&D centers assumed trust and commitment to innovation from members through stock cross-holding and reciprocal contracting (Ishizawa-Grbic, 2000; Oh, 1999; Okumura, 1991; Watanabe, 1992).

Thirdly, the Japanese PIS had overcome the uncertainties of initial R&D investments for a completely new technology and the uncertainties of further R&D investment for upgrading and innovating existing technologies, because the system of private domination of the NIS infrastructure was a unified consensus among policy makers in the Japanese government, reflecting a high degree of cohesion and unity among the public sector leaders. Although a consensus among public sector leaders was reached to initiate new technology developments, this did not always guarantee further investments in technology innovation and/or upgrades. The Japanese government, thus, fueled and fanned intensive market competition between keiretsu firms in order to cause innovation and thereby lower production costs. The invitation of foreign competitors in the Japanese market was another mechanism for pressuring the keiretsu firms to show commitment to innovation (Nishiguchi, 1987, 1991, 1994).

Finally, the Japanese PIS had one unique feature that was absent in both Korea and Taiwan – nonmaterial incentives of productivity for R&D personnel. It was apparent that Japanese corporate workers were paid less than their counterparts in competing countries, although working hours in Japan were longer. The famous corporate welfare system in Japan – along with the three jewels of lifetime employment, payment by seniority, and enterprise union – could not explain high productivity despite low pay and long working hours (i.e., X-efficiency). For one thing, the fall of productivity in the 1990s occurred even when all of these corporate welfare mechanisms were still in place. Instead, we argue that nonmaterial incentives of hard work derived from institutional complementarity between managers and workers, where the latter enjoyed a substantial degree of independence and participation in managerial decision making, were responsible for the success of the Japanese PIS (Nishiguchi, 1991). During the economic upturn, Japanese-style teamwork between workers provided nonmaterial incentives for hard work, although shirking was obvious during recession.

The South Korean PIS was organized only at the behest of the state, because the R&D resources had never been in the hands of the chaebol (with the exception of a brief period in the 1950s). Decisions regarding investments in new technology development could not be made until the state approved initial R&D funding. However, even the state did not know how to create PIS with its own money, as it had to passively accept the US advice of participating in world trade as an American partner in the low end of a product cycle (Ernst, 1997, 1998; Hong, 1994; Kim, 1997). To place the chaebol in the low end of a product cycle, the state actively promoted technology transfers from the Korean-Japanese industrialists first, who agreed to build new factories in their "motherland" (Lie, 1998). The first wave of technology transfer was thus free (i.e., no licensing payments or OEM profit sharing with multinational firms). However, subsequent transfers from established Japanese corporations, did incur some costs.

Korean PIS initially seemed viable, as long as the product cycle continued, and the chaebol could upgrade technologies by purchasing licenses that Japanese firms had just abandoned. However, when the product cycle stopped, and chaebol groups had to compete with Japanese firms in order to secure cutting-edge technologies, no one seemed to be happy to invest money in new R&D PIS. To ameliorate this problem, the state had to provide funds to chaebol groups that were in competition with Japanese firms in one targeted industrial sector. Targeting by definition entailed protection and oligopoly. Electronics, automobiles, and heavy and chemical industries had fewer than four giants in each sector (Lee, 1977). In the case of semiconductors and memory chips, Samsung, alone, accounted for more than half of all exports. This kind of oligopoly later provided one of the causes for the financial crisis in the 1990s.

Nonmaterial incentives for innovation and hard work did not exist in Korea, although the government and the firms alike tried to emulate the Japanese-style labor-management relations. Notably, Korean chaebol groups did not introduce any of the three jewels of the Japanese management or corporate welfare system. Labor disputes with management ensued during every round of wage negotiations. The lack of enthusiasm and commitment to hard work among R&D workers had been noticeable in major government and private laboratories. As a result, inflexible monetary allocations to long-term and short-term projects killed most of the innovative minds, if there had been any. Mediocre minds dominated the industry with mediocre levels of R&D infrastructures. In addition, international PIS networking did not exist in a Taiwanese fashion, not being able to utilize overseas Korean brains in the United States and other countries. In sum, in most part the Korean pattern of PIS relied on knowledge piracy and technology licensing.

The Taiwanese PIS was slow to go through the "taking-off stage," even as late as the early 1980s. This was again due to its NIS policy – i.e., public trust of public R&D, and later, private trust of public R&D. Investment decisions relating new technology development and technology upgrades focused on alliance with the foreign PIS, notably the Japanese and the Silicon Valley PIS. Product cycles transformed Taiwanese family firms and guanxiqiye into suppliers of Japanese OEM products. In addition to this OEM-related technological transfer, innovation came also from Silicon Valley, where Chinese-Americans provided new technologies and R&D manpower to such public research institutes as ITRI and ERSO. The role of the ITRI and ERSO was to set up small-scale semiconductor firms based upon technology spin-offs, such as those of TSMC (the largest foundry service provider in the world) and UMC (the second largest foundry service provider in Taiwan). The technology spin-offs through international networks of PIS proved very successful, even though the role of the government was limited to R&D activities (MOEA, 1999; also, see Chapter 6).

The success of the TSMC and UMC encouraged the PIS in Taiwan, although its magnitude was in no way comparable to that of either Japan or Korea. For one thing, the government had been very reluctant to transfer R&D centers and manpower to the PIS (that is, there was not an easy transition from the public trust of public R&D to public trust of private R&D). Complaints from the large family firms became more vociferous than ever, as public R&D institutes alone could not attract Taiwanese brains back from the United States (Aoyama, 1999; Hsu and Saxenian, 2000).

Table 3.1 Differences of the traditional NIS in three countries

	Government policies	*NIS infrastructure*	*Private innovation systems*
Japan	Private protection of private interests	Private banks and R&D facilities	Private domination of NIS infrastructure
Korea	Public protection of private interests	Public banks and private R&D facilities	Conditional awards of NIS infrastructure to selected firms
Taiwan	Public protection of public interests	Public banks and R&D facilities	Conditional use of foreign NIS infrastructure by small & medium firms

Table 3.1 gives a comparison of the pre-NITR systems of national innovation in Japan, Korea, and Taiwan. During this period, all three countries had produced different NIS structures, depending on the nature of conflicts and consensus between government NIS policies and the PIS over the domination and use of the NIS infrastructures. These three patterns of NIS are now rapidly changing due to a new phenomenon we call "mad" technology.

The changing NIS in the age of mad technology

Mad technology is a bottom-up global revolution that challenges the NIS in each country. Its impetus derives from the internet community, which grew rapidly out of the West Coast in America and was subsequently exported to the rest of the world. A major impact of mad technology on the existing NIS was the destruction of the modern sense of the nation-state, its NIS policies, and the replacement of them with the NITR. In this section, we discuss changes in the NIS focusing on the NIS infrastructure and the PIS in Japan, South Korea, and Taiwan.

Mad NIS infrastructure

The South Korean government responded to mad technology by offering massive financial assistance to the rising IT venture sector, an industry that had never prospered in the past, due to the domination of the chaebol and the NIS. In 1999, the total number of IT venture firms in Korea jumped to 4,256 from 2,042 in 1998 – an increase of 108.4 percent. In the same year, the level of total venture investments increased to over $400 million, an 84.5 percent rise from the previous year (National Statistics Office, 2000). Such dramatic growth is almost unprecedented, since it is normal to expect R&D investments and technology transfers to have a long lead-time. To many observers, this kind of R&D investment decision on the part of the government seemed irrational. It seemed that the government had either failed to understand the nature of mad technology, or that it had deliberately spread mad technologies to gain access to some sort of political capital or simply to accrue irregular funds for politicians' own personal use. Nevertheless, the South Korean IT boom was the finishing stroke to a picture that had already been painted in East Asia – a new breeding ground for emerging mad technologies.

Japan's NIS infrastructure, measured by monetary investments in mad technology, is second only to that of the United States (Kumon, 1996). As we mentioned earlier, Taiwanese high-tech firms are now demanding that the government keep away from their R&D investment decisions. In the East Asian region, the total number of Taiwanese venture firms that incubate mad technologies is currently second only to South Korea. What are the effects of the NITR on NIS infrastructure in East Asia, heralded by what we call mad technologies and new strategies of R&D investments and planning?

First and foremost, all three countries now seem to be rapidly adopting a new NIS philosophy of "private trust of private R&D," a prototype Japanese-style system of innovation. However, this does not amount to a mere imitation of the Japanese NIS and its infrastructure, since the new private trust of private R&D is not intended for big companies, but, rather, for small, innovating, and IT-oriented private venture firms. The East Asian wave of private trust of private R&D represents an amalgamation of Taiwanese corporate size, Japanese corporate mind and brain, and Korean-style corporate muscle.

Secondly, the movement of monetary resources under the NITR and mad NIS infrastructures is from the private financial institutions to the private innovators. This, again, is different from the previous Japanese NIS infrastructure, in that the "private financial institutions" are no longer banks and the "private innovators" are no longer large corporations. A new global network of private R&D investments includes innovators themselves, some "angel" investors (many of them related to organized crime), venture firms in Silicon Valley, Beat Valley (Tokyo), Teheran Valley (Seoul), and Hsinchu (Taiwan), venture capital firms from across the world, and individual stockholders who trade their stocks in internet cafés or on their own company PCs.

However, these R&D investments in mad technologies are somewhat shaky and unstable, with no systematic governmental regulation or supervision. For one thing, shoddy deals and corruption still dominate the market, as shown by a recent scandal in which 66 Korean government officials were found to have received stocks from unlisted IT venture firms in return for receiving venture capital funds (*Korea Herald*, 14 August 2001). In another instance, the so-called Jin Sung Hyun and Chung Hyun Joon scandals rocked the entire country by uncovering under-the-table deals between government officials and venture businessmen to share company profits in exchange for raising IT funds (*Chosun Daily*, 29 December 2000). The biggest IT venture capital firm in Japan, the Softbank Corp., had also been under suspicion by the public for a possible corrupt deal with the government in which it purchased the bankrupt, government-owned Nippon Credit Bank (*Japan Times*, 5 September 2000).

Moral hazards, widespread in mad technology markets, invited a natural consequence of disastrous stock market performances in various nations, where IT ventures stocks produced overnight fortunes for a few, before they were dealt a harsh blow with by disastrous market downturns. For instance, the KOSDAQ indexes for the Korean "dot.com" companies were –23.6 percent in 1998 and –80.23 percent in 2000, with a 235.26 percent market soar in 1999 (*Chosun Daily*, 19 August 2000). The NASDAQ Japan, which opened up its market floor to the public in June 2000, faced a similar fate, as total volumes had fallen for five straight months at an average of 20 percent per month in 2001 (*Japan Times*, 3 August 2001).

Thirdly, manpower in the mad technology industry comes from throughout the world, another point that distinguishes it from traditional R&D firms, in which geographical location was very important. Internet networking, for instance, allows different groups of people from different regions to work together (e.g., 24-hour gambling or chatting). Mad technology innovators are none other than the overqualified corporate workers who were fired in large numbers in the processes of restructuring and downsizing – i.e., "creative destruction," a Schumpeterian dream (see Schumpeter, 1961) most big corporations made into reality in the 1980s in the U.S. and in the 1990s in East Asia. These new mad technology innovators often have ties with US-educated scientists or have educational backgrounds in the United States. The reliance on the national education system has, therefore, become meaningless in the construction of the mad NIS infrastructure.

The mad infrastructure, based on international monetary resources, global R&D institutions, and multinational manpower, has created wide-ranging venture networks between mad technology firms. For instance, the virtual network of Yahoo!, Yahoo! Japan, Yahoo! Korea, and Yahoo! Taiwan is not based solely on a technological hierarchy. Their relationship is more or less an expansion of a computer network of equal partners – in other words, a strategic alliance of virtual firms. They seem to share similar educational, ethnic, and cultural backgrounds (but not nationality). The role of the public sector as a strong contender for NIS infrastructure in tandem with its private counterpart has all but lost its strong regulatory power, simply providing legal and institutional backups for these new mad technology networks.

Mad PIS

The "mad PIS" now defies the authority and the boundaries of the nation-state. The domination of the NIS infrastructure by the mad PIS is not only encouraged but also taken for granted by the public sector. Under the traditional NIS, private corporations had various problems with PIS start-ups, because of the uncertainties surrounding investment decisions. As we explained, the different ways through which they cleared the uncertainties generated very distinctive PIS structures in Japan, Korea, and Taiwan. The mad PIS, however, offers us a very different picture.

Although communication difficulties still exist between venture capitalists and mad technology firms, the flexible supply of R&D money stock lowered market barriers significantly enough to allow many small venture firms to enter the IT market. Venture firms can make quick decisions regarding R&D investments and new technology commercialization, although they now face new hurdles of enhanced competition and short product cycles. In contrast to the previous era, motivation for further innovation derives from the strength of the market and the performance of their stocks. The role of the angel investors and venture capital firms in the innovation decisions has become much stronger than before. In addition, in contrast to the previous era, the internal authority of the chief technology officers (who often cash in on their patented knowledge) and the chief executive officer (who is appointed by venture capital firms) has become more powerful, although the ensuing conflicts between the two are becoming more visible, as IT stock performance has become unstable over the years. Human resource management involves the use of headhunters who are connected to international networks of scientists, engineers, artists, and MBA holders. The motivation of workers in IT firms originates from the flexibility of their working conditions, including incentive payments, stock options, and non-tenured job contracts that provides room for rapid upward mobility.

The downside of this new arrangement is a lack of consistency in R&D and innovation decisions. The small size of the firm, which had worked as a benefit for its flexibility, often turned out to be suboptimal in securing long-term finance. This is mostly because of the need for cross-boundary communication for outside funds that are available only on unfavorable terms (Arrow, 2000: 238). In addition, inexperienced financial managers, who do not possess information about the potential dangers of mad technology stocks, dump IT stocks in the market for overnight cash conversion or trade off conventionally well-performing stock for IT stocks. Since the financial decision at the headquarters of venture capital firms to retreat from investment commitment to R&D and innovation is taken so quickly, this has meant the almost complete absence of any stable source of financial support for long-term planning within young venture firms.

As an overall effect of mad technology, the PIS in Japan, South Korea, and Taiwan are becoming more alike than ever before. In all three countries the interactive and electronic transaction of new knowledge goods and services on a low-cost or free-of-cost basis has been increasing dramatically. Just as Goldman Sachs projected, the size of the 2002 internet-based market for Korea jumped 92 percent to $21 billion (*Chosun Daily*, 25 May 2001). Net users in Japan also increased by 74 percent to 47 million people in 2000, although her internet subscription ratio is ranked 14th in the world (*Japan Times*, 11 July 2001). According to Neilson NetRatings, Taiwan's in 2001 internet market size was ranked third in the Asia-Pacific region,

Table 3.2 Changes in the NIS

Countries	*State–business relations*	*NIS infrastructure*	*PIS*
Japan	Private trust of private R&D	Second largest investment in mad technology	Introduction of venture firms to the new NIS infrastructure
Korea	Private trust of private R&D	Largest investment in mad technology	Venture domination in the new NIS infrastructure
Taiwan	Private trust of private R&D	Third largest investment in mad technology	Venture domination in technology spin-offs and trans-Pacific NIS infrastructure

behind the two leading countries – Japan and Korea (*Taipei Times*, 18 March 2001). Table 3.2 summarizes the changes in the NIS in the three countries.

Conclusion

We have seen from this chapter that the traditional NIS in Japan, South Korea, and Taiwan did not provide the impetus for the development of mad technology. This came from abroad, as restrictions on R&D investment gradually disappeared due to the existence of "casino" capitalism and "mad" money, as we explained in the previous chapter. The NITR emerged at around the same time as "casino" capitalism and mad money were actively seeking new investment markets, and this led to the creation of a fertile environment for "mad" technologies that had all the characteristics of gambling, involving taking enormous risks in the hope of securing substantial overnight profits. This, however, does not mean that mad technology is standing on a wobbly pedestal. It has a strong grounding in technological know-how and innovative minds, all of which will certainly restructure the entire global economy in the not-too-distant future. Three clear advantages enjoyed by mad technology are the increased reciprocal networking power, geographical mobility, and the financial flexibility of innovative activities.

Japan, South Korea, and Taiwan had produced different NIS structures, depending upon their traditional NIS policies, infrastructures, and private innovation system. Notably, Japan guided Korea and Taiwan in all aspects, although its NIS outcomes had hidden problems in the areas of education, recruitment, and financial sectors. We called the Japanese NIS a "private trust of private R&D." South Korea overrode the Prisoner's dilemma surrounding new R&D decisions through a system we termed a "public trust of private R&D." Here, the potential for rapid growth and innovation was realized, although the country clearly suffered from a lack of creative minds, a poor education system, and an overly regulated and corrupt financial sector. Taiwan had never overcome the Prisoner's dilemma, as its system, which we called a "public trust of public R&D," did not depend upon private R&D efforts. Nonetheless, the country has demonstrated its ability to cultivate small firm networks that can tap into the flexible consumer goods and semiconductor markets.

Changes in the global market – in particular, the rise of casino capitalism, mad money, and mad technology – have meant that the NIS of these countries has come under siege. In this chapter, we proposed a model of NIS building, a refinement of Lundvall's, which would place an emphasis on the conflictual relationship between public and private contenders for the NIS infrastructure. Depending upon the nature of such contention between the two opposing groups of actors, the role of the state in forming the NIS differed widely from country to country. The existence of the public sector as a strong contender for the NIS infrastructure is rapidly being replaced by the PIS, which is motivated, organized, and coordinated on an individual basis. The role the private monetary resources play is alarmingly grandiose, resembling the gambling establishments in Las Vegas, Monaco, or Macao.

The future has yet to be written for mad technology and the venture firms which are its hosts. However, we can safely ascertain that the present predicament of the NIS in Japan, South Korea, and Taiwan needs to be resolved through the incorporation of the rise of these "mad" venture firms into their conservative, yet innovative, system – the NIS. Otherwise, these venture firms will have to seek their own ways of survival, which must include alliances between multinational venture firms, with no national boundaries or identities. They are nation-less, border-less, and identity-less cyberspace occupiers who only communicate with each other through domain names and aliases. It is now time that we give some serious consideration to the real potential of both online and offline developments and transactions of mad technology with institutional regulation, long-term views and stable financial arrangements.

4
National R&D Investments in Korea

This chapter offers an empirical investigation of how decisions regarding national R&D investments are made in Korea. We are interested in locating structural problems within the Korean NIS in the face of globalization and mad technologies through a system of dynamic simulation and modeling. In so doing, we intend to devise ways of ameliorating problems within the NIS investment decision-making process by providing policy implications. Korea offers an interesting testing ground for a system of dynamic modeling because of the drastic changes in the NIS sector which have occurred as a result of rapid economic development and its combative response to the threat of mad technologies.

Pavitt (1988) argued that international gaps in researcher qualifications and R&D expenditures can provide countries with catalysts for catching up with a global technology leader or even outstripping such a leading nation. Innovation is an important element of strengthening national competitiveness and productivity, and R&D serve as basic investment resources for innovation (Bozeman and Melkers, 1993). In the past decades, technological innovations have progressed drastically, making it impossible to think of national competitiveness without considering their contribution (Edler et al., 2002). In a similar vein, scholars have emphasized the importance of national innovative capacities that can improve the national technological level and knowledge stocks through a virtuous cycle (Lee et al., 2001). In general, economists have treated technological innovation as a key production factor, responsible for productivity increases, while simultaneously agreeing with the idea that R&D is a fundamental basis of technological innovations (Borrus and Stowsky, 1999).

Throughout the last decade, expenditure increases in R&D among OECD countries have been accompanied by changing trends in how R&D funds were allocated and eventually implemented. It was discerned that R&D needs and opportunities often determined project orientations, while expenditures were implemented in linkage with end-users and their R&D budgets (Webster, 1991; Shin, 2002). American NIS spending, the largest in the world, is also at a juncture, awaiting a final decision by the government regarding future changes to allocation and implementation of R&D funds (Bonvillian, 2002; Korn et al., 2002).

It is obvious that private sector corporations have played central roles in bringing about technological innovations in other countries in the past (Pavitt, 1998). However, in Korea, it was the government that has played a similar role, and it is expected to continue to play this role in the future. In 2002, R&D expenditure in Korea finally reached $11.4 billion (2.91 percent of total GDP) after three decades of efforts by the government and private corporations (MST, 2003). These figures are hardly any different from OECD averages (2.5–3 percent). In addition, OECD countries selected Korea as a model nation for reforming its NIS funding structures to reduce funding overlaps and concentrate resources in a few targeted areas. These areas constitute national strategy fields under the banner of "selection and concentration" (OECD, 1999).

However, the Korean NIS suffers from an inefficient structure that combines high R&D investments with a low level of innovation breakthrough. Why did this structure of "high cost–low efficiency" come into being in the Korean NIS? Is this a short-term effect caused by the rapid expansion of R&D investment that has exceeded the speed of a corresponding increase in R&D capabilities? Or is it a long-term, structural malady resulting from the rapid transition to innovation-first strategies, which might have triggered time-lag effects between new innovation directions and traditional R&D paths?

In this chapter, we want to analyze the system-dynamic structure of the relationships between factors that intervene in the process of making NIS investment decisions in order to map out an unobtrusive structure of dynamism that can be observed in every step of the Korean NIS decision-making procedures. We believe that this analysis will locate some of the policy leverages that can be applied to future decision-making procedures in order to increase NIS funding efficiencies. This chapter presents first a survey of the Korean R&D investment system and its investment dilemmas. This is then followed by the presentation of a simulation model that helps to locate policy leverages based on system-dynamic analyses. The analysis and interpretation of the simulation results will identify what is causing the structural inefficiency of the Korean NIS in the face of globalization and mad technologies. Finally, we will provide policy implications.

R&D uncertainties and investment dilemma

The dilemma of R&D funding size

The scale of R&D funding is important for two reasons. If R&D expenditure is too large, short-term financial stability is endangered. If the expenditure is too small, long-term competitiveness is threatened (Heidenberger et al., 2003). Although it is easy to assume that one's economic size determines R&D expenditures, it is not always certain whether the total funding size, in alliance with corporate end-users and collaborators, will bring about intended short-term financial stability and long-term competitiveness. NISTEP (1999) argues that empirical studies must follow previously ascertained theoretical contours regarding the size of R&D expenditures (e.g., Arrow's socially sub-optimal vs Dasgupta and Stiglitz's redundant investments).

Stewart (1995) points out that NIS policy makers focused on choosing preferred sciences and technologies for the NIS projects, prioritized according to national objects, whereas the existing literature on the subject emphasized both structural and thematic priorities of NIS projects. Although NIS projects are appropriately determined as to their exact funding sizes, a dilemma may occur in determining investment priorities, depending upon where policy makers wish to place the emphasis – on thematic, structural, or preferred area priorities. Heidenberger et al. (2003) finds that budget allocation rules devised to help determine investment timing and funding size did not produce positive results, as various unforeseen problems occurred during budget implementation. Keating et al. (1999) also noticed what he calls "improvement paradox," referring to the failure of efforts to improve quality control and reengineering procedures.

According to *Science and Technology Plans*, published by the Ministry of Science and Technology, the Korean NIS funds two overall types of projects – strategic technological development (STM) and R&D capacity development (RCD). Both types of projects have either one-year (short-term) or three-year (long-term) projects. STM projects are related to the so-called 6T industries (IT, BT, NT, etc.), whereas RCD deals with long-term projects that are designed to support the transition of the Korean economy to a 6T-intensive one. If a funding balance is broken between these two separate project groups, we can foresee that an R&D investment dilemma will occur, similar to the so-called *kaizen* paradox, which results in a continuous reduction in R&D efficiency.

> *Research Question 1*: It is important to prioritize NIS projects without causing R&D investment dilemma, because they will enhance the flow of R&D resources and knowledge depository. However, is it possible to find a balance point for a correct combination of STM and RCD projects?

Dilemmas caused by myopic investment decisions

Uncertainties about the benefit of the current R&D investments to the future national interests invite various conflicts in the process of prioritizing NIS investments (Bloom, 1998). Consequently, a gradual increase in R&D expenditures occurs, as decision makers opt for a larger funding package than that of the optimal level (Lundstrum, 2002). American firms are found to take a myopic posture of investing more in the projects that yield quick profits, than in those that require optimal-level investments.

As Lundstrum (2002) demonstrated, myopic investment strategies produce mediocre R&D results, since they tend to favor projects with quick turnovers and, thus, distort the entire NIS investment policies. This American tendency is a typical example of decisional dilemma caused by myopia. Members of the National Science Council, who determine the final prioritization of NIS projects, face strenuous situations because of R&D uncertainties. A sudden expansion of the national R&D budget, time limits, and the myopic decision-making strategy may result in negative side-effects by lowering the funding size for the NIS projects related to thematic priority groups (e.g., new researcher support, provincial science and technology development, etc.).

> *Research Question 2*: Expansion of the R&D budget, amid unclear investment guidelines, may continue to fund inefficient NIS projects that should have been terminated. Path-dependent investments, profit-oriented investments, and other myopic funding decisions based on the principle of selection and concentration can worsen the final R&D results. Is there any way to detect these problems beforehand and ameliorate the consequences?

Agency problem and decisional dilemma

In administrating and inducing R&D results, conflicts between the initial intention of the government policy and the goal of representing researchers can occur. The so-called 'agency problem' arises because of information asymmetry between principals (the government) and agents (representing researchers). A typical scenario of moral hazards is one in which the principal wants to provide suboptimal funding and the agent delivers R&D results whose quality cannot be easily measured. Information asymmetry leads to two-tiered moral hazards, as the government cannot check on the sincerity of R&D institutions, and the latter cannot evaluate efforts shown by their researchers.

In addition, if the government concentrates R&D resources in high-risk projects, including the development of new and cutting-edge technologies, in order to fight globalization and mad technologies, the expanded R&D budget *qua* slack capital can serve as a buffer to the changing global economic environment. However, prolonged investments in such high-risk projects as nano-, bio-, and information technology development, which have a very low probability of success but may yield a big return if successful, will destroy existing technology stocks, as researchers will abandon traditional projects and take up new high risk items. Therefore, it is doubtful whether the slack capital, invested in cutting-edge technologies, as a buffer to globalization and mad technologies, can perform its intended function, especially when the Korean NIS still suffers from the "high-cost/low-productivity" syndrome.

Research Question 3: Is it possible to find a solution to principal–agent problems that result from the disaccord between the strategic loop that prioritizes NIS projects and the effective loop that induces researcher commitment? Also, is it possible to find a solution to the problem of the inept slack capital?

Prioritizing NIS projects in Korea

Braun (1998) described cognitive development within a scientific body of knowledge as being a complex process of interaction between four subsystems of funding agencies: cognitive traditions and scenarios, the motivations of researchers, and technological development. It was noted that funding agencies receive initial cues from external interests in new technologies. The Korean NIS structure has two separate mechanisms of determining the priority of funding, which is under the purview of the National Science and Technology Council (NSTC), and getting approval of and distributing funding packages to researchers, a jurisdiction of the Planning and Budgetary Board (PBB). Recently, the PBB's role has been reduced to obtaining budgetary approvals from the National Assembly, while NSTC now prioritizes and funds NIS projects. The overall coordination mechanism within the NSTC and the PBB involves a complex and dynamic structure of prioritizing NIS projects according to their structural, thematic, and scientific importance and determining funding sizes in consultation with the PBB.

The actual procedure for prioritizing and determining funding sizes is as follows. First, data are collected from the examination and evaluation of the projects granted in the previous year. Secondly, a new set of criteria and categories of new projects to be granted is pre-negotiated with the PBB, which provides information on the new R&D resource restrictions. Finally, these findings are reported to the president who resides over the NSTC meeting. In the NSTC meeting with the president, final decisions are made regarding the priority of each project to be funded. When the decisions are reported to the PBB, it will begin the final budget allocation procedure. As can be gleaned from this complex decision-making process, national science and technology projects involve many layers of different decision makers, making the entire process both complicated and political (Stewart, 1995). Since this political decision-making process involves several layers of different decision makers, the Korean NIS decision-making system is an area of institutional complementarity (Leoncini, 1998).

Causal nodes of stratified decision making

Hansen et al. (1999) reported that the decision-making process for distributing resources involves a three-tiered structure. The first tier deals with decisions made by public agencies such as the Department of Defense to protect their current capacity and expand their future power. The second tier is about distributing resources for different stages of R&D projects, and the final stratum concerns the decisions specifically made for distributing resources to a project that goes through different stages. The Korean system of decision making involves a complex web of causal mechanisms that determine project prioritization, distribute funds to prioritized projects, and oversee R&D progress.

The causal nodes of stratified decision making can be shown in a diagram as in Figure 4.1, which bears three different loops. The strategic loop determines the priority and funding size of R&D projects through coordination and discussion among PBB agents,

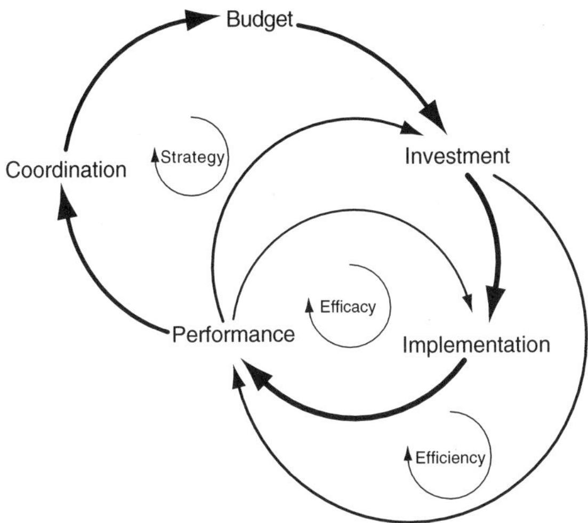

Figure 4.1 Three loops in the R&D investment system

professional R&D institutes, and researchers. Although decisions are based on the actual performance of previous projects and future feasibility of extant projects, bureaucratic inertia, evaluations based on short-term performances, and the trap of targeting and concentration will loom large in this loop. The second one is a structural or efficiency loop that affects the process of making decisions in the strategic loop by providing information on the circulation of R&D resources and on how R&D projects were carried out in previous years. Analyses of the cyclical flow of R&D money and projects can give information on the complex web of individual and group interests in addition to the progress of R&D projects. The third one is an efficacy loop or researcher loop that is related to the correlation between researcher attitudes and R&D investment priorities. For example, the efficacy loop shows how the attitude of a software developer can make the entire R&D project smooth, although the project is actually about developing a new hardware system. Overall, these three loops can measure how external interests – including scientific and technological issues, individual project performance, and researchers' R&D activities – are continuously siphoned into the R&D investment system.

Figure 4.1 indicates that the direction and consistency of the flow are related to the decision makers who prioritized R&D investments in the Korean coordination procedure. This means that the prioritizing system affected lower systems of decision making, as all three loops are connected to each other, while end-results also affected the prioritizing procedure as feedback.

Designing system-dynamic simulation models

As we clarified in the beginning, we intend to resolve the decisional dilemmas noticed in all three loops that we have described above. To do this our system-dynamic model must be able to provide some leveraged indicators to show whether the Korean NIS has to increase or reduce R&D spending. If expansion/reduction is a possible policy alternative suggested by the model, which projects must be further funded and which must be stopped is another issue. Therefore, the choice of system-dynamic modeling has to be justified for our purpose.

It has been noticed that strong correlation coefficients between R&D investment and R&D performance in a multiple regression model do not necessarily indicate that a causal relationship exists between the two variables. Occasionally, reverse causality between variables x and y is also discovered, when correlations are statistically significant (Oh et al., 2002). Also, although mutual dependence of two particular variables can be expressed by a procedural diagram, it simply reflects a still picture of otherwise very dynamic relationships (Senge, 1994). In R&D investment decisions, many different participants make decisions either simultaneously or at different times, while their actions and decisions mutually affect the other participants, and different steps and stages of decision-making procedures are all closely associated with each other.

In order to understand a complex system, we need to master some basic concepts of system dynamics, such as feedbacks, stocks and flows, time delays, and asymmetry (Sterman, 2002). When they attempt to make decisions regarding R&D investments, participants employ different mental models. Subsystems also contribute to the complexity of the overall decision-making system. Changes in one variable will bring about similar changes in other variables of the same feedback loops. Therefore, the use of a system-dynamic model can be justified in the analysis of the Korean R&D investment system.

The first task in the construction of system-dynamic models is to find core factors that affect the working of the Korean R&D investment system. In this chapter, we drew a feedback loop that consists of strategic, efficacy, and efficiency loops, based on our theoretical research and participant observation. We mixed both stocks and flows models in the construction of each loop in order to make it easy for us to generalize our findings in a conclusive feedback loop. In particular, we divided NIS projects into basic, application, and add-on technology types and observed how they changed over time in order to find out policy leverages that are significant for the relationship between each loop. We used the software program STELLA 5.1.1 in the design of each loop.

Strategic loop

This loop coordinates the initial process of decision making regarding R&D investments. Broadly speaking, coordinators are the government (PBB), professional institutes (KISTEP), and researchers. The government was assumed to be the party that makes decisions about the priority and size of R&D funding, whereas professional institutes and researchers were considered to react to, or interact with, the governmental decisions, based on R&D performance and future potential for succeess in new technology development. It is additionally assumed that project priority and funding size are determined by the distribution of power each party has in the coordination process (Lounamaa and March, 1987).

Activity levels intensify when participants have confidence in the future success of the R&D projects. Such confidence is usually based on empirical inference, which is obtained by learning after either intended or unintended consequences occur. This process of learning takes the form of gradient search, because these consequences are a critical starting point of cognitive development. Periodic cognitive developments determine the level of activities taken up by participants in R&D projects.

Learning activities are reinforced by the evaluation of R&D performances. We assume that performance evaluators use only partial rationality or intended rationality to highlight only those aspects of the project that they want to emphasize. For example, researchers want to utilize research results for the next round's funding negotiation, whereas the PBB highlights only research productivity for the money invested. On the other hand, professional research institutes want to take technological capacities into consideration, in addition to financial conditions.

Conflictual interactions between three actors, regarding project prioritizing and funding size, receive final coordination from the government. For instance, the Korean government publishes a guideline of R&D investments to make its policy intentions public (e.g., investment ratios for basic research to total investments), which eventually adds weight to a particular actor's interests and policy preferences. In other words, we devised a governmental decision-making model that is subject to input from external actors. We express this model of distributing funds to each stage of a selected R&D project as follows:

$$T_{kt} = \frac{\sum_{i=1}^{3} f_{kt} A_{ikt}}{\sum_{k=1}^{3} \sum_{i=1}^{3} f_{kt} A_{ikt}},$$

where f_{kt} is added weight on the decision coordination over a new technology of k during the period of t. Although technology had a 1×3 (basic, applied, and add-on) matrix initially, it later becomes a 3 (PBB, professional institutes, researchers) $\times$ 3 matrix, expressed by X. f_{kt} is a weighted value of an X_i factor of the matrix X during the period t.

In addition, we assigned a 1 when each actor perceives opponents' changes in strategic postures. 0 was given when such perception was absent. It is obvious that increased interactions between actors enhance the chances of obtaining perception on such changes. We, thus, assigned the following scores for each actor for a heuristic purpose.

Actors	*PBB*	*Professional institutes*	*Researchers*
Score	0.7	0.2	0.1

Finally, we added logical operators to decision coordination (T_{kt}) in order to reflect the importance of heuristic decision making at the time of the increasing number of current projects in progress with which the government and other participants have to deal. Decision makers often utilize heuristic methods of distributing R&D resources equally to extant projects when complexity increases, due to either too many cases or too many variables. The stocks and flows of the strategic loop, those factors which determine the priority and funding size of NIS projects, is shown in Figure 4.2.

The strategic loop has a central structure that coordinates different R&D intentions held by three groups of participants and players, who set their levels of activities according to limited rationality and the evaluation of previous studies. Individual or group perceptions will determine the outcome of project evaluations. We can produce a model of perceptions using the following stocks and flows models (Figure 4.3).

As Figure 4.3 indicates, performance evaluation of a project, where actual researchers are participating, starts from program performance, which is then diverted into monetary efficiency and knowledge accumulation dimensions. Depending upon which dimension is emphasized by the participants, the performance evaluation

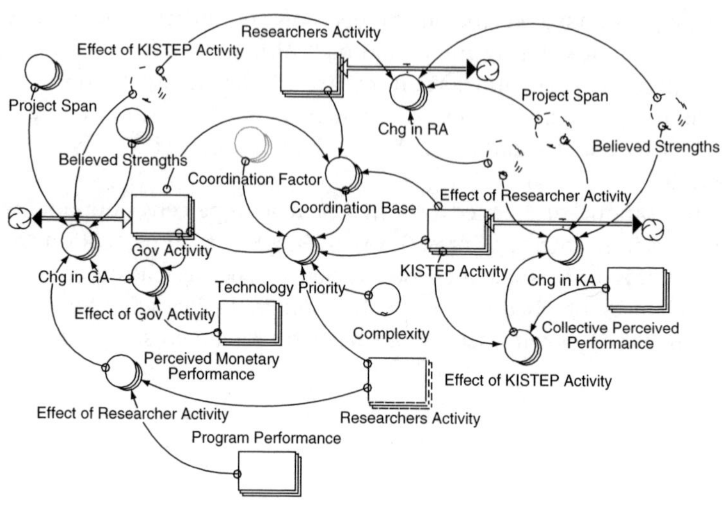

Figure 4.2 Strategic loop

changes. The monetary efficiency dimension refers to the financial aspects of a project that are related to the ratio between project results and total investments. The knowledge accumulation dimension, however, emphasizes capacity aspects of a research project that are related to the ratio between knowledge being created and its relationship to previously created knowledge.

Efficacy loop

We designed the efficacy loop using two dimensions – attitudes toward R&D investments and those toward R&D performance. The first set of attitudes refers to how researchers react to slack resources allocated to their R&D research. Two consequences can occur when slack resources are allocated. First, researchers can be motivated highly, to the extent that innovative research is possible (Cyert and March, 1963). Research organizations with a large pool of slack resources can outperform others in terms of the number of subprojects they can run, which also provides research with psychological motivation to work harder than they would otherwise do. When slack resource pools are absent, researchers rely upon a routinized decision-making pattern, resulting in the adoption of an exploitative,

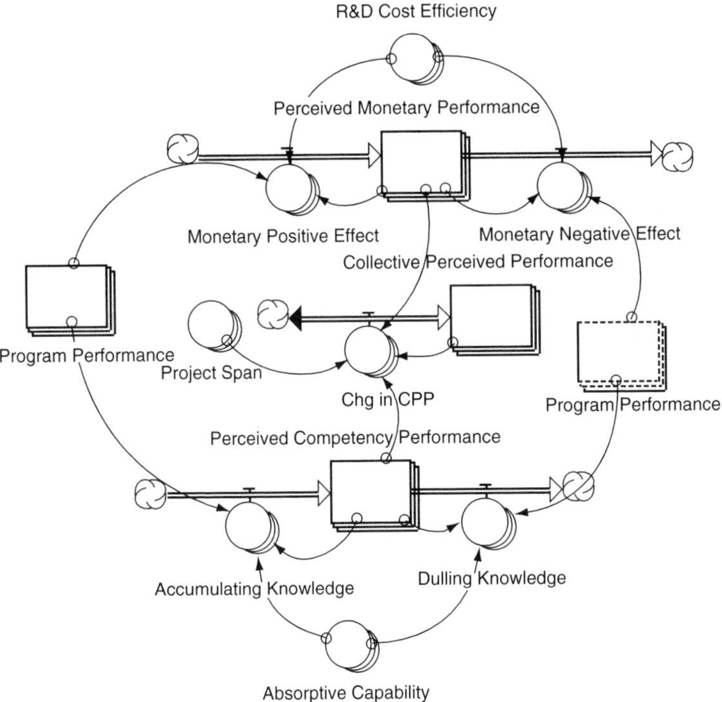

Figure 4.3 Model for perceptions on project evaluation

rather than an explorative, research strategy (March, 1991). Perrow (1984) also argued that big accidents in a complex organization are "normal," since the lack of slack resources blocks any attempt at innovating organizations. In this sense, slack resources are fertilizers for technological and organizational innovation.

Second, slack resources can also motivate researchers to adopt risk-averse postures. Slack resources can unnecessarily prolong project periods, as researchers can try different alternatives to the solution of project problems. Failures of these trials are compensated for by slack resources, making it much easier for researchers to lengthen the project time frame. Therefore, slack resources can have adverse effects on the organization's ability to adapt to changing environments (Thompson, 1967). In addition, in an agent–principal relation, agents can always privatize slack resources for personal use, instead of dispersing it organization-wide for group or organizational benefit, a typical example of moral hazard problems (Holmstrom, 1979; Jensen and Meckling, 1976).

In this context, we can easily show that slack resources can be a cause of both motivational boosts and the pursuit of private self-interest. An increase in slack resources certainly brings about positive reactions among researchers who are highly motivated to take up difficult tasks (Greve, 2003). However, an excessive amount of slack resources can easily create conditions for moral hazards. On the other hand, the absence of slack resources (i.e., a situation in which funding was provided at a sub-optimal level than was initially requested) will make researchers avoid difficulties and dangers, seeking sub-optimal research strategies and even sabotages to cause delays in generating research results.

In our model of R&D efficacy we distinguished capacity-based slack from monetary slack. Capacity slack refers to the amount of R&D funding that exceeds researchers' R&D capacity. Capacity slack can motivate researchers to work harder than they would otherwise do, although it can also be a source of moral hazard problems. We assumed the relationship between capacity slack and researcher confidence in investment support to be asymmetrical as in Figure 4.4.

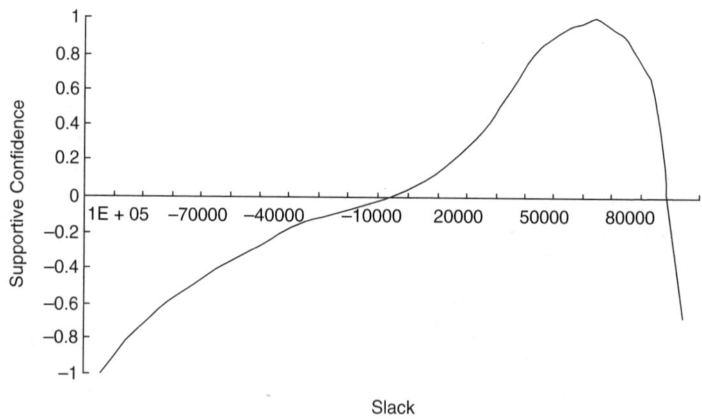

Figure 4.4 Relationship between capacity slack and researcher confidence

Monetary slack occurs when participating parties have different R&D expectation levels and oversupply research funding to researchers. Monetary slack is linked to personal reward expectation, as the oversupplied portion of R&D money is supposed to be converted into personal gain. Individual utility functions show that people take risk-averse strategies when behavioral consequences produce positive gains at the time of decision making amid uncertainty; conversely, they change to risk-taking postures when behavioral consequences are in the negative (Kahneman and Tversky, 1979). In other words, the occurrence of slack resources leads researchers to the expectation of personal gain or reward, which then motivates researchers to be risk averse. On the other hand, when no monetary slack occurred, researchers can take risks, because they might have to spend their own money resources on the R&D project (Sitkin and Pablo, 1992; Wiseman and Gomez-Mejia, 1998). This relationship between personal reward expectation and monetary slack can be expressed as in Figure 4.5.

In sum, slack resources affect researchers' risk preference pattern, which in turn influences researchers' attitudes toward their R&D projects. Since the utility function for risk-averse postures takes a logistic growth function, while risk-taking postures generate an exponential growth function, we devised the following functions:

$$U(P) = 1 - exp(-rP),\ r \geq 0$$
$$U(P) = exp(-rP),\ r < 0,$$

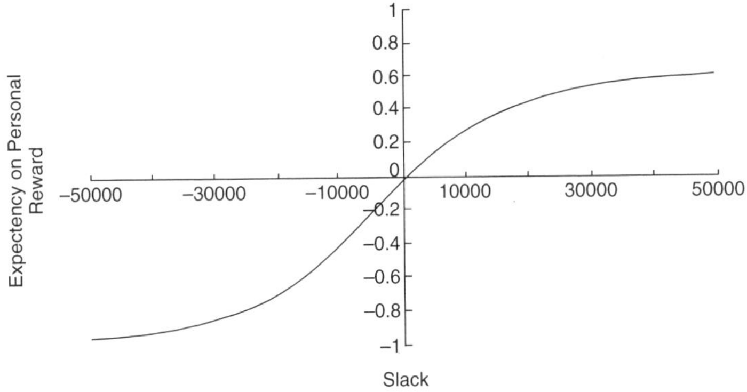

Figure 4.5 Monetary slack and personal reward expectation

where r is a coefficient parameter for risk-aversion. The parameter is positive when researchers are risk-averse and negative when they prefer risks. x refers to monetary performance or project performance. It is thus argued that researchers' attitudes are determined by their confidence in their own research abilities and risk-averse postures toward the resource slack. Its function is:

$$FA(t+1) = FA(t) + U(P)C(Slack)$$

Our next concern, research performance, can be examined by both quantitative and qualitative means. The quantitative option is simply to count all completed projects within a given deadline, while qualitative measurement is presumed to be related to researchers' attitudes, because it is more difficult to utilize than the quantitative measure. Therefore, research performance is measured by the number of completed projects by researchers' actual attitudes. Actual attitudes is a concept that incorporates both will and real activity levels held by researchers and is expressed in terms of the level of confidence about research performance held by researchers multiplied by their actual research activities. We have already assumed that the level of confidence is correlated with researchers' positive attitudes toward their projects. The efficacy loop has the stocks and flow structure shown in Figure 4.6.

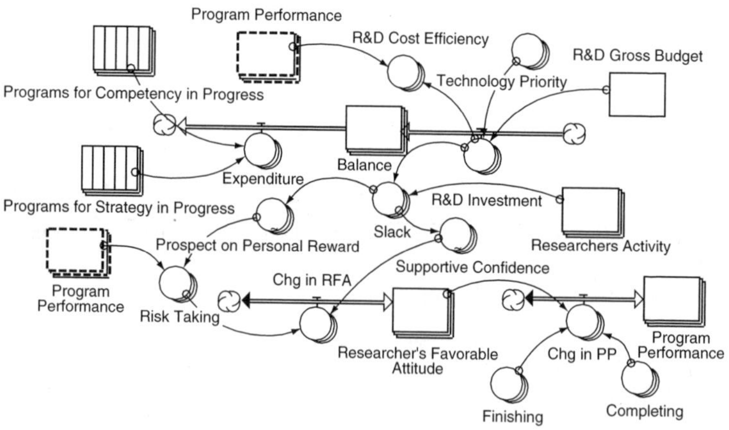

Figure 4.6 Modeling of the efficacy loop

Efficiency loop

We approached the modeling of the efficiency loop from two dissimilar aspects. One is the flow of a program (or project), and the other is the flow of the implementation of R&D budgets and budget decisions for the next fiscal year. As we indicated earlier, NIS projects can be classified into competency-building programs and strategic technology development programs. The process and behavior of each type of project varies from case to case.

Capacity-building programs include basic science, human resource development, and short-term projects. Therefore, we assumed that knowledge accumulation will grow exponentially past a tipping point, although it would not be visible in early stages. On the other hand, strategic technology development programs usually include long-term projects for developing strategically targeted new technologies, although they quickly adapt to changing environments. Therefore, we assumed that the finished results of each project might be very visible, although new technologies can easily become obsolete when the market is saturated. In the long run, strategically developed technologies disappear from the market.

On the other hand, strategically developed technologies maintain linkages between different dimensions of technologies. In a linear relationship between stages of technological development, basic technology serves as a basis for application and add-on technologies. This linear relationship is determined by absorptive capacity, where learning capacity of digesting foreign technologies and applying them to domestic conditions is a key to success (Cohen and Levinthal, 1989, 1990).

Based on the above viewpoints, we propose the following stocks and flow structure. We presumed that researchers are rotated every term for capacity building programs, whereas they are rotated every three terms for strategic technology development programs (Figure 4.7).

The accumulation of new knowledge will serve as a foundation for future projects, which means that technological development corresponds to the number of projects. Innovation occurs after certain periods of time, as paradigms change. A virtuous cycle of technological development, paradigmatic changes, and innovations continues. Figure 4.8 offers a stock and flow structure of this cycle.

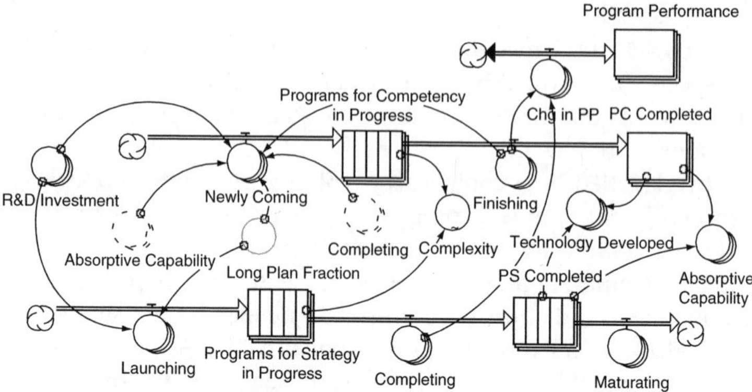

Figure 4.7 Modeling of the efficiency loop

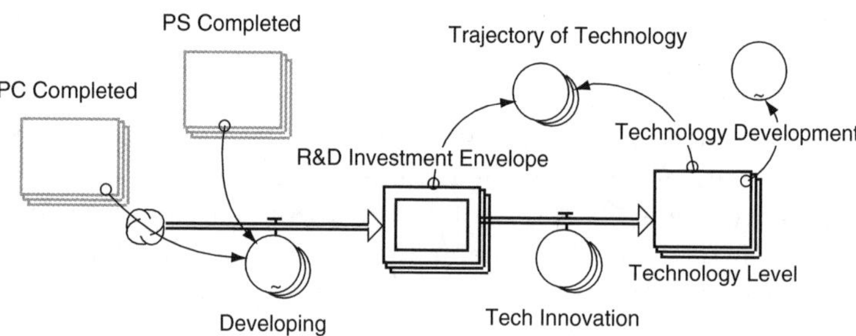

Figure 4.8 Project flow in the efficiency loop

Monetary flows deal with the issue of how research performance affects the distribution of funding to future R&D projects (Figure 4.9). Research performance of a project is measured by its financial performance, using the ratio between productivity and its total expenditures. Financial performance is then a source of decision for future terms. When technological development contributes positively to economic development, an increased economic size can also lead to larger R&D budgets. Decision making based on financial performance usually occurs in the investment of strategic technology development.

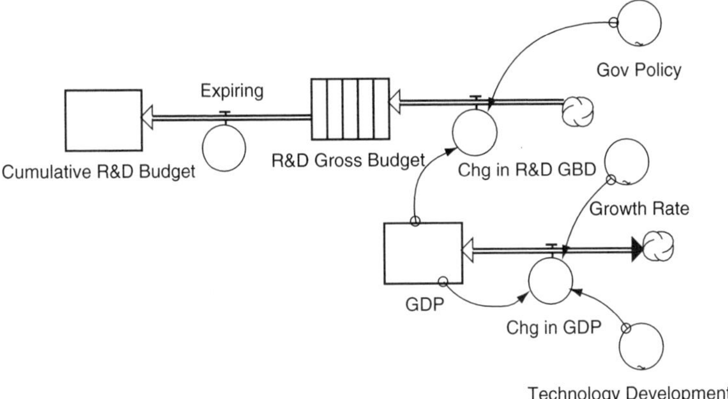

Figure 4.9 Monetary flow in the efficiency loop

Findings and policy implications

In this section we will introduce findings and discuss their implications, using three types of technologies (basic, application, add-on) and three types of programs (capacity building, strategic technology development, and researcher attitudes). These findings will be followed by a short discussion on the policy implications of our findings.

First, we asked a normative question about how to devise desirable decisions at each R&D stage in the strategic loop. This can be done by manipulating coordination factors during each R&D stage, which yields different investment effects and technological innovations. When factors are set to favor basic technologies (i.e., basic, application, and add-on technologies are set at 0.8, 0.1, 0.1), the results are as shown in Figures 4.10(a) and 4.10(b).

Figures 4.10(a), 4.10(b) and 4.10(c) represent basic, application, and add-on technologies respectively. In both technological development and program performance, it is noted that application and add-on technology take off only after basic technologies show rapid increases in terms of technological development and program performance. In particular, Figures 4.10(a) and 4.10(b) show that add-on technologies take more time in technology development than application technologies, although the growth pattern of the former is faster and

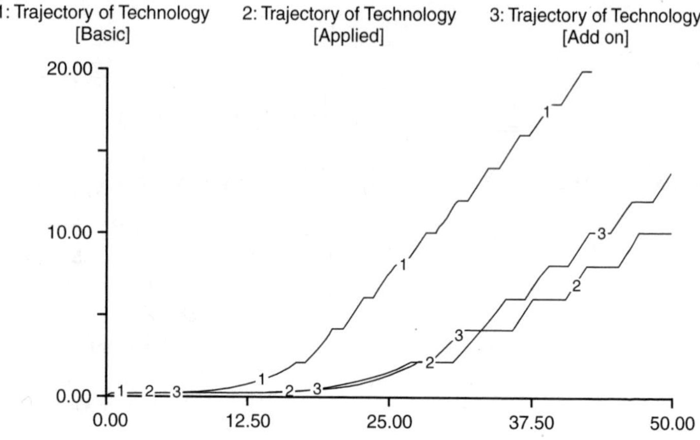

Figure 4.10(a) Technological development (0.8, 0.1, 0.1)

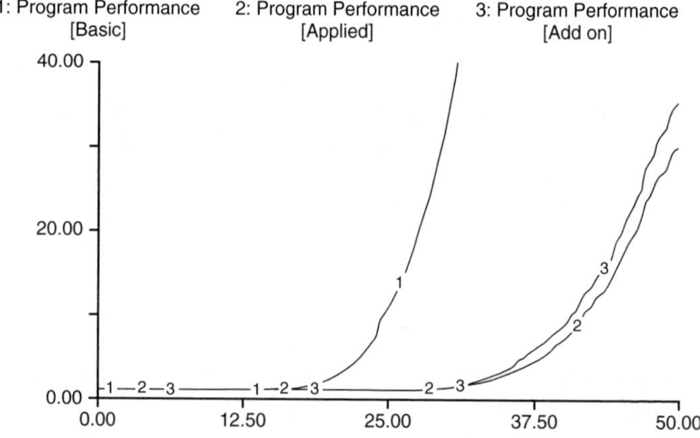

Figure 4.10(b) Program performance (0.8, 0.1, 0.1)

larger than the latter. This means that application technologies produce unintended inefficiencies in technology development.

However, both application and add-on technologies create delays in technological innovation, although short-term developments are clearly noticeable from one stage to another. The reason is that absorptive capacity is affected by the level of basic technologies,

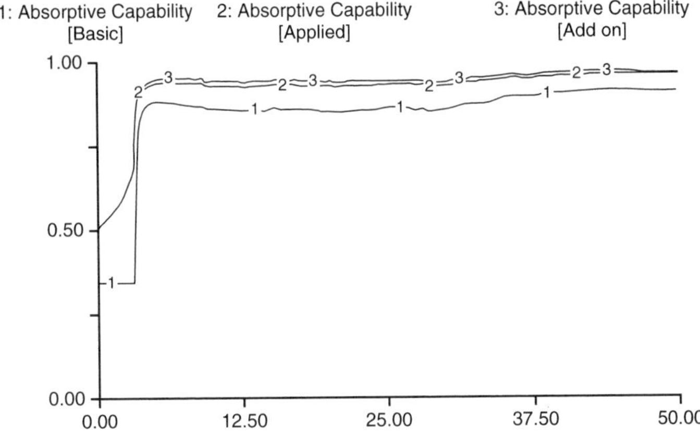

Figure 4.10(c) Absorptive capacity (0.8, 0.1, 0.1)

which in turn affects the growth pattern of application and add-on technologies. As Figure 4.10(c) indicates, the absorptive capacity of both application and add-on technologies drastically increase in the early phase of the project, allowing us to infer from it that innovations in basic technologies bring about developments of application and add-on technologies.

On the other hand, when coordination factors were set to prefer application and add-on technologies, the results are as shown in Figure 4.11. These figures show that technological innovations are retarded, whereas the short-term performance growth of application and add-on technologies is remarkable. Simultaneously, the figures show that basic technologies continue to improve, despite low levels of funding. This supports the argument that the short-term economic gain from application and add-on technologies does not in fact contribute to the real innovative performance of a country, creating the problem of an inefficient allocation of research resources. Figure 4.10(c) also supports this argument, as absorptive capacities of all three technologies increased rapidly, when basic research was heavily funded.

This finding is in accordance with the argument that the traditional Korean policy of favoring application technologies has unnecessarily slowed down developments in basic technologies that are critical in

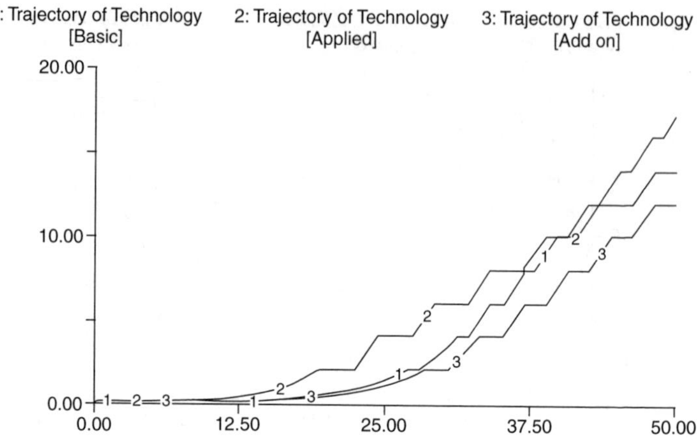

Figure 4.11(a) Development patterns (0.1, 0.8, 0.1)

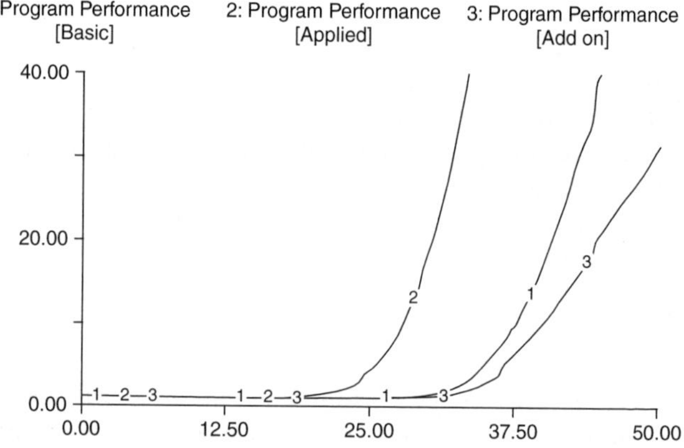

Figure 4.11(b) Program performance (0.1, 0.8, 0.1)

bringing about long-term technological innovations. To avoid an R&D dilemma and to enhance flows and stocks of R&D resources, it is necessary to give priority to basic technologies.

Two of the reasons for R&D dilemmas were: (1) bureaucratic inertia that prohibits participants from canceling some of the inefficient extant projects at the time of R&D budget expansion and (2) myopic

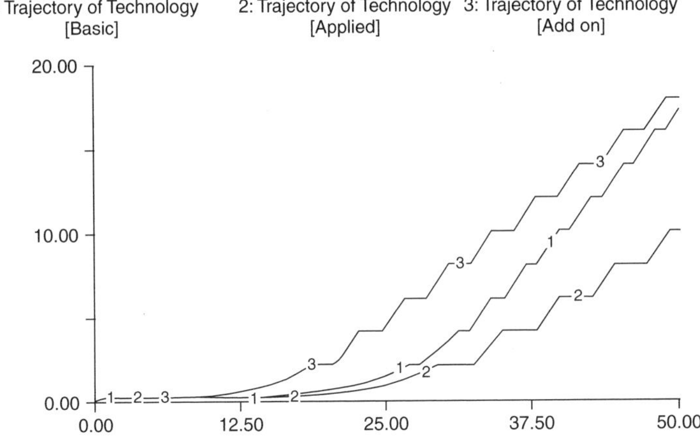

Figure 4.11(c) Development patterns (0.1, 0.1, 0.8)

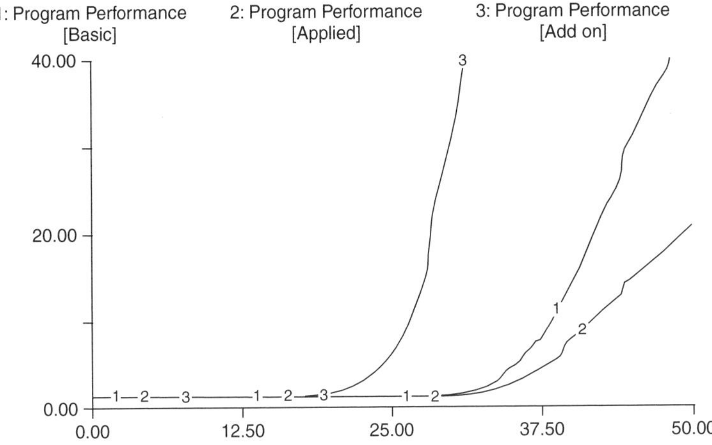

Figure 4.11(d) Program performance (0.1, 0.1, 0.8)

investment decisions that emphasize only short-term performance results. In order to examine the effects of inertia and myopia, we continued to use the concepts of capacity-building projects and strategic technology development programs. Our assumption is that myopia and inertia occur mostly in the latter, while they decrease significantly in the former. We wanted to analyze how technological development changes as R&D projects are differently weighted. We assumed that R&D investment weights are similar across all three technologies, while we produced simulations controlling long plan fraction factors (LP). First, when myopic investment decisions occur (LP = 0.01), the results are as shown in Figure 4.12(a).

If we also introduce graphs of program performance for strategic technology development and capacity-building programs, they are something like what is shown in Figures 4.12(b) and 4.12(c). These figures represent the completion of strategic technology development (4.12(b)) and capacity-building programs (4.12(c)), respectively. As the figures show, capacity-building programs yielded no significant performance results, while strategic technology development programs generated some growth. Even the growth pattern of strategic technology development programs failed to generate a steady pattern of technology accumulation, as different programs appeared and perished from the R&D sector at different intervals. This is because capacity-building programs are undeveloped, retarding the whole process of knowledge accumulation even in strategic technology development programs. This growth limitation fails to produce radical innovations as time elapses. Absorptive capacities also decrease

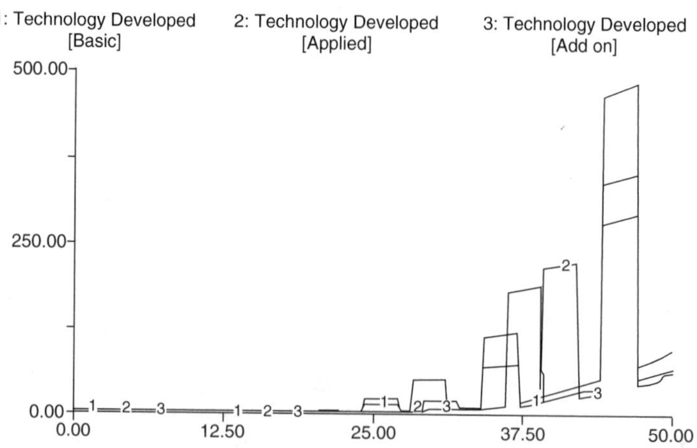

Figure 4.12(a) Technological development due to program performance (LP = 0.01)

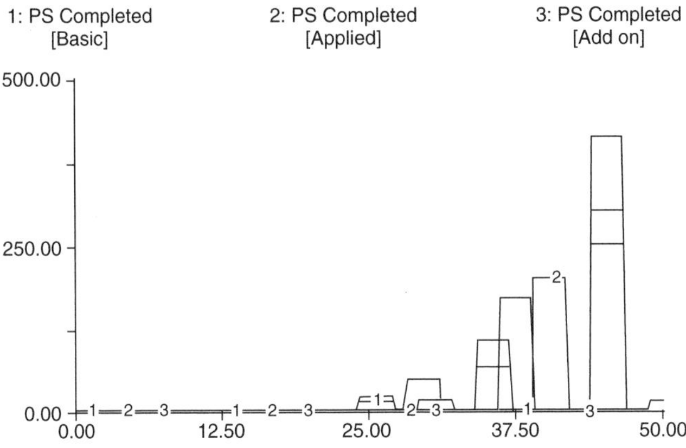

Figure 4.12(b) The performance of strategic programs

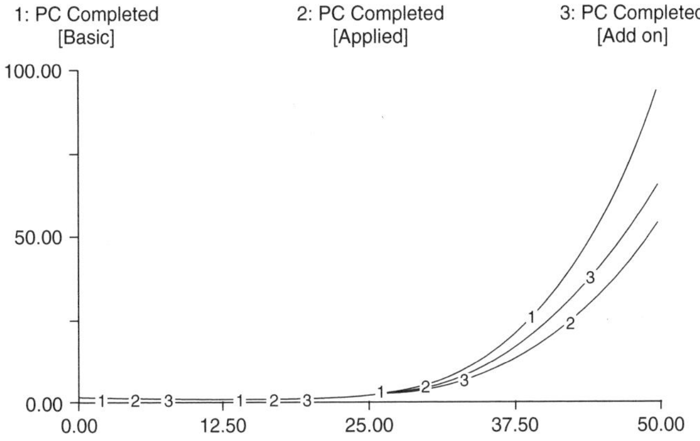

Figure 4.12(c) The performance of capacity programs

during the course of evolution, which reinforces the limitations of strategic technology development (Figure 4.12(d)).

If we take the accumulation of technology and knowledge as being a definition of learning (March, 1991), the erratic fluctuations of absorptive capacities shown in Figure 4.12(d) indicate that technology and knowledge have not been learned or accumulated, but, rather,

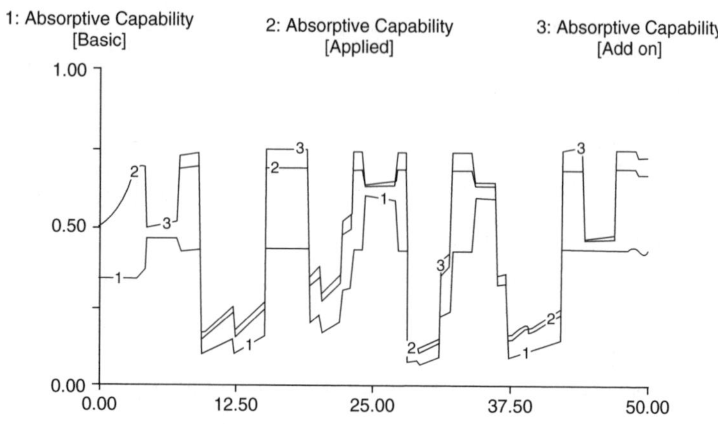

Figure 4.12(d) Absorptive capacity

were stored temporarily at different intervals. When one cycle of the program was finished, the obtained knowledge was emptied from the "storage bin", being replaced during subsequent cycles. Therefore, investment decisions that favor strategic technology development programs only generate a range of unorganized and unclassified knowledge that cannot result in learning due to the lack of capacity building programs. On the other hand, when coordination factors are set to favor capacity building programs (LP = 0.99), Figure 4.13(a) can be derived.

In contrast to the previous graphs, Figure 4.13(a) demonstrates an exponential growth in technological development, after R&D projects go through a certain period of temporal delay. If we further divide up technological development into strategic and capacity building programs, Figures 4.13(b) and 4.13(c) can be obtained.

Although strategic technology development programs suffer from a low level of technological development, capacity-building programs produce a remarkably high level of R&D success in terms of technological development, as Figures 4.13(b) and 4.13(c) indicate. This means that the social and economic conditions of technology development have increased, since capacity-building programs require large sums of investment in fixtures and facilities.

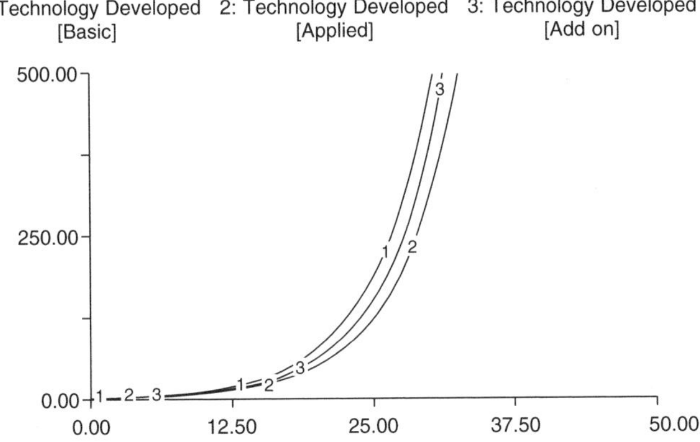

Figure 4.13(a) Technological development due to program performance (LP = 0.99)

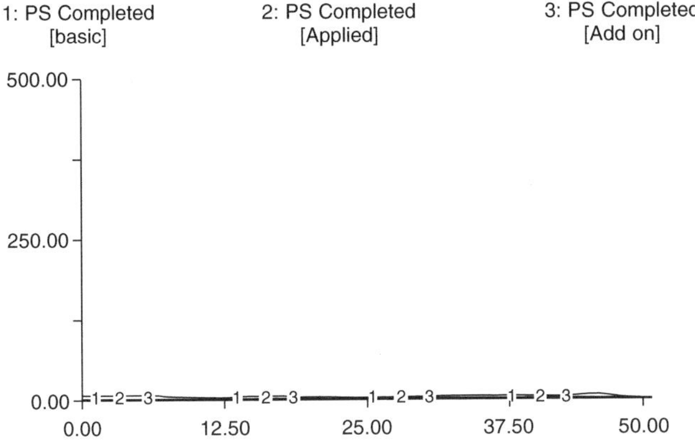

Figure 4.13(b) Strategic programs

In sum, we can confirm that myopic R&D decision making leads to all sorts of errors by focusing only on short-term R&D performances, without taking into account the importance of absorptive capacities. Therefore, R&D investments must accommodate absorptive capacities in their formulae.

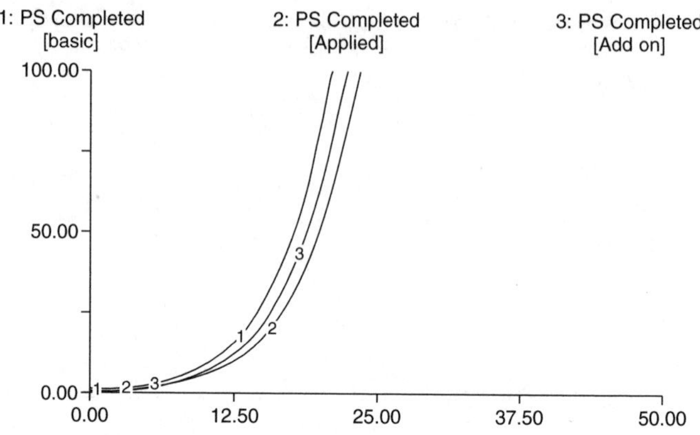

Figure 4.13(c) Capacity-building programs

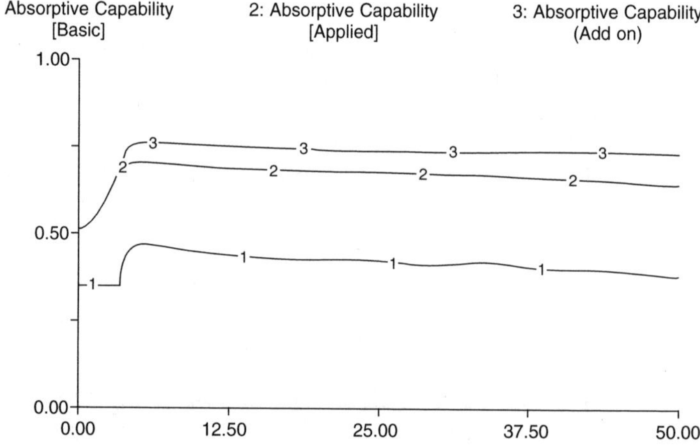

Figure 4.13(d) Absorptive capacities

Having discussed the impacts of different types of technologies (i.e., basic, application, add-on) and different patterns of programs (i.e., strategic technology development, capacity building) on both short-term and long-term R&D performance, we can now analyze the impact of researcher attitudes on R&D performances by changing the size of the initial budget. Since we assume that researcher attitudes change according to the initial size of the funding package, our model is expected to produce some significant simulation results. This model also demonstrates how the mentality side of R&D investment decisions works in the form of researcher attitudes. The following graphs are possible (Figures 4.14(a)–4.14(d)), if we set the weighted R&D proportion to GDP (GP) at one percent (GP=0.01).

The above results show that program performance increases after a certain initial period of delay. Although confidence in getting

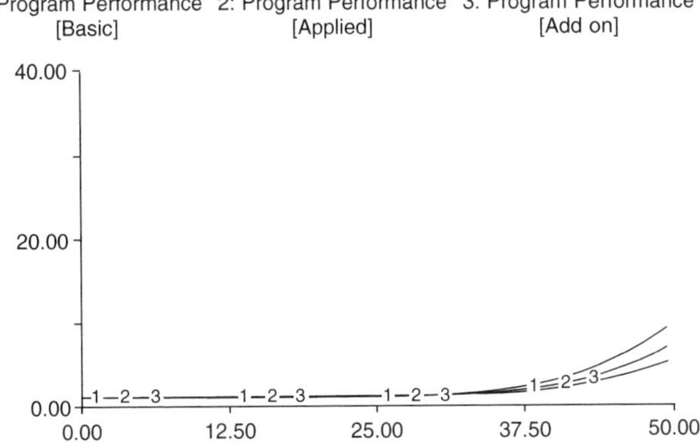

Figure 4.14(a) Program performance

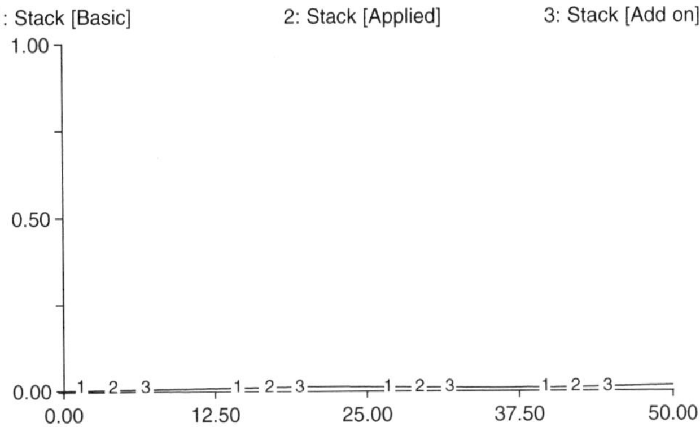

Figure 4.14(b) Slack resources

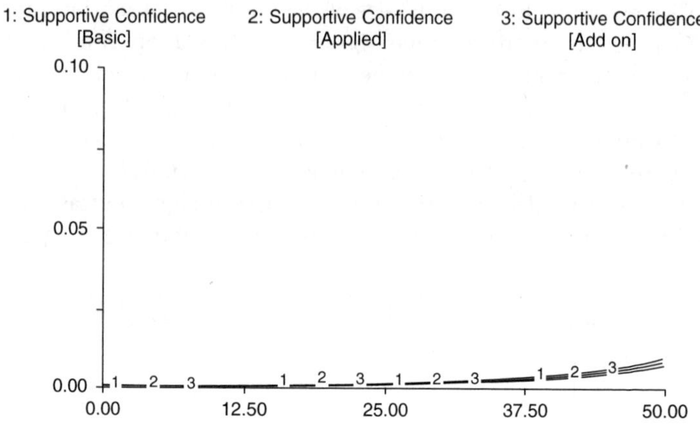

Figure 4.14(c) Confidence in getting support

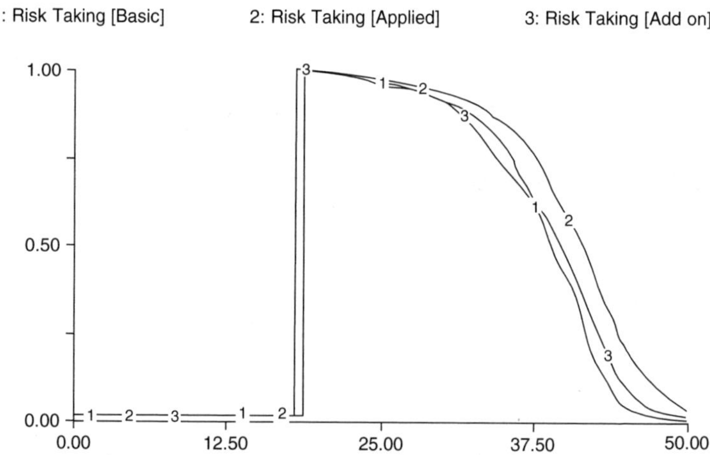

Figure 4.14(d) Researchers' positive attitude

support increases over time, the level remains very low, just like that of program performance. The reason for the increase of program performance at the later stage can be traced to the rapid rise of researchers' positive or affirmative attitude toward their projects in the middle phase, despite the minimal level of support confidence.

However, when the GP was set at 10 percent (GP=0.1), its results are different from the previous one, as program performance increases markedly (Figure 4.15).

The reason for the early drastic increase in program performance is the rapid rise of support confidence among researchers, which resulted

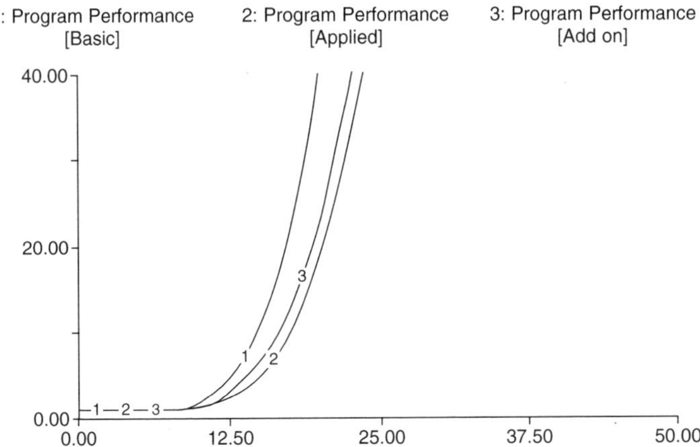

Figure 4.15(a) Program performance

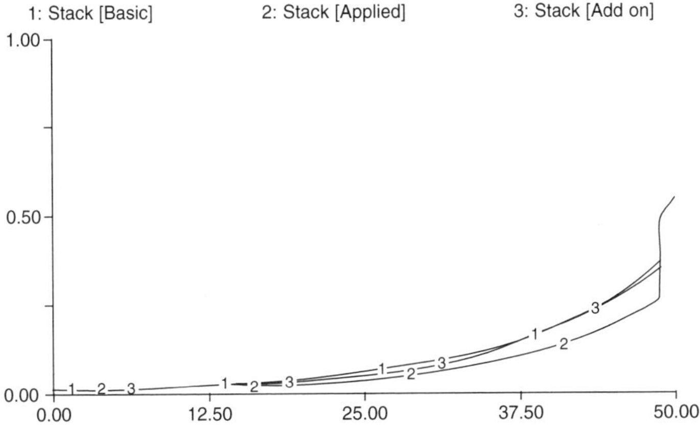

Figure 4.15(b) Slack resources

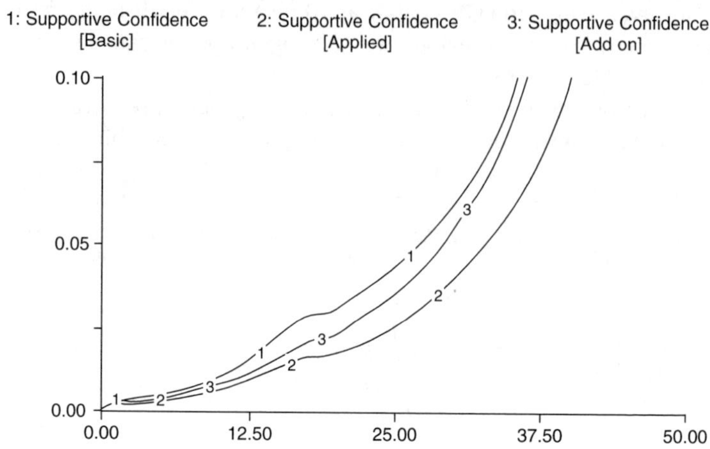

Figure 4.15(c) Confidence

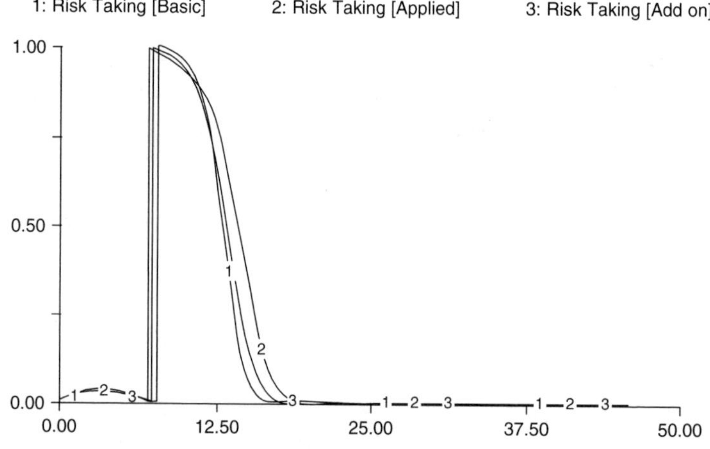

Figure 4.15(d) Researchers' positive attitude

in a similarly rapid increase in researchers' positive attitudes. However, it is also known from the above simulation that support confidence has a short interval of diminishing marginal utility, since the attitude curve falls quickly after it hits the maximum point. In effect, it is found that slack resources would not always result in researcher efficacy. Expanding the funding size to motivate researchers would only lead to other types of inefficiencies. Having discussed the theoretical significance of types of technologies, patterns of NIS strategies, and slack resources in affecting R&D performance in the Korean context, we lastly suggest some policy implications.

Among OECD countries, it is taken for granted that technological innovations play a central role in economic development. These countries are trying to reform the role of the state, so that it can support quick and efficient processes of specialization in the area of new knowledge creation, in addition to providing both short and long term plans for R&D development (Marceau, 2002). The Korean government has continued to play the role of carrying out comprehensive coordination since 1999 for prioritizing R&D investment decisions for the NIS programs. That year coincides with the time when the Korean domestic stock market was invaded and inundated by mad technologies and experienced the subsequent fall of the so-called "dot.com" stocks in 2000.

Our short empirical study suggests that the lack of long-term government plans for developing basic technologies in Korea invited such an economic disaster caused by dot.com companies. As we will show in Chapter 7, Japan had no such problems, due to a strong NIS network that preferred basic technologies. Japan's problem was not being able to find application knowledge using basic technologies. We argued that investment decisions had suffered from some visible dilemmas, mostly due to myopia and bureaucratic inertia. Science and technology are closely related to the NIS budgeting process (Makeig, 2002). This means that the social prioritization of different types of technologies is critical in determining what kind of technological level a society can achieve. For instance, the Korean case shows that universities are mostly carrying out R&D on basic technologies, whereas corporations focus mostly on application or add-on technologies. What can we do to find out an optimal prioritization ratio?

Given that NIS has to be continued, and the role of the state has to be strengthened – in part to resolve dilemmas surrounding R&D investment decisions – we suggest that the PBB must continue to coordinate the investment decision-making process in consultation with other participants. In addition, our simulation results found the following possibilities to ameliorate the Korean situation. First, although investment expansion in application and add-on technologies can bring about quick results, it is much wiser to increase investments in foundational research projects in order to obtain long-term scientific and technological competitiveness and to speed up technological developments. Second, we could identify that short-term and concentrated financial support for strategic technology development programs engenders all sorts of problems and side-effects, because it often disregards the importance of capacity-building programs and their ability to beef up absorptive capacities for most R&D institutes and participants. Strategic programs were also found to provide the initial seeds for commencing a whole vicious cycle of continuous reduction in investment effects. Finally, we found out that new policy leverages must take the dynamic process of R&D decision making into consideration to resolve various dilemmas detected at various stages in the dynamic decision-making system.

Future studies on this topic can focus on the side-effects and structural delays to identify their overall impact on the NIS and their organizational and dynamic sources. Needless to say, we must acknowledge that this chapter failed to devise feasible policy leverages that could overcome the different dilemmas present in the current NIS system in Korea. We need further studies to devise a systematic way of providing policy leverages in the resolution of decisional dilemmas in NIS funding.

5
Innovation Strategies of the Korean Chaebols

In Chapter 4, we empirically identified the effects of external shocks on policy making in the Korean NIS when faced by advancing mad technologies. We called for the introduction of long-term investment plans in fundamental and traditional sciences in order to combat the negative effects of mad technologies. In this chapter, we will discuss how big chaebol groups and their PIS are fighting the encroachment of mad technologies in their traditional markets.

Despite numerous studies of the Korean chaebols and their successes (or deficiencies), one question still remains a riddle – how can centralized family firms (in terms of financial ownership and concentration of decision making) be a source of innovation for the entire Korean economy, which is being invaded by mad technologies? Cases of innovation that the top five chaebol groups have introduced to the global market are by no means few and far between, although the actual number of patents is far smaller than that possessed by Japanese or American firms. Hyundai's automobile and engine technology, Samsung's memory chip technology, SK's telecommunication technology, and LG's display panel and plasma technologies are globally approved, successful innovation cases.

Only one argument suggests that the Korean chaebol is a favorable setting for innovation – one-man control can be quicker and more decisive in making R&D investments of large sums than corporations which have decentralized decision-making structures (Kim, 1993; Kim, 1998; Kim et al., 1999). However, the majority of arguments do not suggest that the chaebol is a favorable setting for innovation and survival. Product differentiation and challenges from global competitors in innovation and product development require disintegrated structures. These were not suited to the chaebol, which pursued economies of scale and the mass production of standard models (Abernathy and Clark, 1985; Chesbrough and Teece, 1996; Teece, 1986, 1988; Nonaka and Takeuchi, 1995; Nooteboom, 1999, 2000; Volberda, 1998).

What we have to establish through the cases of radical innovation (that is, creative destruction through organizational innovations) that occurred in the chaebols is a theoretical framework that can explain the mechanism of organizational complementarity toward innovation, despite family ownership and centralized decision-making structures. The assumed absence of functional complementarity within the chaebol (i.e., no Fordism), especially between divisions, also refutes the argument that the chaebol induced innovation through specialized teamwork. However, the lack of functional complementarity in centralized family firms does not mean that the chaebol has utilized teamwork among generalists in order to induce technological complementarity between divisions (i.e., no Toyotism). The chaebol is clearly a different group of firms from its Japanese counterpart, whose keiretsu governance structures readily allow teamwork of generalists between keiretsu firms. What would be a chaebol's organizational advantage in inducing innovation and technology commercialization? In order to approach the issue of innovation within the chaebol we need to adopt a new perspective regarding the chaebol organization itself.

To enliven otherwise anemic organizational studies about chaebols' innovation structures, we intend to initiate a theoretical discussion that explores possible conceptual tools with which to identify chaebols' innovation structures. We start from the assumption that the governance structures of firms are closely related to their innovation potential. This assumption is substantially different from the prevalent economic wisdom that firm size (rather than corporate governance per se) is the key to innovation success/failure. More definitely, we can argue that firm size is also reflective of particular governance structures. Once innovation is perceived to be a problem of governance, we can then proceed to assess the plausibility of the impact of the following four variables, all of which seem to be critical in innovation studies (Nooteboom, 2000) – (1) contractual characteristics; (2) the mode of conduct between contractual partners; (3) the culture/institutions of organizations; and (4) the intervening variables (specific investments, switching costs, value of the partner, room for opportunism, and inclination to opportunism).

The first three variables concern governance, specifically transactional governance – a term we will clarify later (see also Chapter 8) – and organizational sense making (culture/institutions). Our second assumption, therefore, is that governance is closely related to organizational sense making, a cognitive process of identifying and memorizing characteristics of the organization and educating organization members about them. The intervening variables are idiosyncratic environmental factors that make organizations of one market sector similar to one another in relation to their organizational sense making. We believe that these intervening variables are, nonetheless, decisive, especially in the case of the chaebols, in either inducing or discouraging innovations of all kinds. The intervening variables produce different innovation outcomes in tandem with the variables of organizational sense making, or the transactional governance variables. This chapter intends to develop these assumptions further to produce some propositions, using the chaebol as its case.

A short discussion of governance and transactional governance

The need to distinguish between these two terms derives from the puzzling observation that the chaebol governance structures have changed little over the years, in spite of external pressures from the government and NGOs. The overall chaebol organizations, however, have changed tremendously in recent years. As a family firm, the chaebol organization has evolved from a one-man ownership and control style of corporate governance into a complex organization, in which a number of division heads also play important roles in decision making. In addition, domestic suppliers, foreign investors, and other strategic partners have further complicated the control aspect of the structure. In other words, the actual corporate governance of the chaebol remained more or less unchanged (that is, there was continued family ownership and governance), although the web of transactions between divisions and external partners grew to the point where the chaebols needed to enter yet another round of organizational innovations.

Therefore, transactional governance is a structure of governing all sorts of transactions between chaebol member firms and divisions on the one hand and between the chaebol and external firms on the other. It is a corporate traffic control of the flow and distribution of monetary resources, employee power and responsibilities, and human resources. Chaebols' day-to-day dealing with the government and other regulatory agencies is another important aspect of transactional governance. On the other hand, corporate governance simply refers to an internal corporate organization that oversees the distribution of power and responsibilities among corporate agents. We posit that a chaebol's transactional governance differs from one chaebol to another, as we take into account the wide differences in their organizational sense-making procedures. Although this chapter cannot provide empirical evidence of: (1) the relationship between transactional governance and organizational sense making; or (2) how each chaebol has different transactional governance systems, transactional governance will play an important role in constituting the model of innovation in the chaebol. Further investigation should be done to collect empirical evidence of (1) and (2).

Organizational and technological innovation as a governance problem

In this section, we will introduce our dependent variables (that is, organizational and technological innovations) and will start to discuss their relationship with the independent variables (organizational sense making and transactional governance). We will also operationalize innovation into five different forms – (1) transaction cost (transactional governance innovation); (2) production cost (technological innovation); (3) product differentiation (technological innovation); (4) incremental innovation (technological and transactional innovations); and (5) creative destruction (technological, transactional, and organizational innovations). The significance of these five forms of innovation will be discussed in the next section.

The view that organizational and technological innovations are intertwined is an old one. For example, Schumpeter noticed how social and corporate organizations had changed in England as the result of technological innovations in navigation (discussed in Kirzner, 1985). An opposite case of technological innovation occurring as a result of organizational evolution is also possible – for example, the product differentiation boom in US automobile industries following the emergence of the multidivisional form (Chandler, 1962).

Given that the chaebol's governance structure has changed little over the years, despite technological advances, it would appear to be ridiculous to argue that the chaebol's technological innovation had any significant relationship with its organizational innovation. However, we need to distinguish carefully between governance structures and organizational innovation at this point. Despite the resilient chaebol governance structures, organizational innovation evolved continuously over the years, including such developments as the introduction of the divisional system, supplier networks, international joint ventures, and teamwork (between generalists and professionals). Although ownership and control as a narrow aspect of corporate governance has not really changed in the chaebols, the transactional governance structures that have been devised to control subsidiaries, suppliers, divisions, workers, and foreign partners have developed substantially over the years. This implies that transactional governance can commence organizational innovations, if not the changes in corporate governance and their impact on different sorts of organizational innovations. Therefore, we cannot easily discard the hypothesis that the chaebols' technological innovation also had a great deal to do with organizational innovation that has some causal relationships with transactional governance, or vice versa:

> Proposition 1. Organizational innovations can occur in two ways – either through innovations in corporate governance or through innovations in transactional governance.
>
> Proposition 1a. Innovations in transactional governance can occur in many different ways, although we cannot discard the hypothesis that technological innovations are one important cause of the innovations in transactional governance.
>
> Proposition 1b. Similarly, we cannot discard the hypothesis that innovations in transactional governance can also induce technological innovation.

What is more important than understanding the exact causal mechanism between technological and organizational innovations is to construct a theoretical framework of why organizational innovation is important in the discussion of technological innovation and commercialization. This is so, as long as our terminal goal is to figure out the mechanism for successfully arriving at technological breakthroughs and/or radical innovations at times of external shocks and changes in the global market. As we said earlier, it is our tentative thesis that the reason for the importance of organizational innovation is the existence of transactional governance. It is fairly safe to assume that the evolution of transactional governance triggers organizational innovation, if the latter accompanies new organizational devices of controlling transactional partners. In the evolution of transactional governance, the above four variables – contractual characteristics, the mode of conduct between contractual partners, the culture/institutions of organizations, and intervening variables (specific investments, switching costs, value of the partner, room for opportunism, and inclination to opportunism) – loom large. We further explain why this is the case.

A model of organizational innovation

In this section, we discuss why our independent variables play a significant role in explaining the dependent variables. Organizational literature has long been concerned with types of organization and innovation, as is shown, for example, in debates between economists and management scientists about the issue of size and innovation. In most case-oriented and quantitative studies, empirical evidence tends to dismiss economists' R&D production function in favor of organizational diversity (see, inter alia, Langlois and Robertson, 1995; Nooteboom, 1989; Rothwell and Zegveld, 1985; Tushman and Anderson, 1986: ch. 6). However, organizational economics, such as transaction cost analysis, still ignore some of the achievements in psychology that take seriously the premise of organization as sense making (see Choo, 1998; Schein, 1985; Volberda, 1998; Weick, 1979, 1995). Although transaction cost economics takes first-order learning as a stepping stone for innovation, it elides the importance of second-order learning, inclusive of such germane processes of innovation as exploration, experimentation, and discovery (Nonaka and Takeuchi, 1995; Volberda, 1998).

If organizations cannot survive without proper forms (flexible size, decentralization, plasticity, cross-boundary teams), the notion of taking organization as sense making opens up a new genre in innovation studies that allows us to chart different ways of formulating organizational strategies of survival. Simply put, organizational managers and their subordinate members must figure out what kind of organization they are operating and managing and what kind of organization they wish to create in the future. If both piecemeal and radical innovations are necessary for organizational survival, finding out successful organizational identities for future innovation is a starting point for organizational innovation (Choo, 1998). In fact, contractual characteristics, mode of conduct, and culture/institutions of organizations are important conduits that lead to the identification of organizational sense making. The intervening variables are no longer central in the model, although they used to be in the economic and other organizational literature (see Figure 5.1).

Therefore, the following propositions are also possible:

> Proposition 2. Organizational sense making is a necessary, albeit not a sufficient, condition of organizational innovation for survival.

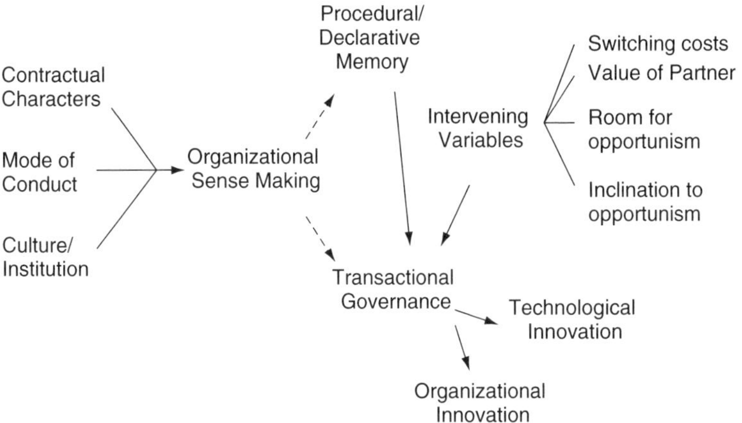

Figure 5.1 Innovation model

Organizational sense making needs a separate study in order to determine its exact learning mechanism, process, and education. Tentatively, for our heuristic purpose, we argue that two ideal types of organizations exist – one that emphasizes procedural memory and the second that stresses declarative memory (Moorman and Miner, 1998; Nonaka, 1990; Winter, 1987). Following the extant studies, we believe that the procedural memory organization will be useful in transferring tacit knowledge (in our case encrypted cultural messages), whereas the declarative memory organization will be beneficial for the transfer of coded knowledge (in our case coded cultural messages). Both memories seem to produce innovation results, although we are not sure which one is better for promoting organizational innovation (i.e., creative destruction).

> Proposition 2a. Two types of organizational sense-making processes occur, either procedural or declarative, to a degree that they are inculcated into memory among organizational participants, and both of them have a significant impact on organizational innovation, as long as the memory procedure involves education (i.e., transfer of knowledge).
>
> Proposition 2b. There is an undeniably strong relationship between organizational sense making and transactional governance, although the exact causal path between the two variables is not known.

If organizational sense making is carried out, corporations will activate the transactional governance system in order to devise better ways of controlling transactional participants, including workers, suppliers, and even foreign business partners. In this sense, organizational sense making can be considered to be a software program that provides the contents to and runs transactional governance. On the other hand, however, the evolution of transactional governance does not necessarily invite either organizational or technological innovations, although it is certainly possible that changes in transactional governance can lead to organizational innovations in the long run. Even then, transactional governance must trigger some sort of technological innovation or vice versa, before organizational innovation can occur at pace with the evolution of transactional governance.

Therefore, our innovation model is incomplete without an analysis of the impact of intervening variables on innovation outcomes.

In previous studies, we found that the chaebol's organizational innovation was a strategic response to the uncertainties of the intervening variables – switching costs, value of the partner, room for opportunism, and inclination to opportunism (Oh, 1999; Oh and Park, 1999, 2001). For the chaebol, the most important external partner in transactional governance was the state and its financial agencies, including the banks. Both the state and the chaebol found the value of all of the intervening variables to be very high, which forced the chaebol to adopt a strategy of diversification – the so-called "too big to fail" myth (Oh, 1999; Oh and Varcin, 2002; see also Chapter 3 of this book). In the remainder of this section, we will further clarify the role of the intervening variables in organizational innovation.

To reiterate, the intervening variables are specific investments, switching costs, value of the partner, room for opportunism, and inclination to opportunism. We think this is the right time to expound on these concepts. Specific investments refer to a firm's financial commitment to employee education. Knowledge can be either tacit or coded, making firms invest substantially high amounts of money in employee training, if knowledge is tacit. A typical example is the Japanese system of "on-the-job" training. Switching costs can increase if specific investments are high, meaning that educational sunk costs make firms shy away from short-term employees. Business partners are in the same category, as the value of the partner changes depending on whether mutual learning requires long or short periods. Room for opportunism is a legal and institutional framework that intends to deter opportunistic behavior, whereas inclination to opportunism is the choice employees or partners make regardless of the institutional framework. Therefore, these intervening variables are specific indicators of the organizational sense-making variables.

Earlier, we operationalized innovation into five categories: (1) transaction cost (transactional innovation); (2) production cost (technological innovation); (3) product differentiation (technological innovation); (4) incremental innovation (technological and transactional innovations); and (5) creative destruction (technological, transactional, and organizational innovations). The significance of these five categories of innovation lies in the degree of knowledge either created or transferred (Nooteboom, 2000). For example, the knowledge needed to reduce transaction costs can either be coded or tacit, whereas the knowledge required to reduce production costs can be often, although not always, coded, as in Fordism. Incremental innovation also occurs as the result of codifyng knowledge that was previously tacit. The most complicated knowledge is the one for creative destruction, which covers technological, transactional, and organizational levels of innovation. Although operationalizing these variables may involve some difficulties, we can at least measure the success of organizational performance and its subsequent survival in terms of these five categories.

A full matrix of organizational sense making variables and intervening variables with regard to these innovation effects can be conceptualized, although it is somewhat complicated. For our purposes, we will compare only the Korean outcome with other representative cases.

The chaebols' innovation system in a comparative perspective

Based on the matrix discussed above, we can discern several types of organizations in terms of their innovation capacities. Among these, four types stand out – American, German, Japanese, and Korean innovation systems (Table 5.1). Although German and Japanese systems differ only with regard to room for opportunism and production cost, these are important differences, since the Japanese system utilizes the just-in-time system with competitive network ties to reduce the room for opportunism and also production costs. Important propositions can be derived from these cases, although they are not our immediate concern at this stage.

The Korean innovation system is based on an organizational sense making that is much more complicated than its Japanese or German counterparts. Looking at the sense-making variables, we notice that Korean chaebol groups have limited legalistic orientation in establishing contractual relationships, a finding that is similar to that observed in Japanese or German types. However, the contract duration is neither short (as in the United States) nor long (as in Germany and Japan). The Korean case reveals a strong tendency toward short contract length in the IT industry and the venture sector, whereas the chaebol sector maintains either long or medium contract lengths.

This means that the Korean mode of contract conduct has a tendency of using the exit option as often as the voice option. Strong union movements in Korea increasingly exhibit the new tendency of relying on voice instead of exit in the mediation of industrial or contractual conflicts.

However, these findings do not mean that the majority of the contractual behavior is voice oriented, because exit continues to play an important role. Therefore, we can assume that the Korean culture is more individualistic than its German or Japanese counterparts as declarative memory is more important than procedural memory in most Korean business organizations. However, this does not mean that procedural memory is neglected, as it plays an important role, especially in making Korean organizations more collectivist than its American counterparts (Park and Ungson, 1997). What Table 5.1 suggests, however, is that successful chaebol groups want to actively utilize, or at least to introduce, short-term contracts with options of exit open to most participants in order to neutralize the effects of mad technology in the same market.

Intervening variables show other interesting differences. As long as exit is an important option for contractual participants, specific investments are medium in Korea, much lower than those of either Germany or Japan, but higher than those of the United States. This automatically means that switching costs and the value of the partner should also be medium in Korea. Room for opportunism is as high as in Germany, because neither are legal institutions as highly developed as those of the United States, nor is there any consensus of lifetime employment or norms of long-term reciprocal relational contracts as in Japan. Since everyone knows that the exit option is very likely to be utilized by participants, inclination toward opportunism is also high in Korea.

Steering a middle course between the US and German (Japanese) extremes gave the chaebols an advantageous stance for producing large quantities of low-quality products. However, it also allowed the chaebol to experiment with product differentiation and still maintain high quality. In mass production sectors, production costs were lower, although they were medium in product differentiation sectors. Transaction costs were medium. Due to legal mechanisms, firms had to establish to control opportunism. We posit that transaction costs in product differentiation sectors were still high. Product differentiation

Table 5.1 International comparison of innovation systems and performance

	United States	*Germany*	*Japan*	*Korea*
Characteristics	Formal, short	Limited, lasting	Limited, lasting	Limited, medium
Mode of conduct	Exit	Voice	Voice	Exit/Voice
Culture/institutions	Individual, large, legal	Groups, networks, group ethic	Same	Individual, groups, large
Specific investments	Low	High	High	Medium
Switching costs	Low	High	High	Medium
Value of the partner	Low	High	High	Medium
Room for opportunism	Low	High	Medium	High
Inclination to opportunism	High	Low	Low	High
Production cost	Low	High	Low	Medium
Transaction cost	High	Low	Low	Medium
Product differentiation	Low	High	High	Medium
Incremental innovation	Low	High	High	Medium
Creative destruction	High	Low	Low	Medium

was in the medium level, like incremental innovation. Most importantly, the Korean system was more effective than its German or Japanese counterparts at introducing creative destruction (i.e., organizational innovation). This was due to the flexibility in making and destroying alliances, new ventures, and cooperation between firms, although their magnitude was lower than the US performance level. The chaebols' ability in manufacturing organizational innovations is clearly a strategic response to mad technology.

The chaebols' innovation system – problems and advantages

Our findings suggest that pursuing a middle course in developing innovation systems (i.e., combining organizational sense making, developing transactional governance, and strategically responding to intervening variables) can be useful in realizing both incremental innovation and creative destruction. Although room for opportunism and the inclination to opportunism were both moderately high, the Korean system could reduce transaction costs in the chairman's office or structural coordination office. By allowing flexibility in organizing and destroying partnerships and ventures (or allowing the adoption of short-term contracts), the chaebol could also induce creative destruction or organizational innovation.

Taking the middle course usually yields the benefits of reducing uncertainties, while still allowing one to enjoy some of the benefits that the two extreme cases can offer. However, the Korean system of innovation may be not good for product differentiation or for any other innovations that require application knowledge, which the Japanese or American systems could maximize. Indeed, the Korean system fails to produce global technological standards or to introduce new application knowledge using existing innovations to the global market (with the exception of some limited cases in the IT industries). In other words, the Korean system may be a good innovation organization for growth economies through medium-level performances in incremental innovation and creative destruction; however, it is not suitable for a leading economy that requires application knowledge or creative destruction. Furthermore, by emphasizing both procedural and declarative memories to the employees, Korean organizations can face the problem of cultural anomie, especially when corporate leaders do not know when to emphasize which type of memories. Finally, the coexistence of exit and voice makes firms unnecessarily strenuous in dealing with the problems of internal labor negotiations, which can often be militant, and of specific investments that are lost due to employee exits.

As we argued in Chapter 3, the NIS of Japan and Korea are becoming more similar to one another than before as a response to the invasion of mad technologies. The Korean PIS can also be seen as becoming similar to its Japanese counterpart. The chaebols are clearly making efforts to reform their innovation strategies in order to resemble more closely those of the Japanese keiretsu groups. This trend indicates, as we also argued previously, that both Japanese and Korean PISs are in fact emulating the American innovation machines that had generated mad technologies in the first place.

Discussion and conclusion

The innovation model introduced in this chapter yielded two interesting results. First, it helped us to recognize the relationship between organizational variables and innovation, while also allowing us to unravel some of the thorny matters involved in the definition of organizational and technological innovations. Secondly, our model offered a partial explanation of why the Korean system of innovation has been successful, and what problems it may encounter in further reforming the system.

Among the remaining issues are the causal relationship between transactional governance and technological (and organizational) innovations. Our purpose in introducing the concept of transactional governance was to trace the patterns of making and dissolving contractual and other business relations with transactional partners. The concept of corporate governance that we could find in the literature of transaction cost economics does not discuss this issue. In the discussion of the Korean chaebols we found that the concept of corporate governance was less important than that of transactional governance. However, the usefulness of the concept did not lead us to any logical conclusion as to whether or not organizational sense making was more important than intervening variables. For now, it appears that the intervening variables are heavily dependent upon how one conceptualizes his or her organizational sense making. If this holds true, then we can devise a simpler model of innovation that excludes intervening variables. However, this is a development that must be left to further case and empirical studies.

In the case of the chaebols, taking a middle course in organizational sense making, by maximizing tolerance to induce the fusion of two different cultures, was a strategic response to the intervening variables. However, by failing to realize the necessity of homogenizing the organizational sense making, the chaebols have faced many problems of labor instability and production inefficiency, resulting in poor levels of organizational innovation. The stalled organizational innovation, especially regarding the role of the chairman's office, is a problem that the chaebols probably can never resolve fully. However, it has been noted in some successful cases of innovation in the IT sector that chaebol groups can emulate both Japanese- and American-style technology management in order to produce genuine breakthroughs. Such advances would strengthen Korea's ability to withstand the threat of mad technology.

6
The Semiconductor Industry in Taiwan

Taiwan's semiconductor industry was the result of carefully orchestrated long-term planning by the government and private firms. It offers an evident example of how the interplay of domestic policy and international supply networks can fend off the encroachment of mad technologies. However, this statement poses three questions that warrant attention from network theorists. First, do small firm networks, such as the family firm networks that exist in Taiwan, despite their limited financial reserves, have hidden network resources that can support risky diversification into semiconductor industries? Secondly, do small firm networks, with severely restricted marketing capabilities, have other network resources that encourage the commercialization of new technologies? Thirdly, if the network resources of Taiwanese family firms have overcome the above two difficulties in innovation and technology commercialization, what are the unique organizational advantages that have made their success possible?

Family firms, or any other small firms based on strong ties, face many difficulties in securing the detailed information that networks of weak ties can easily generate (Granovetter, 1973). This disadvantage, however, can be offset by alliances with other firms based on trust, regional proximity, shared interests, and relational subcontracting (see, inter alia, Hsu and Saxenian, 2000; Lazerson, 1988; Perrow, 1992; Perry, 1999; Sabel, 1992, 1995; Uzzi, 1997). Such structures are labeled domestic policy networks. If domestic policy networks are designed to maximize the utilities of structural holes, family firms can also enhance their information gathering and processing capabilities (Burt, 1992). However, even if trust is obtained by the above organizational contingencies, it is still questionable whether or not small family firms can invest large sums of money in high-technology industries such as the semiconductor industry. This is why we argue that an international supply network is also necessary in such circumstances.

Typical organizational characteristics of the Taiwanese family firms entail difficulties of diversifying financial sources due to their small scale and simple organizational structures (Redding, 1995). Arrow notes that small firms often acquiesce to a sub-optimal scale of development expenditures, because "capital will be available from the outside only on unfavorable terms" (Arrow, 2000). This is the case in part because cross-boundary transmissions of communication always suffer from considerable degradation.

Once a new technology is developed, the next question is: how can it be exploited commercially? In marketing a new product, Taiwanese family firms face the same problem of communication degradation, because they have to market memory chips and display panels through distributors who are neither hierarchically nor horizontally integrated into their firms. A substantial number of integrated circuit (IC) chips are in fact marketed across several different countries, not alleviating the level of uncertainties surrounding product commercialization (Aoyama, 1999).

Existing studies emphasize two institutional mechanisms that have fended off the danger of uncertainties surrounding R&D investments by small family firms in Taiwan, especially when the threat of mad technology was present – policy networks and international networks (see, inter alia, Aoyama, 1999; Asamoto, 1996; Asamoto and Liu, 2001; Chu, 1999; Saxenian, 2000; Wang, 1998). Although policy networks attenuate opportunism among market participants by offering incentives to cooperate, especially between governmental research units and family firms, policy networks can also be found in South Korea and Japan as well, where large firms dominate R&D (for policy networks, see Asamoto, 1996; Chu, 1999; Doner, 1992; Kim, 2000; Wang, 1998). In a similar vein, competing firms in Japan and South Korea, both of which maintain large firms, can straightforwardly replicate the process of forming international networks to reduce commercialization and marketing uncertainties (for international networks, see Aoyama,

1999; Saxenian, 2000). What, then, are the small-firm-specific network mechanisms that render efficient R&D investments and commercialization decisions in the semiconductor sector?

This chapter assumes that organizational structures exert important leverages on firms' decisions on R&D investments. This is Arrow's innovation process model (Arrow, 2000). We, however, want to refine the model by providing organizational evidence relating to why and how small firms can also minimize decisional uncertainties surrounding R&D investments. Briefly, Taiwanese family firms ensure low levels of risk by swapping products and services among themselves in Taiwan on the one hand and with their counterparts in Silicon Valley on the other. The reason for choosing firms in Silicon Valley was due to the location's advanced IT technology, a strategy of blocking the invasion of mad technologies at their source. In addition, many of these Silicon Valley participants were in fact Taiwanese engineers. In combination, these two factors led to the involvement of Taiwanese small firms with their counterparts in Silicon Valley. Networks of this kind maximize the comparative advantage of small firms by minimizing the level of uncertainties. A relational division of labor between firms is a predominant mode of networking among Taiwanese semiconductor producers, while they simultaneously create and exploit structural holes in the networks, on both sides of the Pacific, after a long period of trial and error. These kinds of small firm networks provide each member with information relating to R&D investments, technology transfers (i.e., reducing investment uncertainties), product development, and marketing (i.e., reducing commercialization uncertainties).

In order to substantiate these observations, we will first explain the concept of the relational division of labor, before moving on to the issue of policy and international networks. After the theoretical discussions, we will focus on one leading – albeit not representative – firm in the semiconductor sector (TSMC) in order to illustrate how policy and international networks reduced the uncertainties of mad technologies under the governance structure of small firm networks. The methodological assumption is basically empirical, although no rigorous statistical methods were adopted (in large part because the Taiwanese high-tech sectors are generally closed to foreign researchers). The desire to protect her industry from the scholars of competing countries, especially South Korea, is very strong. The entire analysis of this study is based on interviews, primary and secondary sources, and governmental archives.

Relational interfirm division of labor in the high-tech sector

The interfirm division of labor raises a number of questions as to whether it can be sustained for a considerable period, unless the legal institutionalization of exchanges of goods and services between partner firms is firmly established. When risks are unbearably high due to asset specificities and switching costs, the interfirm division of labor faces untenably expensive transaction costs (Nooteboom, 1999; Williamson, 1985). However, as Piore and Sabel (1984) demonstrated, the interfirm division of labor turns out to be a feasible project, as long as the interfirm division of labor leads to the flexible specialization of core technologies that can develop their own corresponding markets (Aoyama, 1999).

The source of mutual benefit for the interfirm division of labor among closely located firms is reciprocity or relational contracting, where participants constantly promote information sharing and maintain the network through the exchange of goods and services. The entire network is based on the premise that all members shall exchange goods and services with each other, switching the roles of suppliers and buyers in every consecutive round of transactions. This is why the networked division of labor leads to both technological specialization and market creation.

In addition, since a pair of suppliers and buyers constantly exchange goods and services in each round of transactions, demands for further innovation are mutually reinforcing, as long as: (a) supplier–buyer relationships are bound by a perception of strong market potential; (b) long periods of networked cooperation are necessary to fight back or neutralize threats from international competitors or mad technologies of foreign origins; and (c) a leader firm in each network cultivates structural holes in which both domestic and international competitors can participate (Burt, 1992; Smitka, 1991; Uzzi, 1997).

In sum, the interfirm division of labor is complete when the divisibility of technologies into small firm units runs out and the number of surviving small firms is not too few to reduce the total number of structural holes. The interfirm division of labor completes a cycle of innovation, labor supply, production, and market creation through product swapping over a period of time (Aoyama, 1999; Chen, 1994; Sato, 1996; Shieh, 1992, 1993). The consequences of the relational interfirm division of labor are the flexible specialization of the in-house task structures, which are fine-tuned to the changing environment and financial sources; the reduction of initial investment costs; rapid cycles of innovation and product commercialization; and the minimization of redundant network ties (i.e., small size).

Although the relational interfirm division of labor theoretically allows small firms to diversify into high-technology and knowledge-based industries, it still falls short of explaining how these small firm networks can become efficient in obtaining external financing and can eventually be successful in innovation and commercialization. Placing a firm in an environment in which the demand for innovation is constantly high is not always congruous with actual success in innovation, the securing of external financing, and commercial success. The networked division of labor is therefore a necessary condition, rather than being a sufficient one. Although environmental uncertainties are drastically reduced in the networked division of labor, other institutional incentives, must also play a role in securing external loan packages that are often large, especially in the case of setting up foundry factories for IC chip production.

A typical institutional arrangement for a large-scale IT investment is a policy network linking public sector agencies and private sector firms. Here, we need to explain how small firms institutionalize policy networks that are significantly different from their counterparts in the markets dominated by large corporations. In Chapter 3, we noticed that significant differences in policy networks existed between Japan, South Korea, and Taiwan. Japan had a typical dual structure market of big firms with small suppliers – the keiretsu. By contrast, Korea had a single market characterized by big firm domination – the chaebol. Taiwan maintained a dual market of large-scale public corporations and small-scale family firms – the guanxiqiye. In contrast to Korea and Japan, Taiwanese family firms do not enjoy a resource pool that is large enough to lobby the government or to set up their own R&D labs geared to generate innovations for import substitution and subsequent exports. The intention of the government to intervene in this innovation process model, thus, seems much more apparent in Taiwan than it is in Japan or Korea (Chu, 1999; Wade, 1990).

However, the Taiwanese government surprisingly took a noninterventionist attitude vis-à-vis the local industries organized and run by indigenous Taiwanese capitalists, for reasons of national security and separatist policy directives (Chu, 1999; Orrù, 1997; Wade, 1990; Wang, 1998). Indeed, this institutional obstacle worked against the development of high-technology industries, such as the automobile, because no policy network provided local car assemblers with incentives for developing automobile engine technologies. This is in stark contrast to its Korean and Japanese counterparts, where indigenous car industries not only replaced foreign imports in the domestic market but also obtained large market shares in North America, Europe, and Asia (Doner, 1992).

The lesson to be drawn from the failure of the Taiwanese automobile industry was the necessity of instigating appropriate policy networks, which are suitable for the small firms that are common throughout the country. The creation of the National Science Council, Hsinchu Science-based Industrial Park (HSIP), Industrial Technology Research Institute (ITRI), and Electronics Research and Services Organization (ERSO) was intended to promote competition, rather than to impose heavy market regulation (Aoyama, 1999; Chang and Hsu, 1998; Chang et al., 1999; Mathews, 1998). Therefore, redundant networking was common as a result of the low barriers to market entry. Since the government has discouraged R&D investments by private firms in semiconductor technologies, the ERSO could exercise enormous power over these networks of small firms – leading to greater benefit from structural holes than any other governmental organizations in the policy networks could enjoy.

Once decisional uncertainties with respect to R&D investments had disappeared at the firm level, it was a straightforward process to group production facilities on the basis of relational interfirm division of labor between small firms on the one hand and between the firms and the ERSO on the other (Aoyama, 1999; Chang and Hsu, 1998; Chu, 1999). The relationship between the ERSO and the firms was based strictly on technological spin-offs and manpower transfers – two important elements in the Taiwanese venture firms that we will consider further in subsequent sections. Thus, for example, major semiconductor firms in Hsinchu are joint ventures between the ERSO and private investors (ERSO, 1999; ITRI, 1998).

Although R&D investment and technology spin-off decisions were under the control of the ERSO, firms' initial commitment to facilities investments remained uncertain. Over the years, family firms have diversified their financing sources, eventually moving away from the parochial and often uncertain tradition of extended family financing. The catalyst for changes, particularly in the high-tech and information technology industries, was the wave of venture capital firms based around the Chinese-American communities that began to invest in Taiwanese financial markets. The policy network in Taiwan swiftly introduced tax breaks for venture capital firms (Chang, 1999; Saxenian, 2000). Dramatic increases in the number of venture capital firms in Taiwan were witnessed during the latter half of the 1990s, repeatedly signaling the Taiwanese characteristic of innovation by individuals, rather than by the government. In addition, the traditional ties with the Japanese multinational corporations continued. However, the encroachment of international venture capital firms was carefully regulated and incorporated into the greater innovation network in Taiwan, as most of the firms were owned by Taiwanese living in the Silicon Valley area.

The complete picture of the Taiwanese relational, interfirm division of labor includes a multitude of actors and institutions. First, small firms, experiencing stiff competition from both domestic and overseas suppliers, break down the entire production task structure to small, discrete tasks. This is to reduce set-up and overhead costs and to enhance reciprocity with other members of the network. These firms exchange markets as buyers and suppliers to motivate each other toward innovation. Secondly, the government reduces uncertainties with respect to R&D and technology spin-off (commercialization) decisions for these firms by establishing national and centralized research institutes that are also in stiff competition with international suppliers of technological innovation. These government labs are strategically placed near the small firm networks. Thirdly, venture capitalists provide funds to the small firms, on the condition that they are linked with both their customers and the government agencies through trust-based networks, which offer substantial incentive opportunities. Finally, industrial associations, such as the Taiwan Semiconductor Industry Association, provide an institutional arena in which all participants concerned with the relational interfirm division of labor can share fine-tuned and detailed information. In combination, these dense networks of firms, labs, and overseas investors continuously strengthen the level of trust among the network participants.

International division of labor in the high-tech sector

The international division of labor between Taiwanese small firms and their counterparts in Silicon Valley has the following components: (1) task specialization and an international division of labor; (2) market swapping with a myriad of structural holes; and (3) international policy networks with transnational capacities. Although we have already explained them in the preceding section, these components require further examination, especially in the international context.

First, task specialization and the international division of labor involve wholesale technology transfers. Traditionally, cooperation between Taiwanese family firms and Japanese multinationals in the labor-intensive sectors has involved an unequal relationship of power (Bernard and Ravenhill, 1995; Hatch and Yamamura, 1996). Transfers of technology from larger firms in Japan to smaller firms in Taiwan depended upon the needs of the Japanese marketing priorities and rarely addressed the needs of Taiwanese firms that were striving to achieve innovation in order to catch up with the foreign multinationals. Even when technologies were transferred, they were done so on a piecemeal and/or "need-to-know" basis.

The picture changes dramatically when a couple of small firms interact together on a common ground of swapping goods and services. Indeed, in the international division of labor with small firms in Silicon Valley, two important environmental changes occurred – (1) sophisticated technologies were shared by thousands of small firms in Silicon Valley, easing the access to new technologies for Taiwanese firms; and (2) many of these firms were in fact owned by Taiwanese living in the United States (Saxenian, 2000). Instead of being the disastrous effects of mad technologies, these two conditions augur similar or equal relationships of power between Taiwanese and Silicon Valley firms in terms of transactional relations, assuring widespread technology transfers. However, we need additional explanations to be able to assert this.

Albeit sophisticated in their own right, the technologies possessed by these small firms would have little commercial benefit unless they were combined with other production processes and technologies. The division of labor looms large in this process. For example, a Silicon Valley firm that produces IC chips would not generate much value, unless they were able to obtain supply contracts with other small firms that produce components such as motherboards, modems, sound cards and scanners. Similarly, a modem-producing firm cannot survive in the market without having a long-term relationship with a company producing IC chips. It is clear that within this sector technologies are specialized, and their scales are reduced, all for the purpose of innovation, however, they cannot survive without a certain degree of interdependency (Hsu and Saxenian, 2000; Saxenian, 2000).

Why would firms enter into an international division of labor? The international division of labor among small firms in high-tech industries has a number of objectives, such as market creation (i.e., goods and services swapping on a global level), technology transfers, cost reduction, and the shortening of product cycles. Among these, we argue that the shortening of product cycles is the most important outcome. As was mentioned above, the survival of small firms depends upon their capacity to respond flexibly to changing demands in the market (i.e., short product cycles). Small firms in the information and technology intensive sectors increasingly feel the need to share innovation with others in the same sector (see Chapter 3). Briefly, new knowledge cannot automatically generate its own value without first circulating in the market, especially among the competitors (Yoneyama, 2000b). Innovators realize that end-users in the market sometimes understand more about the potential of new technologies than do the inventors themselves. The more widely new technology is circulated in the market, the better the chance of commercialization, eventually shortening the product cycle of the technology. In an era of short product cycles, the end-users of a new technology are often international firms that strive to shorten the cycle even further.

Since the overseas Chinese, who run small firms in Silicon Valley, have already compartmentalized their technological specialty and production lines, they would normally search for alliance partners in Taiwan, where small firms have also compartmentalized their core technologies. This, however, is done only through a multitude of networked interdependence, which involves a network of overseas

Chinese associations in Silicon Valley, venture capital firms on both sides of the Pacific, and the policy networks in Taiwan.

Secondly, the relational international division of labor requires a guarantee of market creation, given that small firms on both sides of the Pacific establish a smooth interdependent relationship as a result of their technological compartmentalization and a seamless fusion of two or more technologies in a loosely networked mode of production. Although product swapping in a domestic market may work as an important means of market creation over a long period of time, this may not hold true for the international market. An important additional condition is the existence of industrial leaders in the strongest markets, who can combine all of the swapped products into a final commercial unit for mass consumption – examples include Microsoft for software products and IBM for hardware equipment. One comparative advantage for Taiwan is the ongoing interdependence between overseas Chinese firms in Silicon Valley and the US market leaders. OEM (Original Equipment Manufacturing) and ODM (Original Design Manufacturing), thus, are two dominant means of trade in Taiwan, whereas OBM (Original Brand Manufacturing) is prevalent in Japan and Korea.

International market swapping in the IT (information technology) sector through OEM or ODM also involves many small firms in the United States. Most small firms in Silicon Valley are closely interdependent and rely on larger firms to market their products. In fact, Taiwanese small firms supply more parts to these small firms in Silicon Valley than to the giant finishers in the United States. In turn, these Silicon Valley firms provide their Taiwanese trade partners with finished products and new technologies. An important distinction to be made here is that small firms in the Silicon Valley import finished Taiwanese products with their own brand names (i.e., OBM), which will then be installed on a larger IT machine that bears a US brand name (OEM and ODM). Thus, the size of market-swapping partners sometimes determines the type of interdependence that exists between them. This is also true in the case of small Japanese and Korean venture IT firms that supply finished products to US finishers who will then use their own original brand labels, although, in contrast to their Taiwanese counterparts, these Korean and Japanese small firms are not invited to participate in the national policy network or the NIS.

Thirdly, policy networks usually manage human resources and information sharing within the marketplace. There are three groups of Taiwanese talent in the trans-Pacific network of high-tech industries: (1) those who permanently stay in Silicon Valley and run small firms, high-tech firms, or private R&D institutes; (2) those who have moved back permanently to the mother island and opened up IT venture firms in association with the ERSO; and (3) those who travel back and forth across the Pacific to bridge the gap between Silicon Valley and Taiwan (Saxenian, 2000). The Taiwanese who are residents in Silicon Valley have formed several professional associations of their own, which are closely related to the policy network in Taiwan. These include the Chinese-American Semiconductor Professional Association and the North American Taiwanese Engineers Association, which have played a significant role in setting up the HSIP, the ITRI, and the ERSO. The Monte Jade Science and Technology Association (MJTA), founded in 1989, focuses on sending Taiwanese scientists and engineers to the HSIP and the ERSO, illustrating the formal institutionalization of the transpacific Taiwanese policy networks. Although formal sources deny such a role and the funding by the Taiwanese government, informal sources all confirm that close ties exist between the government and the MJTA (Saxenian, 2000). The number of Taiwanese professionals recruited by the HSIP firms and R&D labs in 1997 was ten times larger than the figure for 1989, the year in which the MJTA was founded (Aoyama, 1999; Saxenian, 2000).

When they move back to Taiwan, these professionals usually do one of two things – work for labs or open up a venture firm. Manpower transfers from the ITRI/ERSO to IT venture firms resemble the Japanese-style *amakudari* (literally, "descending from heaven," but meaning a substantial retirement package for high-ranking bureaucrats). However, former scientists of the ERSO, in contrast to the retired Japanese bureaucrats, carry advanced scientific and research knowledge with them when they commence new jobs (usually, as chief technology officers) at thriving venture firms such as TSMC. For example, the former ITRI chairman, Chang Zhong Mo, moved to TSMC, the biggest semiconductor company in Taiwan; and, similarly, Tsao Hsing Chung (Robert Tsao), former vice chairman of the ERSO, took the chairman's position at UMC, the second biggest firm in Taiwan (Aoyama, 1999). Many similar cases could also be cited.

The most important "go-between" group is the venture capital firm. Of course, those at other subgroups in the Taiwanese international policy networks travel trans-Pacific all the time, as in the case of the famous National Development Conference, annually hosted by the Ministry of Economic Affairs to maintain global Chinese connections. Yet, it is the venture capital firms that maintain business bases on both sides of the Pacific. As we explained earlier, the handshake between the trans-Pacific venture firms and the Ministry of Finance, which offered tax breaks, finalized the Taiwanese international policy network and the institutionalization of the semiconductor industry in the HSIP. All of the venture capital firms that invest money in high-tech industries in Taiwan receive tax breaks on 25 percent of total investments for five years (Saxenian, 2000). The go-betweens provided resources for the Taiwanese family firms, so that they could address the issue of building export-oriented IT industries in Taiwan.

The Taiwanese international division of labor strengthens trans-Pacific technology transfers, the international reciprocity of market creation through product swapping, and reverse brain drain and cash inflow in the form of venture capital from the United States to Taiwan. All of these were made possible by the fact that firms involved in the international division of labor were small in size, networked under ethnic and national commonalities, and guided and financed by government agencies. Therefore, the Taiwanese mode of innovation is "smallness and international networking first," a rare phenomenon in the literature of the East Asian models of development (O'Riain, 1999).

A small-firm model of innovation and commercialization

Two axes of efficiency in the Taiwanese mode of innovation are, on the one hand, the relational interfirm division of labor in the domestic market and, on the other hand, the international market. The huge network of small firms in Taiwan is connected to the similarly large small firms' network in Silicon Valley, all very rich in structural holes. In Burt's words, entrepreneurs are those who succeed in linking two similar, yet conflictual, networks together – i.e., the *tertius* (Burt, 2000). Taiwan's small firm model of innovation and commercialization offers a close fit to Burt's definition of entrepreneurship, although we don't know who the *tertius* was. We can merely conjecture that the Taiwanese *tertius* were the first Taiwanese students who went to the United States to pursue advanced degrees in engineering.

Why the linkage was possible and who made it possible are important questions with which we have to deal later in a separate analysis. For now, we will confine ourselves to an explanation of why this linkage was efficient. Based on the lengthy discussion on the HSIP and Silicon Valley networks, we find some new insights on innovation that are not always congruous with Arrow's innovation process model (Arrow, 2000). The model basically assumes that the firm size is critical in determining the outcome of innovation results, a premise that we also adopted in this chapter. The most significant difference between the multidivisional firms and small firm networks in general is that "large firms will have a disproportionately larger and more stable internal capital supply than smaller firms will" (Arrow, 2000).

In addition, small firms will suffer from a sub-optimal level of R&D investments, although they will be, simultaneously, well aware of the development possibility function – i.e., the function used to calculate the expected profitability for any given level of development expenditure (Arrow, 2000). This is mainly because of the degradation of information that occurs when funding is sought from outside the firm, although the development possibility function is better understood in small firms than it is in larger ones. Therefore, small firms will exceed the achievements of large firms only in a market where development expenditures are relatively small and research projects are novel in content.

Since research results determine development expenditures, small firms tend to undertake a line of research in which results will optimally involve much larger development expenditures than it is prepared to undertake. This is because no one can be sure that research results – which often require huge development expenditures – will be commercially valuable. Given the restriction on R&D funding among small firms, they usually abandon such research altogether or downsize development plans to a scale that is much smaller than the optimal level.

In contrast to Arrow's innovation process model, however, the disadvantages of small firms in financing R&D disappear when two conflictual networks of shared interests are combined through a *tertius*. In the case of the HSIP the *tertius* was the ITRI/ERSO that linked together the two networks of engineers in Taiwan and Silicon Valley. Funds for joint ventures came from both government banks and private investors. Once the success of joint ventures of this kind became apparent, more private investors rushed to the HSIP for further networked division of labor (Aoyama, 1999; Chang and Hsu, 1998; Saxenian, 2000).

As Figure 6.1 shows, the small firm model of innovation process involves an evolution of networks. During the inception of the semiconductor industry in Taiwan (1975–79), the network had three participants – the ERSO, Taiwanese engineers, and RCA (along with Taiwanese engineers in the United States). The ERSO operated as a broker, connecting the linkages between RCA and Taiwanese engineers in order to transfer technologies from the United States. The network was very simple and tightly connected, with no structural holes. The second phase of network evolution (1979–83) incorporated the first Taiwanese semiconductor firm (UMC), a commercial spin-off from the ERSO. Even during this phase, the network between UMC, ERSO, and Taiwanese engineers in America was simple and tightly connected, with few structural holes. The third period of network evolution (1983–88) succeeded in creating structural holes, because Taiwanese firms in Silicon Valley joined Taiwanese firms in the HSIP through the ERSO. This period marked the completion of the model of innovation process for Taiwanese small firms.

The third stage of network evolution greatly increased efficiency through creating structural holes, which the ERSO could exploit in its effort to sustain optimal levels of developmental expenditures. However, size is always a mixed blessing (Burt, 2000). Engineers and semiconductor firms are still connected to the ERSO in the HSIP and Taiwanese-owned firms and engineer associations in Silicon Valley are still connected to the ERSO. The biggest change over the years was the initiation taken by small firms in the HSIP to solicit technology transfers from Philips and Mitsubishi that are not related to the ERSO. In addition, venture capital firms in the United States and Taiwan participated in this network, although they are still linked to the ERSO.

Therefore, we can deduce that the ERSO took innovative actions when it linked the two separate networks in the United States and Taiwan, whereas it is now the small firms in the HSIP that are taking

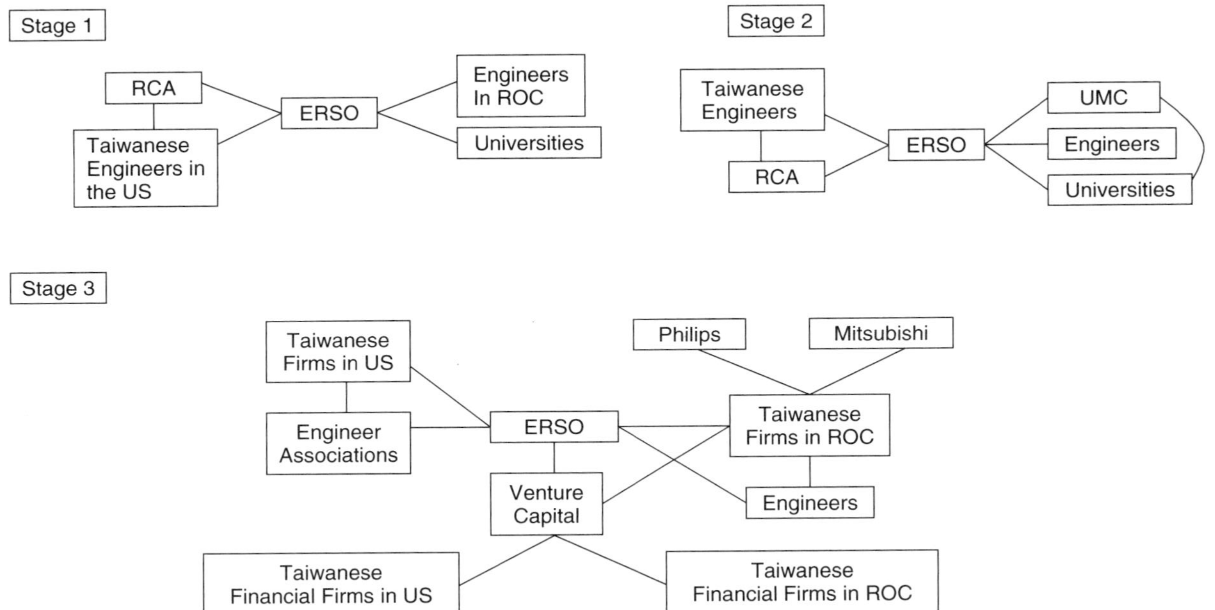

Figure 6.1 The stages of network evolution in the Taiwanese semiconductor industry

more innovative actions by linking their networks to such external companies as Philips, Mitsubishi, and venture capital firms. We can anticipate that a fourth form of network evolution will be possible, in which the role of the ERSO will be assumed by leading Taiwanese firms in the HSIP that will maintain the connection with their American partners in addition to their networks with venture capital firms and multinational leaders in technologies.

The case of TSMC

Taiwanese high-tech companies demonstrate clearly that small firms with limited financial and marketing capabilities can overcome these difficulties through creating and enhancing dense networks of firms, labs, and overseas investors. In contrast to the arguments presented by Arrow's model, Taiwanese small firms manifest the possibility of successful innovation and commercialization, despite their disadvantageous size. The case of Taiwan Semiconductor Manufacturing Company, Ltd. (TSMC), the most successful high-tech company in Taiwan, provides empirical evidence of such phenomena.

TSMC was founded in 1987 as the ITRI's technology spin-off. TSMC started as a joint-venture firm, with 30 percent of its total investment originating from Philips, and is now the largest semiconductor manufacturing firm in Taiwan (Aoyama, 1999). TSMC focuses on foundry services (that is, wafer production), while maintaining the relational interfirm division of labor with Taiwanese small firms and multinational firms in North America, Japan, and Europe.

A typical domestic division of labor within a foundry involves the following processes: IC design, photo masking, wafer production, wafer probing, IC assembly, IC testing, and IC packaging. TSMC specializes in photo masking, wafer production, and wafer probing, while designing, assembling, testing, and packaging processes are outsourced under the principle of relational interfirm division of labor. For example, Global UniChip and Goya maintain strategic alliances with TSMC for design and ASE for IC assembly and testing (Aoyama, 1999; TSMC, 2002). As shown in Figure 6.2, TSMC achieved a central position in the market by linking up important manufacturing units that were densely networked with other small firms (i.e., rich structural holes).

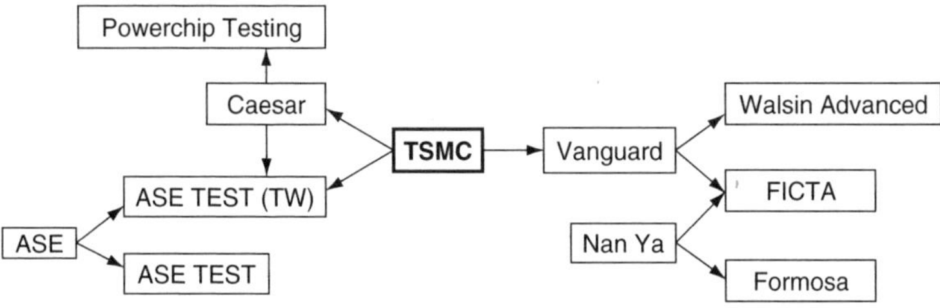

Figure 6.2 TSMC's network with structural holes

TSMC established "Virtual Fab," a networked division of labor between TSMC and its customers. Virtual Fab allows small firms with new IC designs to have access to TSMC's flexible foundry service without the requirement of investing large sums of money in developing their own foundry fabs (i.e., virtual fab). TSMC's comparatively small size also makes it possible to produce wafers that meet customers' new design needs, an advantage that is not easily replicable by large foundry service providers (TSMC, 2002). TSMC's customers fall into three main categories: fabless semiconductor companies, integrated device manufacturers, and system companies.

The key to the success of TSMC depended to a large extent on the speed of product delivery and the creation of newly designed IC chips for the upgraded versions of integrated products. Consequently, product cycles have to be shortened in order for TSMC to be competitive in the market. Information sharing in Virtual Fab was accelerated in part due to the weak ties prevalent among partners in the network. Since task specialization was so clear between network members, information sharing toward innovation resulted in mutual benefit rather than mutual destruction. In fact, at the TSMC headquarters in Hsinchu, it is not uncommon to meet engineers of customer firms working closely with TSMC engineers. Furthermore, TSMC engineers are often seconded to customer firms in Silicon Valley for substantial periods (Saxenian, 2000).

In addition to technology transfers and information sharing toward innovation, manpower shifts across the Pacific have been common at TSMC. For example, the chairman of the company, Morris Chang, moved from the ITRI to assume its current position. Furthermore, vice president Steve Tso came from AMD, a leading Silicon Valley firm that specializes in foundry materials. These human resource networks lead to networked cooperation between TSMC and the ITRI/ERSO on the one hand and between TSMC and AMD on the other. These two people thus served as the *tertius*, linking the two networks.

TSMC receives financing from a wide range of sources. In addition to Philips, the Taiwanese government (via administrative development fund) invested 48.3 percent of total capital in the company at the time of inception. The government later sold its shares to private investors, reducing its stake to 23 percent in 1998. Although it faced enormous difficulty in soliciting investments from venture capital firms and other private investors during the 1980s, TSMC's success, along with other semiconductor firms that were also spun off from the ITRI/ERSO network, reversed the situation dramatically. Both domestic and international venture capital firms are now significant investors in the company (Aoyama, 1999). Thus, it is clear that the role that finance officers played in bringing external investors into TSMC's network was pivotal.

Innovation records at TSMC have been remarkable. Organizational innovations include the creation of Virtual Fab and the Design Center Alliance. If Virtual Fab is concerned with the cooperation with customers and their local production networks, the Design Center Alliance focuses on cooperation with producers. TSMC's Design Center Alliance is a global affiliation of qualified IC design centers, which include 26 companies, employing more than 2,500 people. They are dedicated to creating and verifying real product designs in TSMC silicon (TSMC, 2002).

Technological innovations include the commercialization of the industry's first 0.13 μm mixed-signal production process in 2001, along with the 0.15 μm technology in 2000, the 0.18 μm technology in 1999, and the 0.25 μm technology in 1998. In addition, the company also retains BiCMOS technologies (TSMC, 2002). As was predicted, the product cycle was very short; less than a year in R&D and about a year in commercialization. The record of R&D and commercialization thus did not fall behind its competitors of big firms in other parts of the world. As a result of these advances, at the time of writing TSMC is the largest foundry service provider in the world.

Conclusion

This chapter attempted to clarify why small firms can be successful in technology-intensive industries such as semiconductor (IC chip) production. Using the case of TSMC in Taiwan, we provided evidence of innovative efficiency among small firms in the semiconductor sector, despite the encroachment of global mad technologies. Arrow's innovation process model was refined to indicate how small firms could also ameliorate the problem of overcoming sub-optimal developmental expenditures due to information degradation in the process of acquiring external funding.

In this process, relational interfirm division of labor in the domestic and global markets appeared to be central to the explanation of the innovative efficiency of these firms in Taiwan. Relational interfirm division of labor was possible in Taiwan because of their compatibility in size with firms in Silicon Valley. The effects of the networked division of labor were: an increased volume of information exchange with little degradation, increased accuracy in the development possibility function, and increased chances of securing funding and manpower for large projects that could otherwise be deemed inappropriate for small firms.

Future studies of the innovation capacity of small firms in the high-tech sectors can focus on actual entrepreneurs who take innovative actions when there are more structural holes in a network to be exploited. This concept of innovators as people who make new networks by linking two or more conflictual networks of non-proximity has turned out to be extremely useful in explaining the success of the Taiwanese semiconductor industry, a sector dominated by small firms.

7
Japan's Commercialization Problem

In the preceding chapters, we saw how some Korean and Taiwanese firms overcame the threats of global mad technologies and succeeded in developing and commercializing new technologies. In this chapter, we want to consider why Japanese corporations are experiencing commercialization problems and what can be done to change this situation.

Although Japanese companies have invested aggressively in R&D and, as a result, have amassed abundant technological knowledge, they are now facing a serious and unanticipated, problem. Japanese corporations have a poor record in the commercial exploitation of new technology. A considerable amount of technological knowledge that Japanese corporations have created in the past remains unexploited, a clear signal that their technological potentials do not bear as much fruit as might be expected. The purpose of this chapter is to explore why new technologies become dormant during this era of flourishing mad technologies, and how companies can overcome the problem in order to facilitate the process of new technology commercialization in the Japanese context.

Although there are several reasons why companies fail in technology commercialization (discussed, inter alia, in Bower and Christensen, 1995; Christensen, 1997; Cohen et al., 1979; Eldred and McGrath, 1997; Iansiti, 1998; Mueller, 1963; Prasad, 1997; Quinn et al., 1996; Wood and Brown, 1998; Yoneyama, 1999, 2000a), we approach the problem from the perspective of knowledge integration capabilities. This perspective holds that new knowledge must be combined with complementary technologies and market knowledge in order to generate profits through commercialization (Eldred and McGrath, 1997; Harryson, 1997; Iansiti, 1998; Leonard-Barton and Doyle, 1996; Teece, 1986; Tripsas, 2000). It is known that capabilities of knowledge integration exert considerable leverage on successful technology commercialization, especially when products and services are complex and systemic (such as in the development of digital home appliances).

Traditionally, Japanese keiretsu group firms had demonstrated a salient organizational advantage in generating profits through technological innovation and commercialization. The source of the organizational strength in delivering innovation and commercialization was the rich complementary asset (Teece, 1986). However, the decade-long high dormancy ratio implies that there is a lack of knowledge integration capabilities within Japanese corporations, as they were often criticized for generating low profits. Our purpose is to show that this problem can be offset by appropriate integration capabilities.

A survey of 59 Japanese corporations ascertains that knowledge integration capabilities underpin the success of the process of technology commercialization. The visibility of knowledge and the organizational mechanisms are two factors that boost knowledge integration. The process of integration involves two step: (1) locating usable knowledge within an organization; and (2) establishing new organizational mechanisms for integrating existing knowledge. We also find that these two steps of integration lead to enhanced corporate performance.

In this chapter, we first offer a brief sketch of the current position of Japanese R&D and clarify the gap between the active creation of technological knowledge and the corporate performance of Japanese companies. Next, we consider why the gap came into being and why the enormous potential of technological knowledge has remained unexploited, all using the concept of knowledge integration capabilities of a firm. The second half of this chapter offers a survey analysis of 59 Japanese corporations, through which we address the importance of the integration capabilities in enhancing corporate performance.

R&D activity and corporate performance

As shown in Figure 7.1, in recent years Japanese companies have invested aggressively in R&D, the total expenditure having increased about sixfold in the period from 1975 to 1996, with a temporary

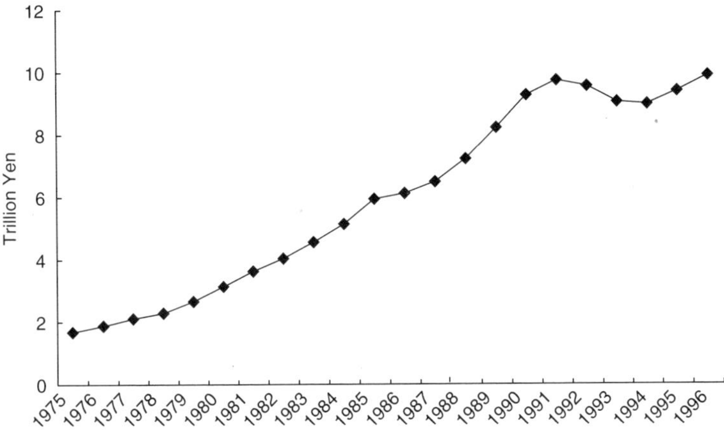

Figure 7.1 R&D investment of Japanese companies
Source: Kagaku Gijutsu Chô (1998).

setback from the bursting of the bubble. The ten trillion yen figure recorded in 1996 is almost the same as total US expenditure on private R&D, and is about twice the level of German national R&D expenditures (Kagaku Gijutsu Chô, 1998).

As discussed in Chapter 3, Japanese NIS maintained a strong commitment to private R&D, as Japanese companies had actively created new pieces of technological knowledge (Mowery and Teece, 1993; National Science Foundation, 1988; Pavitt and Patel, 1988). In 1998 alone, more than 400,000 patents were applied and about 150,000 were registered, of which about 80 percent were possessed by Japanese companies (Tokkyo Chô, 2000). Similar phenomena can be observed in global patent markets. Table 7.1 shows how Japanese companies fared in the acquisition of patents in the US market. In 1996 alone, eight of the top ten companies with the most number of patents in the United States were Japanese companies: Canon, NEC, Hitachi, Mitsubishi Electric, Toshiba, Fujitsu, Sony, and Matsushita Electric.

Figure 7.2 summarizes the trend of the total number of patents that Japanese private companies, universities, government research institutes, and individuals have received from overseas patenting authorities in recent years. Taking into consideration that about

Table 7.1 Top 10 patenting organizations in the United States

Rank	*Number of patents*	*Organization*
1	1,867	IBM
2	1,541	Canon
3	1,064	Motorola
4	1,043	NEC
5	963	Hitachi
6	934	Mitsubishi Denki
7	923	US government
8	914	Toshiba
9	869	Fujitsu
10	855	Sony

Source: United States Patents and Trademark Office (2002).

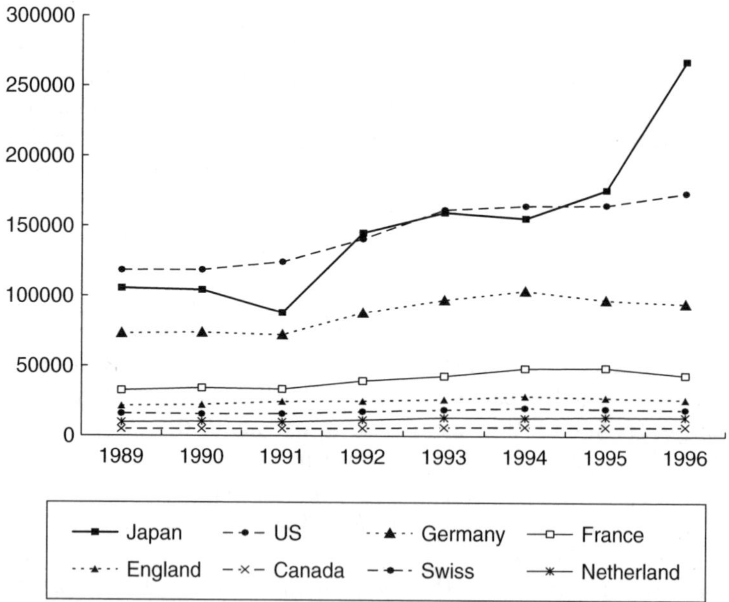

Figure 7.2 International comparison of patent rights
Source: Tokkyo Chô (1990–97).

95 percent of all Japanese patents belong to private companies, we can see how rich Japanese companies are in terms of technological assets (Tokkyo Chô, 2000). The numerical success of Japanese corporations in obtaining patents in the global market, however, did not come at the sacrifice of quality. For example, as highlighted by Narin and Frame (1989), based on the patent citation data in the United States, the quality of Japanese patents was much higher than statistically expected.

Japanese companies are clearly global leaders as far as technological innovation is concerned. The problem, however, is that a considerable amount of this knowledge remains unutilized. According to research conducted by the Commission on Intellectual Property Rights in the 21st Century, only 33 percent of all technology patents are put to any practical use (The Commission on Intellectual Property Rights in the Twenty-first Century, 1997; Kagaku Gijutsu Chô, 1998). Of the unutilized 67 percent of all patents, as much as 44 percent are reported to have little prospect of ever being used, and the rest are viewed as being retained as defensive patents or for future implementation. This tendency shows that companies with rich technological knowledge do not necessarily achieve high levels of corporate performance. Table 7.2 illustrates that there is little correlation between the number of patents and sales growth or operating profit growth, although there is a positive correlation between R&D expenditures and the number of patents obtained by different industries (Yoneyama, 2000a).

Table 7.2 Knowledge creation and corporate performance

	n	*R&D/ Patent*	*Patent/ operational profit*	*Patent/ sales growth*
Electronics	46	0.337*	0.129	0.205
Precise machinery	31	0.472**	0.204	0.224
General machinery	41	0.338*	0.224	0.140
Steel	14	0.530***	0.039	0.177
Pharmaceutical	34	0.249	0.162	0.140
Chemistry	45	0.530**	0.108	0.054

** = $p < 0.01$, * = $p < 0.05$, *** = $p < 0.1$

Since it is very difficult to locate comparable international data about dormancy ratios, we have used international corporate performance data for the dependent variable. Our premise is that new technology commercialization has a high correlation with corporate performance. It is theoretically possible to argue that even a small decrease in the dormancy ratio would generate a considerable increase in corporate performance.

Technology commercialization and knowledge integration capabilities

Many studies have addressed the problem of why companies often fail to commercialize new technologies and how they can overcome the dormancy problem (see, inter alia, Bower and Christensen, 1995; Christensen, 1997; Cohen et al., 1979; Eldred and McGrath, 1997; Iansiti, 1998; Leonard-Barton and Doyle, 1996; Nevens et al., 1990; Prasad, 1997; Quinn and Mueller, 1963; Wood and Brown, 1998; Yoneyama, 1999, 2000b). Quinn and Mueller (1963), for example, emphasized the failure of coordination between research and development organizations (see also Cohen et al., 1979; Eldred and McGrath, 1997; Prasad, 1997; Wood and Brown, 1998). Communication between research and development centers is often discouraged, due to their dissimilar short-term objectives, different sense of time and cost in project works, and the varying degree of predictability (Wood and Brown, 1998). Informal means of communication and bonding were believed to help organizations to establish a clear common goal and to synchronize inter-group tasks (Cohen et al., 1979; Eldred and McGrath, 1997). In addition, the rotation of researchers and engineers at regular intervals with a concurrent use of IT tools eliminates communication barriers (Geisler and Kassicieh, 1997; Harryson, 1997; Prasad, 1997).

Bower and Christensen (1995) and Christensen (1997), however, approach the problem from a different point of view. They attribute the failure of the technology commercialization process to one of the most popular of the recent management dogmas: stay close to the customer. New technologies, especially the most disruptive ones, which introduce a very different set of attributes from those that customers usually expect, will often perform far worse than conventional commodities. As a rule, mainstream customers are unwilling to use products that utilize disruptive technologies (Bower and Christensen, 1995). In addition, since the commercialization of new technologies involves creating a new organizational mechanism that is significantly different from the conventional one, the rule of "stay close to the customer" will also discourage commercialization.

Another approach pays attention to the interpretive flexibility of technology (see, for example, Yoneyama, 2000b; Yoneyama and Kato, 2002). As technology is equivocal (Weick, 1990), and it is an artifact with interpretive flexibility by its own nature, the future orientation of its application cannot be determined *ex ante* (MacLoughlin, 1999; Pinch and Bijker, 1987; Yoneyama, 1999). Even if companies aim at a certain application field at the starting point of the commercialization of new technology, this field is not necessarily the final destination. It is often the case that technology is more successfully introduced to an unexpected field (Jewkes, 1969; Ohkouchi, 1992; Quinn, 1985). In this sense, technology commercialization is the process of exploring an appropriate application field that is inherently indeterminate in the beginning. As we mentioned in Chapter 2, this is one critical indicator of mad technologies. From such a multidirectional view, Yoneyama and Kato (2002) argue that determining an application field in the early stage of the commercialization process can spoil the potential of a new technology. Companies are encouraged to learn a new technology's opportunities and threats through exposing it to the public and/or implementing it experimentally into different applications.

There is no doubt that all of these studies offer some insight to Japanese companies aiming to manage the complicated process of technology commercialization. However, we need also to consider other factors, including the knowledge integration capability of a company. This is because technology does not work in isolation – it works in conjunction with other technologies. Technologies create value only as integrated systems (Iansiti, 1998). Therefore, the successful commercialization of a technology needs certain complementary technologies, ensuring effective integration between them. In addition to these complementary technologies, relevant market knowledge and information also need to be integrated. Leonard-Barton and Doyle (1996) point to the importance of linking an adequate understanding of user needs to technologies in order to achieve the successful commercialization of technology (also Quinn and Mueller, 1963).

According to these arguments, successful commercial exploitation largely depends upon the existence of complementary technologies and market knowledge and, more importantly, the capabilities to integrate all of the knowledge a company possesses to achieve the commercialization of new technologies.

The notion of technological complementarity provides many useful insights when assessing Japanese keiretsu firms that possess a great variety of technological and market-related knowledge. These firms are endowed with rich complementary assets, a starting point for a smooth transition to new technology commercialization from knowledge depositories (Teece, 1986). The failure of keiretsu firms to lower the dormancy ratio, especially following the rise of global mad technologies, suggests a lack of knowledge integration capability within Japanese companies.

Knowledge integration capabilities are an organizational capacity that combines and synthesizes existing, yet unstructured bodies of technological and market-related knowledge. The concept of integration is a familiar one in organizational theory and management studies (see Clark and Fujimoto, 1991; Galbraith, 1973, 1977; Lawrence and Lorsh, 1967). According to these studies, integration is usually carried out through such organizational mechanisms as lateral organizations, integration groups or teams, and project managers. In addition to these organizational mechanisms, we argue that the visibility of knowledge within a company is also important for knowledge integration.

In knowledge integration, each of the company's work units has to know what kind of knowledge has been stored within the company and where it is located. Even if a company carefully prepares effective organizational mechanisms, knowledge integration would not be complete without the presence of a knowledge infrastructure. The visibility of knowledge is a prerequisite to the development of knowledge integration capabilities. When corporations are big, decentralized, and complex, as is the case with many of the keiretsu firms, the visibility issue is critical. On the other hand, even if corporations maintain a high degree of visibility of knowledge, it is difficult for them to integrate knowledge in the absence of any effective organizational mechanism. Therefore, the knowledge integration capabilities of a company will be considered in terms of both the visibility of knowledge and the organizational mechanisms of integration.

Companies can enhance the visibility of knowledge by holding regular and frequent meetings, introducing intranet information technologies, building knowledge management (KM) systems, and other similar measures. Simultaneously, such informal or social devices as informal communication between members of different divisions and work units, job rotations, and spontaneous workshops are also important (Ichijo et al., 2001; Konno, 2002). Informal social relations between organizational members also encourage information sharing (Nonaka, 1991; Nonaka and Takeuchi, 1995). This means that knowledge visibility can be evaluated from structural and social aspects.

As is shown in Figure 7.3, knowledge integration capabilities can be split into four dimensions. Simply constructing a lateral organization or a cross-divisional project team will not be sufficient to enhance the integration capabilities. Companies are required to maintain social relationships between members and to pay close attention to the visibility of knowledge. As mentioned earlier, one of the difficulties faced by Japanese companies in the process of technology commercialization is their lack of knowledge integration capabilities. Although other organizational approaches to facilitating the process may exist, we posit that knowledge integration capabilities are particularly effective for large organizations such as many of the Japanese corporations. The relationship between integration capabilities and performance is clear. In the next section, we examine the effect of the capabilities on corporate performance, based upon a questionnaire survey carried out among Japanese manufacturing companies.

	Visibility	Integration mechanism
Structural	e.g. Introduction of IT-based intranet system and knowledge management	e.g. Designing lateral organization and project teams
Social	e.g. Facilitating informal communication and spontaneous meetings	e.g. Building corporate culture for collaborating with different divisions

Figure 7.3 A framework of knowledge integration capabilities

Survey

The primary purpose of this questionnaire survey is to examine the effect of knowledge integration capabilities on corporate performance. The basic hypothesis is simple: the higher the degree of the capabilities, the higher the corporate performance. We also intend to analyze the differing impacts of visibility and organizational mechanism variables on new technology commercialization. Moreover, we are interested in finding out if there is any cross-industry difference in the impact of these two variables. In this sense, this survey purports to generate hypotheses for future corroboration.

Measurement

Our independent variable, knowledge integration capabilities, was operationalized into four factors just as in the 2×2 matrix presented in Figure 7.3. Several questions were written as corresponding to each factor and answered by respondents on a 4-point scale: 1 = not true at all, 2 = not necessarily true, 3 = true to some extent, and 4 = absolutely true. For example, as for the visibility × structural factor, the upper left quadrant of the Figure 7.3, we asked, "Is an information system, like intranet, fully up and running in your company?", "Is the knowledge data base regarding its content and location well maintained?", and "Is a special group or team for knowledge management organized in your company?" Each factor was then evaluated by the sum of the points, and the total points of the four factors were used to measure the knowledge integration capabilities.

With regard to corporate performance, our dependent variable, we chose to consider sales growth rates from 1994 to 1997 of the sample companies. We calculated the average growth rates during this period, when the effect of mad technologies was visible. Although sales growth is influenced by many factors, it is thought to represent the success of technology commercialization, or the success of new product and service development. Contrary to other indexes, like profitability or ROE, sales growth is not affected by the so-called restructuring (or downsizing) efforts that occurred widely in Japan during the period under consideration.

Data collection

Our questionnaire was mailed to the corporate planning divisions of 388 Japanese manufacturing companies. This sample excluded non-manufacturing companies from a list of participants in the Management Academy of the Japan Productivity Center for Socio-economic Development. Of the 62 companies that returned our survey, three were excluded because they failed to answer some of the most vital questions. The sample 59 companies were well-known ones that could be viewed as representative of the Japanese manufacturing sector. Although these companies operate in several different sectors (e.g., electrical equipment and electronics, general machinery, automobile, steel and nonferrous metals, chemicals, and pharmaceuticals), they could be broadly divided into two categories: assemblies and materials (28 companies belonged to the former category, and 31 to the latter). The sales growth data were collected independently from the questionnaire survey, mainly from their annual reports, from which we compiled a data set for the fiscal years 1994–1997.

Research findings and discussions

The research results are summarized in Table 7.3. In the total sample ($n=59$), the knowledge integration capability was closely related to the sales growth of the companies ($r=0.591$, $p<0.01$). In particular, integration by social factors and visibility by social factors contributed more to performance ($r=0.567$, $p<0.01$; $r=0.519$, $p<0.01$, respectively) than other matrixes. Notably, the correlation coefficients changed greatly according to industry types. While assembly industries demonstrated a strong correlation between knowledge integration and performance ($n=28$, $r=0.634$, $p<0.01$), material-related industries

Table 7.3 Knowledge integration capabilities and sales growth (1)

	n	*Aggregate*	*St-V*	*St-C*	*So-V*	*So-C*
Total	59	0.591**	0.338*	0.482**	0.519**	0.567**
Assemblies	28	0.634**	0.293	0.660**	0.531*	0.638**
Materials	31	0.334	–0.001	0.188	0.492*	0.330

** = $p<0.01$, * = $p<0.05$

Table 7.4 Knowledge integration capabilities and sales growth (2)

	n	*Aggregate*	*Visibility*	*Combination*	*Structural*	*Social*
Total	59	0.591**	0.508**	0.574**	0.469**	0.629**
Assemblies	28	0.634**	0.471*	0.717**	0.569*	0.645**
Materials	31	0.334	0.315	0.281	0.109	0.493*

** = p < 0.01, * = p < 0.05

did not (n=31, r=0.334, not statistically significant). Also, in the assembly industries, integration by structural, integration by social, and visibility by social factors had considerably strong relations with the corporate performance (r=0.660, p<0.01; r=0.638, p<0.01; r=0.531, p<0.05, respectively), whereas only visibility by social factors contributed to performance in material-related industries (r=0.492, p<0.05).

Table 7.4 addresses the issue of which factors are the most important for corporate performance – the visibility of knowledge vs organizational integration mechanisms, and structural vs social approaches. In our sample, integration mechanisms, rather than the visibility of knowledge, and the social approach, rather than the structural approach, turned out to be the most important factors in improving corporate performance. The contribution of the social approach to performance is particularly noteworthy (r=0.629, p<0.01). This trend is almost the same in the sample of assembly industries, where the integration mechanism and the social approach have a strong effect on corporate performance (r=0.717, p<0.01: r=0.645, p<0.01, respectively). In the material industries, however, the social approach alone has a significant positive relation with performance (r=0.493, p<0.05).

Among the matrixes of the knowledge integration capabilities (visibility by structural, integration by structural, visibility by social, and integration by social), positive, but weak, correlations were observed. Since the correlation is not statistically significant (p>0.05 or more), the matrixes can be regarded as independent from each other.

The research results support our basic hypothesis that knowledge integration capabilities have a significant impact upon corporate performance. Simply possessing rich technological knowledge does not lead automatically to high corporate performance, even though companies had performed well before the rise of mad technologies. Enhancing the capabilities of knowledge integration, a key strength of mad technologies, is also necessary in order to facilitate the commercialization of knowledge and, thus, improving performance. In enhancing integration capabilities, designing effective organizational integration mechanisms, such as cross-divisional or cross-functional project teams, special integration groups, powerful project managers, and cooperative organizational culture, is critical.

Another interesting finding is the contribution of the social devices to corporate performance in all of the sample sets. It is clear from this study that the structural devices should be complemented with social devices, such as informal communication between organizational members, information circulation in the organization, spontaneous workshops, and the breeding of cooperative culture. The social device may well be the core competence of a company (Hamel and Prahalad, 1994; Prahalad and Hamel, 1990). Although such structural devices as intranet communication systems, knowledge management systems, cross-divisional project teams, and integration groups are relatively easy to emulate (i.e., mimetic isomorphism), social devices are hard to construct. This is why mad technologies can quickly enhance knowledge integration capabilities through the use of cyber-networks. However, once constructed, social devices, *qua* core competence, would improve corporate performance in the long run.

The relationship between knowledge integration capabilities and corporate performance is more prominent in the sample of assembly-related industries than in their counterparts in the material-oriented industries. It is predictable that the capabilities are of greater importance in the assembly industries, where the effective and efficient integration of component technologies is the key success factor in product development (Clark and Fujimoto, 1991). Knowledge integration is expected to be more important in the future and will be stretched beyond divisional and functional boundaries, as products and services in these industries become more complex and systemic.

In the Japanese context, one implication of our findings is that integration capabilities play an important role in enhancing corporate performance, provided that they are coupled with comprehensive technological knowledge. Korean and Taiwanese firms do not have a strong depository of technological knowledge, making it somewhat harder to defend their NIS bases from the impact of mad technologies. Conversely, even if there is a large amount of detailed technological knowledge, it cannot be readily commercialized in the absence of integration capabilities. Korean and Taiwanese firms seem to have more developed integration capabilities than their Japanese counterparts, because of strong on- or offline social networks. According to our analysis, therefore, the development of integration capabilities is a key managerial issue for all technology-intensive Japanese companies.

Conclusion

In this chapter, we have described the R&D activities of Japanese companies and their apparent problems in achieving successful technology commercialization. While Japanese companies have invested aggressively in R&D and, as a result, have amassed much technological knowledge, they have failed in the process of new technology commercialization. It is often the case that companies with substantial technological knowledge do not enjoy high levels of corporate performance in the marketplace. We explored why new technologies become dormant and how Japanese companies can overcome the problem of facilitating technology commercialization. For our endeavor, we relied mostly on the perspective of "knowledge integration capabilities." Technology does not work in isolation; rather, it works in conjunction with other technologies. Technologies add value only as integrated systems. Although there may be other organizational approaches to technology commercialization, we emphasized that the concept of knowledge integration capabilities was especially important for big and decentralized complex organizations as the large Japanese corporations.

We proposed a conceptual framework of knowledge integration capabilities, which highlights both the visibility of knowledge and also organizational integration mechanisms. Based on this framework, we examined the impact of the capabilities on corporate performance. We generated data using a questionnaire survey of Japanese manufacturing companies. The research results generally supported our original hypothesis that the higher the degree of the capabilities, the higher the level of corporate performance. In particular, the effect of the capabilities on corporate performance was prominent in the assembly-related industries. Although the degree of the impact can be different among industries, they are thought to play an important role in enhancing corporate performance.

8
Why Governance Reforms are Not Effective

In the previous chapters, we discussed how large firms in Japan, Korea, and Taiwan have been defending their technological advantages in an age of globalization and mad technology. We noticed that the NIS structures in these three countries were becoming increasingly alike and that Korean and Taiwanese firms are quickly changing their R&D strategies by adopting some of the main features of mad technologies. Korean firms were particularly effective in obtaining knowledge integration skills for new technologies (i.e., commercialization), while Taiwanese firms had proven remarkably successful in organizing international networks of specialized and reciprocal division of labor. Japanese firms were found to be very efficient in knowledge patenting, although they were slow to adopt quick knowledge integration skills.

However, these countries continue to face further threats from globalization and mad technology, as the so-called "dot.com" companies went belly up, mostly in 2000 and 2001, after undermining investors' confidence in the traditional stock markets in Japan, Korea, and Taiwan. The IT failure was an added effect to the ongoing economic recession due to the Asian financial crisis and the bursting of the economic bubble. The governments in these three countries have been pivotal in leading reform efforts for the entire economy in general and corporate governance structures in particular, to ameliorate economic problems. In all three countries, but most particularly in Japan and Korea, foreign investors also asked corporations to change traditional corporate governance structures drastically in order to introduce Anglo-American-style corporate governance. The top-down reforms, however, made little difference, especially in Korea, where family members still own and control the chaebol groups. This chapter discusses why corporate governance reforms are not performing very well in Korea (or possibly in Japan and Taiwan, either) and why large firms are avoiding corporate governance reforms in order to defend their technological advantages from mad technologies and globalization.

This chapter offers a case study of Samsung Electronics, which has successfully defended its core technologies from mad technologies on the one hand and has also strengthened transactional governance through interdivisional teamwork on the other. Samsung Electronics, however, was not active in reforming corporate governance of the Samsung group. The focal points of this chapter are the processes of establishing, changing, and defending transactional governance at Samsung. We also discuss factors of successful interdivisional networking in the Korean context.

The theoretical background

The environmental impact on the changes of corporate governance has received little scholarly analysis, although extant arguments maintain that environmental uncertainties shape corporate governance structures. For instance, despite the lack of empirical testing, the concepts of technological and institutional complementarity explain the role that uncertainties of the systemic environmental parameters play in the introduction of teamwork that brought about the worker-controlled corporate governance structure in major Japanese firms (Aoki, 2000; Lincoln, 1990; Tachibanaki and Taki, 2000; Williamson, 1985).

This complementarity argument, however, suffers because of its inability to predict when systemic environmental uncertainties induce changes in corporate governance structures. During the Asian financial crisis, many Asian firms faced drastic changes in their systemic environments that dictated changes in the corporate governance. However, many firms tenaciously retained their traditional corporate governance of one-man control, as in the case of the Korean chaebols (Fukagawa, 2000; Oh and Park, 2001). The resilience of the traditional corporate governance necessitates re-evaluating the significance of environmental factors.

We assume that the complementarity thesis took as its starting point a broadly defined view of corporate governance, and this has resulted in an overly simple conclusion about the relationship between the systemic environmental parameters and the evolution of corporate governance structures. A more accurate view of corporate governance would distinguish it from transactional governance (Argyris and Liebeskind, 1999). Transactional governance is a term that analyzes the governance structures of interfirm transactions and relation patterns, whereas, strictly speaking, corporate governance deals with the control of managers in one firm (Geringer and Herbert, 1989; Jensen and Meckling, 1990; Nooteboom, 1996; see also Chapter 6). If Asian firms did not change their corporate governance structures despite external pressures, it may mean that internal governance resilience was offset by changes in transactional governance relations to neutralize external threats.

Therefore, the main goal of this chapter is to clarify the environmental contingencies of transactional governance, if systemic environmental uncertainties do not readily change corporate governance. Samsung's success in maintaining one-man control and simultaneously securing high levels of corporate performance is not the result of an efficient corporate governance structure, but rather results from an efficient innovation in transactional governance. Interdivisional cooperation or teamwork, which many feel contributes to the success of Samsung Electronics, is in fact the result of the transactional governance structures. We also argue that organizational memory is an important internal mechanism that intervenes in the process of shaping transactional governance when the environmental parameters are controlled. We will discuss germane theoretical aspects of this chapter in order to generate some propositions.

Corporate governance, transactional governance, and environmental parameters

Corporate governance is broadly defined as the institutionalized control of employees to ensure that managers follow the interests of shareholders (Berle and Means, 1932; Nooteboom, 1999; Vives, 2000). Control is carried out by institutional means (e.g., majority equity holding) for the stockholders who have great stakes in an organization (Coase, 1991; Fama and Jensen, 1983; Williamson, 1996). This concept assumes that governance takes place within a firm, although it is not clear as to whether the term can be applied to the governance of several different firms that do business together as a group or a team.

A more appropriate term than corporate governance for the reference of multilateral teamwork in more than one organization may be transactional governance, a term that emphasizes the institutional governance of transactions between divisions of a corporate group or between different firms (see, inter alia, Alter and Hage, 1993; Dubini and Aldrich, 1991; Gerlach and Lincoln, 1992; Granovetter, 1994, 1995; Kreiner and Schultz, 1993; Larson, 1992; Liebeskind et al., 1996; Miles and Snow, 1986, 1992; Powell, 1990; Williamson, 1996). If corporate governance takes a single corporation as its unit of analysis, transactional governance takes one interfirm relation as its unit of analysis.

From the Korean chaebol's point of view, no obvious corporate governance problem existed, because a single owner of the chaebol, *qua* CEO, controlled the entire enterprise group (Chang et al., 1998; Fukagawa, 2000; Kim, 1998; Park and Kim, 1997; Woo-Cumings, 1998). However, problems of coordination arose because the chaebol usually had more than twenty subsidiary firms or several divisions in different markets (Interview with Samsung). A traditional governance mechanism was to deploy family members to divisional head positions. Over the years, the death of Samsung's founding father led to the secession of the chaebol into small groups, as his sons and daughters assumed the full ownership of each subgroup. Consequently, some of the divisional heads at the mother firm were increasingly non-family members who had received advanced degrees from American universities and other international business experience.

Professional managers occupied the divisional CEO posts, if not the group CEO position, a change in the control of the chaebol divisions which may lead to increasing difficulties in coordinating interdivisional teamwork. Traditionally, Samsung and LG groups, the two most prominent chaebols in Korea at present, have relied on the chairman's office to promote interdivisional coordination. This, however, ended in 1997 as a result of pressure from the government that forced these groups to shut down the office in order to accelerate the diffusion of ownership and control of the chaebol.

External pressures of governance reform, especially during the financial crisis and IT venture failures, constituted an important source of systemic environmental uncertainty. Theoretically, systemic environmental uncertainty leads to teamwork with increased levels of interdivisional communication and information sharing (Aoki, 2000; Aoki and Saxonhouse, 2000; Tachibanaki and Taki, 2000). However, it is not certain whether or not interdivisional communication and information sharing lead to the reform of corporate governance. Despite the external pressures, Samsung and LG did not change their corporate governance structures – the Chairman's Office merely changed its name to Structural Coordination Office. In the context of Samsung and LG, we notice that the role of the CEO as owner-controller of the chaebol did not change despite the shifts in systemic environmental parameters.

We need to operationalize two environmental parameters and changes in corporate and transactional governance before developing propositions regarding their relationships. First, as shown in Table 8.1, changes of corporate governance in the chaebol suggest the delegation of decision-making power to professional managers, while the diffusion of ownership is likely to proceed to the extent that there will eventually be no single owner of each group and/or intra-group divisions. Changes of transactional governance in the chaebol's case includes the restructuring of the chairman's office into a structural coordination office (or any other structural reform in the coordination team of the entire group) and the establishment and destruction of new or existing interdivisional teams, whose functions are mostly concentrated in the area of governance of interdivisional transactions. The previous statement assumes that diversification has already made considerable progression in these groups. Transactional governance, thus, does not consider ownership and control of the entire group as important. What is at stake is the governance of interdivisional transactions, i.e., teamwork between divisions.

Secondly, systemic and idiosyncratic environmental parameters deal with information on how environmental uncertainties affect groups. For instance, if the uncertainty affects only one subgroup or division, then the environmental parameter is considered to be idiosyncratic to that group alone. If the uncertainty affects all subgroups

Table 8.1 Operationalization of governance and environmental parameters

Corporate governance	*Transactional governance*	*Systemic environmental parameters*	*Idiosyncratic environmental parameters*
• Institutional means (e.g., equity holding; board of directors) of controlling managers and workers of a firm • Internal organization after mergers and acquisitions of different firms • Ownership and control structures (E.g., family capitalism vs. managerial capitalism)	• Governance of transactions between divisions or member firms within a group or a network • Central coordination unit (e.g., Chairman's Office; Structural Coordination Office) • Teamwork between divisions, subunits, or firms within a group or a network	• Overall financial and consumer markets • Governmental policies (changes in tax and interest rates) • Global political and economic changes • Advancement of mad technologies and IT ventures	• Environmental uncertainties that affect core technologies • E.g., Innovation within an electronic sector • E.g., Changes in the demand of electronic goods • E.g., Advancement of mad technologies and IT ventures
Observed phenomenon:	*Unexpected consequences due to resistance to SEP and IEP*:		
Resistance to both systemic and idiosyncratic environmental parameters	• SEP → Interdivisional competition (specialization) • IEP → Interdivisional cooperation (teamwork)		

and divisions, it is seen as systemic to the entire network. The nature of uncertainty can change from one industrial sector to another, or from one country to another.

It is difficult to measure the extent of environmental uncertainties. For heuristic purposes, idiosyncratic uncertainties refer to the problems that arise in the maintenance of core technologies (Thompson, 1967; Aoki, 2000). By contrast, systemic uncertainties occur mostly in the area of financial and consumer markets, although governmental policies, such as the changes of tax and interest rates, also constitute substantial threats to business enterprises (Aoki, 2000). In the Korean case, domestic governmental policies of chaebol reform have played a major role in reforming the entire chaebol (Oh and Park, 1999). The gray area lies in the source of uncertainties that affect both core technologies and the entire group (Kusunoki and Numagami, 1996; Tachibanaki and Taki, 2000). An example would be the progress of a particular core technology that affects the entire network of subsidiaries in the different traditional markets (e.g., digital technologies and the production of mobile phones and internet game machines).

We can theoretically predict that the consequence of systemic and idiosyncratic uncertainties is the organization of governance structures. Uncertainties of idiosyncratic environmental parameters lead to the specialization of subgroups or divisions, discouraging teamwork or collaboration between subgroups or divisions (i.e., scientific management). Uncertainties of systemic environmental parameters lead to teamwork or collaboration between different subgroups or divisions (Aoki, 2000; Gerlach, 1987; Kusunoki and Numagami, 1996; Tachibanaki and Taki, 2000). The gray area is the case when idiosyncratic uncertainties spill over to other subunits that do not have to share information about their core technology with other subunits (e.g., the development of digital technology that leads to cooperation between the semiconductor division, the camera division, and the mobile phone division to produce a digital mobile phone with a digital movie camera).

What is also ironic in the case of Korea is the unexpected consequence of resistance to governmental reform policies and foreign pressures for governance reform. Governmental policies, *qua* systemic environmental uncertainty, led to intra-group specialization, not intergroup teamwork. Moreover, it was the mad technology, *qua* idiosyncratic uncertainties, that reinforced interdivisional teamwork in the case of the chaebol (Table 8.1).

The shaping of teamwork or the specialization of divisions does not change corporate governance structures. Changes in corporate governance structures involve a shift of power relations between stockholders and managers, or the annulment or creation of governance or agency problems (Mone et al., 1998; Nooteboom, 1996; Williamson, 1996). As we discussed above, the specialization of divisions or teamwork would not create governance problems as long as ownership and control are in the hands of the chairman. However, the organization of interfirm transactions still creates governance problems, a central theme of transaction cost economics (Argyris and Liebeskind, 1999; Dyer and Singh, 1998; Noorderhaven, 1996; Nooteboom, 1996; Williamson, 1979, 1981, 1987).

The central concern is whether to have a teamwork-based interfirm relation that is dominated by generalists or to have a decentralized division of labor between firms, dominated by specialists. The creation of the multidivisional form has been common in the case of transactional governance problems, although that has been discouraged in the case of the chaebol for fear of competition between divisions. In other words, the chaebol did not favor scientific management or the specialization of divisions (Lee, 1993). Like the Japanese keiretsu, the chaebol preferred teamwork, and we wish to understand why. Briefly, the answer is already given, since chaebol groups' reaction to government policies and/or foreign pressures led to the unexpected consequences of reinforcing interdivisional teamwork (i.e., close-tied diversification) and discouraging intra-group specialization. Intra-group specialization occurred only as a façade or as a temporary strategic measure against governmental policies. Having unpacked the concepts of corporate governance, transaction governance, and environmental uncertainties, we now move on to the question of their structural relations.

Environmental factors and governance

Scholars take the transaction cost economics understanding of corporate governance as an evolutionary entity too literally to expect the resistance of old governance structures, such as the family capitalism of the chaebols. Structural or environmental contingencies, for instance, were thought to have almost automatic impacts on the choice of a governance structure. Any interfirm alliances would fail if they resisted these internal or external factors of the market. However, transactional governance gives a different perspective on the mechanism of governance changes.

The operationalization of factors and initial fieldwork with Samsung reveal that teamwork – an important organizational device for organizing, coordinating, and controlling transactional governance – changes when idiosyncratic environmental parameters pose more serious uncertainty problems than the systemic environmental parameters. The usual managerial strategy of controlling the uncertainties of idiosyncratic parameters has been divisional specialization. Although it is very tempting to withdraw from such an unstable market, this option cannot be pursued if the division is really important – as is the case with Samsung Electronics. The specialization of the division with professionals changes the ongoing transactional governance within an enterprise group, as the power of the specific division increases. In the case of Samsung, the establishment of a functional team with professionals demanded almost unconditional support from the chairman's office in the past and the structural coordination office at present. Therefore:

> Proposition 1. An increase in the uncertainty of idiosyncratic environmental parameters intensifies systemic environmental uncertainties, if the division that faces idiosyncratic environmental uncertainties is a core unit of an entire interfirm network.

> Proposition 1(a). The expansion of the idiosyncratic uncertainties of one division to other divisions as a chain reaction that leads to teamwork.

The spread of the idiosyncratic uncertainties of a core unit into other divisions is often met with resistance from the latter. It is an organizational defensive measure by the peripheral divisions to protect their ongoing transactional governance patterns. New teamwork, created by the uncertainties of idiosyncratic environmental parameters, changes the transactional governance patterns. Therefore:

> Proposition 1(b). The teamwork of Proposition 1(a) reflects a new transactional governance of interdivisional cooperation, and it is

most likely that the core unit will dominate the teamwork, when the spread of idiosyncratic uncertainties of the core division into other divisions proceeds despite intragroup resistance.

In theory, systemic environmental uncertainties lead to teamwork (Kusunoki and Numagami, 1996; Aoki, 2000; Tachibanaki and Taki, 2000), although it is not clear as to when systemic uncertainties cause transactional governance changes. Our assumption is that systemic environmental changes do not trigger reforms in either transactional or corporate governance structures. This is due to the resistance from corporations to systemic environmental changes. As in the example of the financial crisis, which did not bring about reforms in corporate governance, we realize that transactional governance changed through division swapping among chaebols (Fukagawa, 2000; Woo-Cumings, 1998). Division swapping was possible, as when the government forced LG to give up its memory chip division and sell it to Hyundai, because the government thought the memory chip division would be more efficiently exploited in Hyundai than in LG. In other words, systematic uncertainties could increase intra-group specialization more than corporate governance reform. Therefore:

Proposition 2. Systemic environmental uncertainties change transactional governance structures, if external agents, such as the government, accelerate the process of prioritizing the importance of divisions within an interfirm network.

Proposition 2(a). Governmental intervention in the change of transactional governance structures results in changes in corporate governance when division swapping and mergers between interfirm networks occur.

Proposition 2(b). Interfirm networks tend to defend their firms from Proposition 2(a) by concentrating governance power in a core division.

The consequence of transactional governance changes either through Proposition 1 or through Proposition 2 only strengthens the power of the core division. In other words, environmental parameters do not explain the success or failure of a governance reform, although they do explain the central position of a core division in interdivisional teamwork. Since our focus is also to explain the success of teamwork at Samsung, we need to find other factors, apart from environmental parameters alone, which do not seem to fully explain the success of Samsung's teamwork. In the past, we understood the success of teamwork in terms of complementarity. Technological complementarity, for instance, resulted from a generalist labor force with lifetime employment in Japanese corporate organizations. Also, the existence of main banks in Japan was the reason for institutional complementarity (Aoki, 2000; Aoki and Saxonhouse, 2000; Hoshi and Kashyap, 2001). However, these are not universal factors of teamwork success. Team diversity studies report the success of teamwork in specialist firms with no lifetime employment (Harrison et al., 1998; Hogg and Terry, 2000; Jackson, 1992; Jackson et al., 1995).

Findings that emphasize team diversity as an important factor of teamwork success, however, tend to fall into the trap of cultural essentialism, where teamwork is a result of specific cultural traits. For instance, teamwork poses severe difficulties in the coordination of interfirm alliances, when demographic diversity among team members is great (Hogg and Terry, 2000; Jackson, 1992; Jackson et al., 1995). In the Korean chaebol, the diversity among senior managers poses such a threat to the governance of transactions. Culture, defined in terms of individualism or collectivism (Hofstede, 1983), is said to have benefits in reducing such a threat (Park, 2002).

However, if culture is important in the shaping of teamwork, we must expect similar teamwork effects to occur in a single-cultural zone. As we will discuss below, Samsung and LG had a far better teamwork-based transactional governance structure than Hyundai. Why did such differences occur in one cultural spectrum? Cultural essentialism elides the importance of environmental factors and transactional governance structures, which we believe affect teamwork formation and success. To clarify the relationship between institutional factors and teamwork success, we introduce another variable – organizational memory.

Memory and teamwork

From our fieldwork, it was apparent that Samsung had far better interdivisional teamwork than existed in any other chaebol. For instance, there was almost no interdivisional teamwork at Hyundai

(Yoon, 1995; Yoon and Chang, 1996; Interview with Samsung). Why do we observe these differences within the same cultural zone?

Following the model developed by Moorman and Miner (1998), we propose that organizational memory, in alliance with environmental factors, plays an important role in the formation and success of interdivisional teamwork. Organizational memories are twofold – procedural and declarative. Procedural memory shapes routines and governance resilience in an organization, whereas declarative memory induces changes and innovation within an organization (Cohen, 1991; Cohen and Bacdayan, 1994; Moorman and Miner, 1998; Nonaka, 1990; Winter, 1987). It has been suggested that declarative memory helps organizations to establish teamwork, although the exact contingencies of declarative memory leading to teamwork has not been found (Moorman and Miner, 1998; Walsh, 1995). Since the definitional assumption implies that organizational memory as a collective phenomenon defies individual defection in the participation of learning and internalizing memories of all kinds, organizational memory has limitations of its own, since it carries the additional assumption that organizational memory is a voluntary phenomenon. The assumption that learning – which involves memorizing facts and the routines of an organization – is always voluntary can be viewed as irrational. However, it can be applied to organizational leaders, who may own a company or run a company as an agent.

When organizational learning through memorizing history occurs among leaders, we should make a distinction between their procedural and their declarative memories. If leaders were subsumed under the traditional scheme of maintaining their organizations using established procedures that have been handed down by their predecessors, we would not expect any organizational innovation. However, an innovative leader would provide a new meaning of an organization by interpreting organizational experience in a revolutionary way, so that he or she can successfully reorient the entire organization in a new direction. When leaders assume an innovative role, we expect an intergroup effort to collect new information and sharing among different groups. Therefore:

> Proposition 3. When leaders emphasize organizational learning through reinterpreting the past, i.e., declarative memory, they initiate the organization of teamwork among different divisions.

Added to this organizational memory issue is the question of when the leaders should emphasize declarative memory. Our initial investigation into the Samsung group affirms that leaders took the role of redefining the history of their organizations at times of external threats or during the rapid change of systemic environmental parameters. Therefore:

> Proposition 3(a). The uncertainties of systemic environment encourage organizational members to prefer leaders who provide declarative memories that can strengthen organizational core technologies.

Proposition 3(a) is also linked to Proposition 1 as long as systemic environmental uncertainties can be caused by core divisions' idiosyncratic environmental uncertainties (i.e., the spill-over effect or external threats from mad technology). Among various examples of chaebol success and failure stories, we notice that the surviving interfirm groups in Korea usually had leaders who were declarative and innovative in their beliefs about future organizational orientation or goal setting. This leads to our final proposition that

> Proposition 3(b). The success of interfirm alliances through adaptive and innovative changes in transactional governance ensures the epochal survival of the group, whereas the failure of initiating innovation in transactional governance leads to the destruction of the entire group.

Because of the last proposition, we can safely argue that the Williamsonian prediction on the evolution of corporate governance should be upheld, only when we realize that we have to introduce the distinction between corporate and transactional governance.

Governance, environmental factors, and organizational memory – discussion

It has been argued repeatedly that corporate governance is important in the guidance of measuring the efficiency of organizational hierarchies vis-à-vis markets (Chandler, 1962; Masten, 1993; Monteverde and Teece, 1982; Ouchi, 1977; Simon, 1991; Williamson, 1973). However, due to the weaknesses of our empirical evidence regarding this simple truth, we have often been misled by two general criticisms of our understanding of capitalist corporate organizations. The first was a very strong neoclassical argument which states that markets must replace hierarchies (Becker and Murphy, 1988, 1992; Fama, 1980), and the second was that hierarchies should be guided by signals from the market, giving all the power and prestige to stockholders who monitor such market fluctuations (Demsetz, 1988; Jensen, 2000).

We started this chapter by adopting a very humanistic view of organizations, suggesting that organizational members have all the rights in ameliorating their fate through establishing and innovating their governance structures. The interaction between human beings and their environmental parameters was deemed to be very humanistic to us, because the notion of the market as an invisible godly hand or human beings as mere observers of the market was too florid for us to take it literally. Instead, this study suggested finding an analytical model which will allow us to approach the issue of how different interfirm alliance networks resolve the confrontation between environmental factors and their organizational fate through adopting and amending governance structures.

In so doing, we noticed that a useful distinction could be drawn between corporate and transactional governance structures, especially when we had to trace the evolution of governance structures of an alliance of multiple divisions or networks. Transactional governance was defined as day-to-day management of transactions between different firms in one network or group. This means that when we talk of transactional governance we are not referring to the governance of transactional costs that occur between suppliers and buyers or transactions between unrelated firms. The internal organization, by way of administrative fiat or relational contracting, cannot be applied to an interfirm alliance that is owned and controlled by one man, as is typical in cases of the chaebol. However, one-man control did not resolve the problem of coordination between divisions, especially when the Confucian-style family ownership and control could not be adopted across all of its divisions. The rise of high-tech industries necessitated the delegation of power to professional managers, who cut their teeth in their own specialty markets.

Divisional managers face idiosyncratic environmental uncertainties that they think they must convey to the chairman or his staff, so that they can reaffirm their significance within the interfirm alliance. If all of the divisional managers call for attention from the central office about their unique environmental parameters, organizational noise or coordination problems ensue. When systemic environmental parameters are not uncertain, this coordination problem can be resolved by the chairman and his immediate staff at the central location – administrative fiat. However, systemic environmental uncertainties lead to other problems, such as "Who is the real controller of our interfirm alliance?" We mentioned that external organizational actors, including international financial organizations, mad technology, and the government, can be dictatorial in their unified demand for organizational or governance reforms (see Figure 8.1).

When external environmental parameters are uncertain, the simultaneous uncertainty of idiosyncratic environmental parameters can be a burden that requires the immediate prioritization of the significance of each division in a group. The failure to defend themselves in this situation results in forced mergers of divisions with other groups. However, the success of some divisions in this situation is a result of collective defense of divisions that maintain solid teamwork to begin with. Teamwork as such can be established according to centralized administrative fiat in times of peace. However, in times of external threats, organizational memory looms large. We

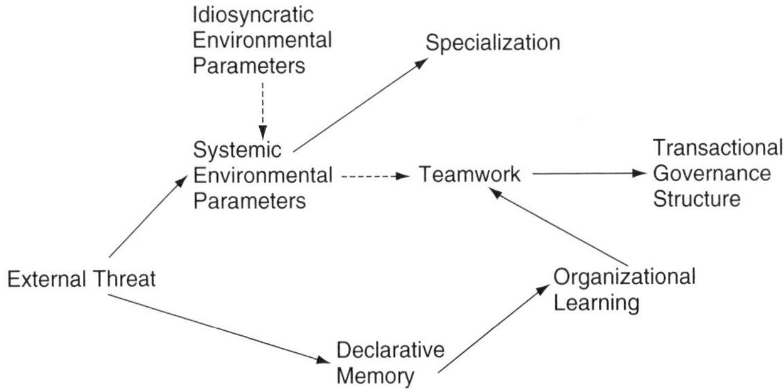

Figure 8.1 A model of environmental factors and transactional governance

argued that declarative memory acquired by a leader could be critical in the shaping of an organizational culture that emphasizes teamwork instead of functional specialization.

The separation of corporate and transactional governance allows us to draw some policy implications. External threats, in the form of governmental prerogatives for changing corporate divisional boundaries through swapping between groups, can only strengthen the power of the core division within a group or an interfirm alliance when corporate leaders tend to utilize declarative memory. This may change transactional governance structures, but will not affect corporate governance. Hyundai's failure to strengthen its core technology was due to a lack of leaders who possessed declarative memory. If the government wants to introduce a more diffused and responsible corporate governance structure (or even purports to replace family capitalism with diffused stock ownership and professional management), it has to stop relying on external threats, which actually produce only unexpected consequences.

Conclusion

The need to separate corporate governance from transactional governance was apparent in our analysis of those firms that tend to resist any form of external influence to change their corporate governance. In the case of the Korean chaebols being faced with governmental efforts at reforming its corporate governance during the 1997 financial crisis, firms did change their transactional governance structures but left their corporate governance structures intact. This chapter generated some propositions concerning the mechanism of the changes of transactional governance structures. It also provided some explanations as to why corporate governance structures remain resilient in the face of external threats and environmental changes. We found that transactional governance structures can be an important source for successful teamwork, although they can also be a source of resistance to change within the corporate governance structures. Further studies are warranted to determine the relationship between corporate governance and transaction governance, and the factors that change the former.

9
Prospects for East Asian Economic Governance

The previous chapter discussed how large corporations in Korea are defending their technological advantage from external threats, including mad technologies, by reinforcing transactional governance through a policy of constant organizational innovation. In our case study chapters, we discovered that the private sectors in Japan and Taiwan are also strengthening their capacities to undertake technological and organizational innovations in order to fight back against mad technologies. All of this indicates that macroeconomic governance by the public sector is weakened to the extent that it no longer seems to be able to regulate global economic contingencies, as the Asian financial crisis of the late 1990s clearly indicated.

For several decades preceding the mid-1990s, Japan, Korea, and Taiwan had recorded remarkably high levels of economic growth. However, the 1997 Asian financial crisis, spawned in Thailand, quickly dismantled their miracle economies, and severely dented investors' confidence. Although the three states now appear to have resumed an economic growth curve after a short period of readjustment, these signs of recovery are derived from the expectations created by macroeconomic expansionist policies and massive stimulation packages. Furthermore, these three countries have made little progress to recast their governing frameworks and an institutional nexus, which had been designed for a high growth era, and which precipitated the 1997 economic crisis.

The pre-crisis governance framework and nexus, a highly integrated and centralized system, had created economies that were far too rigid to adapt to the globalized economic system that encroached upon these three countries in 1997. As a consequence, Japan, the world's second largest economy, has experienced stagnant growth for most of the past decade. It is clear from this that Japan's economic problems were not cyclical; they reflected institutional weaknesses at its economic core. On the other hand, post-1997 economic reforms in Korea fueled one of the region's most dramatic reversals, although later developments in the political realm and other international economic factors seem to be slowing down the entire recovery and further growth. By contrast, Taiwan initially escaped the worst of the crisis. However, it failed to generate a political consensus for future development, because of the limited capacity of its minority government to oversee the economy.

These three East Asian economies also face significant geopolitical factors such as competition from China, an unexpected slowdown in global IT demand, oil price fluctuations, uncertain economic prospects in the United States and the European Union, and South American economic vulnerability. China is poised to go beyond the regional territory the East Asian states have claimed over the past few decades. Furthermore, rising oil prices could stoke inflation and interest rates, thereby increasing corporate and financial restructuring costs. The timing and strength of any economic recovery clearly depend in part on economic conditions across Asia and the world.

Many scholars have debated the viability and vulnerability of the East Asian model of capitalism and its economic governance framework (see, inter alia, Chang et al., 1998; Deyo and Doner, 2001; Flynn, 1999; Haggard, 2000; Kang, 2002; Kim, 2000d; Mathews, 1998; Oh, 1999; Pempel, 1999). Some blamed the recent crisis on the weakness of the governance framework, characterized by crony capitalism, a collusive state–business alliance, a poorly regulated financial system, government-controlled capital allocation, and non-transparent corporate governance. Others have argued that market failures in over-liquidated and under-regulated financial markets encouraged an overreliance on short-term international capital and speculative investments.

We focus on the analytical linkage between two institutional levels – the governance framework within which economic transactions occur and the institutional nexus within which it emerges and functions – to address the question of how to recast East Asian economic governance for continued growth. First, we argue that the state, as the main governing institutional nexus, must reassert its institutional capacity as a locus of economic governance in the face of globalization and financial liberalization. Even though "destatization" of national economies under neoliberal economic reforms has attenuated the developmental state model (Ohmae, 1995; Strange, 1996), the state must continue to play a central role, even in engineering economic governance reforms (Gamble, 2000; Jayasuriya, 2000; Kim, 2000a, b, c; Vogel, 1996). Secondly, we argue that East Asian states requiring market reforms must change the framework of economic governance and adopt facilitative and regulatory capacities for managing the national economy and coordinating with the private sector. In these countries, both the state and the private sector need to reconstitute the framework of economic governance. Instead of interventionism, a regulatory state should recover its institutional capacities of management and coordination toward the establishment of a suitable regulatory and legally governing framework, while the private sector minimizes rent-seeking behavior and monopolistic market power by adopting global standards of liberal capitalism with transparent management, removal of moral hazards, and sound corporate governance.

Institutional nexus and the East Asian economic governance framework

Governance as a user-friendly umbrella concept originates from the Greek *kybernetes*, or navigation (Frischtack, 1994; Kim, 2000a), containing the notion of both management and coordination (Dhonte and Kapur, 1996; Frischtak, 1994; Frischtak and Atiyas, 1996; Kim, 2000a, b, c; Kooiman, 1993; Williamson, 1996; World Bank, 1992: 1). Economic governance refers to a credibly established institutional nexus and framework among, as well as for, economic agents to organize and transact goods and services through competition or cooperation inside and across economic system boundaries (Davis and North, 1971; Deyo and Doner, 2001: 5; Gamble, 2000; Hollingsworth et al., 1994; Kim, 2000a, b, c; Willliamson, 1985, 1996).

As we have demonstrated in previous chapters, despite similarities among the three countries – heavy state involvement in industrial development, export-oriented development strategy, Confucian cultural heritages, and poor natural resource endowment – they have varied markedly in the nature of the economic governance that has been adopted (Hamilton and Biggart, 1988; Kim, 1993, 1994). Korea has emphasized large-scale production across a wide range of industries (Amsden, 1989; Jones and Sakong, 1980). This bias created a concentrated and vertically integrated market structure mostly dominated by business groups – chaebols. By contrast, Taiwan has endorsed decentralized economic governance in which small and medium-sized family businesses predominate and are highly integrated through informal patrilineal networks in both domestic and export sectors (Redding, 1990; Wong, 1985), whereas Japan has relied on a third system – small enterprises and business groups with a pervasive, symbiotic network of long-term and hierarchical subcontracting (Fruin, 1994; Gerlach, 1992).

What accounts for such cross-national differences that belie any necessary move within high growth states toward economies of scale, industrial concentration, monopolistic markets, corporate hierarchies, and decline in small-scale firms? We argue that the institutional nexus of the developmental state and its governance framework have significantly influenced the way of shaping economic governance. In other words, the divergent pre-crisis economic governances were embedded in their distinctive institutional nexuses and their governance frameworks which provided coherent and disparate logics for the structuring and coordination of economic activities (Clegg, 1990; Hollingsworth and Boyer, 1997; Kim, 1994, 2000a; Maurice et al., 1980; Rose, 1985; Whitley, 1992, 1999). In this argument, "embeddedness" does not mean that the nexus determines all aspects of economic governance or deny the significance of competitive pressures in economic environments. It rather emphasizes that different organizational trajectories are integrated within a broader institutional nexus. We further argue that the regional economic crisis itself has derived from the institutional nexus and its governance framework. Thus, we must recast both the institutional nexus and its governance framework in order to find the path back to sustainable growth.

We propose that an institutional perspective best unravels the causal primacy of the institutional nexus and its governance framework. Moreover, it explains divergence in economic governance in high-growth conditions and suggests how to achieve post-crisis sustainable growth. This perspective assesses the state as both an actor and a network of institutions (Haggard, 1990; Kim, 1994; Wade, 1990). As an actor, the state defines problems and implements a strategic course of development. As a network the state endorses formal rules, compliance procedures, and standard operating procedures (March and Olsen, 1989). The network constrains both the agents' policy choices and offers opportunities for action (Elster, 1979).

As actors, the East Asian states favored either a strategy of big business consolidation or a small-scale strategy of industrial order (Fields, 1995; Kim, 1994). For example, Korea favored a big business consolidation strategy for rapid economic growth. Such a strategy of economies of scale and industrial concentration involved shifting some private sector risks to the state and an expansionist vision for industrial restructuring and export upgrading. For this, the state tolerated heightened inflation and external indebtedness to underwrite large-scale investments. This growth strategy favored concentrating resources on a few, proven economic actors. By contrast, Taiwan preferred industrial dispersion and fragmented economic units. It shifted risks to the private sector and emphasized economic stability and redistribution. This strategy endorsed a pluralistic economy and polity that buttressed state power bases, as well as favoring parametric policy instruments to provide a regulated framework and infrastructure.

As networks of institutions, East Asian developmental states developed quasi-internal and hierarchical policy networks to cooperate with the private sector in policy making (Hollingsworth et al., 1994; Kim, 2000a). Viewed as relations of "reciprocity" (Amsden, 1989; Wade, 1990) or types of "quasi-internal organizations" (Imai and Itami, 1984), these networks functioned like arms of the state and formed an institutional basis for minimizing transaction costs between the state and individual firms. East Asian growth-oriented networks worked well during the period of rapid economic growth in the region, but all transformed into rent-oriented ones when the private sector gained momentum and penetrated into policy making in the face of financial liberalization and deregulation.

Coming into the 1990s, the three East Asian states embraced deregulation policies such as the liberalization of exchange rates, the abandonment of tariff barriers and protectionist industrial policies, and the liberation of capital to enhance market competition in order to establish so-called "fair" markets in the face of globalization. They imposed no proper regulatory governing framework while they executed deregulation policies, and while mad technologies and other unregulated commodities invaded into local markets (Lee and Kim,

2000). By withdrawing the protection and support that had been hitherto bestowed upon domestic capital, they inadvertently dismantled the institutional basis of economic governance. Unrestricted capital deregulation attenuated states' power to prevent private sector monopolies. Businesses took advantage of relaxed regulation and diversified their lines to maximize market power, creating a highly leveraged financial structure that was over-reliant on short-term capital and speculative investments. To accompany deregulation and liberalization, the states should have established new regulatory institutions to strengthen state monitoring and disciplinary prerogatives (Gamble, 2000; Jayasuriya, 2000; Kim, 2000a; Lee and Kim, 2000; Vogel, 1996).

Weakened regulatory frameworks and the forced decentralization of public power created the 1990s East Asian economic governance crisis (Jayasuriya, 2000; Kim, 2000b, c). The state forfeited a meaningful institutional nexus when structural rigidity attenuated its monitoring and disciplinary capacities and its ability to ensure secure economic development in the face of globalization and financial liberalization. Development thus evaporated when the coordinating governance framework between the state and private sector was replaced by rent-oriented public policy, dictated by the latter. Furthermore, due to extensive private penetration of interest group politics in the social policy arena, the state became a captive of societal interests, reflecting its loss of credibility.

To resume sustainable growth and yet embrace liberal capitalism, neoliberal reform programs must not simply promote market-oriented policy; they must also recast the governance framework within which economic transactions occur and the institutional nexus within which the framework emerges and functions. East Asian states must establish new institutional nexuses to strengthen state monitoring and disciplinary prerogatives and foster market reforms by assuming new facilitative and regulatory – rather than directive and interventionist – roles, while, simultaneously, the private sector must adopt global standards of liberal capitalism that minimize rent-seeking behaviors and monopolistic market power. In other words, the state-controlled, highly regulated governance frameworks, including collusive state–business alliances and opaque financial systems, need to be reshaped. Most importantly, the key lies in the fact that the states need to be responsible agents and need to create responsible modes of governance through neoliberal reforms (Kim, 2002a, b, 2004a).

Recasting East Asian economic governance

Our cross-national comparison of institutional change helps us to generalize contingent principles that are claimed to link state institutional nexuses to modes of economic governance. It explores the compatibility of a given, distinctive institutional nexus and a particular form of economic governance, focusing on the issue of how to recast the institutional nexus of the developmental state and its corresponding governance framework in order to resume sustainable growth.

Recasting the institutional nexus and economic governance in Japan

The Japanese economy, which began showing signs of serious deflationary recession in the early 1990s, continued to plummet even when the pro-reform cabinet, led by Koizumi Junichirô, assumed control of the government in April 2000. The Koizumi cabinet promised to transform the economy through further deregulation and drastic restructuring and to open up the entire political process to public scrutiny, although whether meaningful change has actually begun or not remains debatable. A public consensus has it that Japan must abandon the state-controlled, highly regulated governance framework that created a three-decade-long post-war economic miracle, but is ill-suited to current global conditions. It is increasingly clear that the Japanese government has exhausted all of the policy tools that could offset domestic contraction. After a decade of generous public spending since the collapse of the 1980s bubble, the ratio of debt to GDP is around 130 percent – the highest in the industrialized world and Japan's most pressing long-term economic problem. Moreover, Japan is caught in a cyclical downturn that involves a slow, deflationary economic shakeout. For instance, bankruptcies are rising, and unemployment was pushed to a post-war record of 5.5 percent in December 2003 (MOFA, 2004).

Japan is navigating its worst post-war recession with a banking system saddled with massive bad loans after a decade of economic stagnation, record unemployment, and near-record bankruptcies.

Banks, bailed out in 1998, have balance sheets of eroding quality as chronic deflation pushes corporate debtors into bankruptcy and default. Confidence in the banking system was further shaken by serial bank failures, involving those of the Industrial Bank of Japan (also known as Long-term Credit Bank), the Hokkaido Takushoku Bank, the Tokyo Bank, and other regional and small banks. Banks have been slowly writing off bad loans – creating more than 72 trillion yen in provisions since 1992. As quickly as past bad loans were resolved, however, new ones surfaced. The state may soon have to provide sizable public funds to prevent further bank failures, as evidenced by the recent problems surrounding Risona Bank. This would thwart financial deregulation, although it would also have the effect of avoiding any further loss of confidence in banking that could dampen consumer spending and economic recovery.

Changes remain elusive, however. The proportion of financial flow through vast state-controlled financial institutions is rising, not falling, while private banks continue to support politically important companies, such as construction groups. Most consumers thus continue to place savings in bank deposits or state institutions. The level of new private bank lending to firms has plummeted with demands for new credit in a contracting economy, while investors prefer government bonds. As a result, the banking system does not create credit, but rather circulates liquidity back into government bonds, which expands the monetary base but not measures of money supply.

Over the majority of the past five decades, Japan has not practiced free-market capitalism guided by rational price and risk assessments. Instead, banks have loaned to particular companies, according to a sense of national duty. Almost half of all financial flow has been channeled through state-controlled financial institutions (*Financial Times*, 25 September 2001). This quasi-socialist system of finance served post-war Japan well for decades. However, after the economy matured, banks extended credit to high-risk real estate projects during the 1980s asset price bubble. When prices plunged, under-capitalized banks and over-leveraged borrowers both collapsed.

Japan's long-term and mutual institutional interdependence between the state's organizational element and the private sector's market element was unique (Dore, 1986; Imai and Itami, 1984; Okimoto, 1989). However, structural rigidity expedited its downfall, when this institutionally legitimate mechanism of exchange confronted globalization. The network provided the private sector with ad hoc or informal advice from ministries, but was problematic for international businesses outside the established bureaucratic relationships and for domestic firms who would have preferred a more transparent system. They favored the predictability that clear regulatory frameworks can provide and the flexibility that deregulation can offer in a competitive global market.

State-regulated economic governance orchestrated Japan's period of rapid economic growth (Kim, 1994, 2000a, b). The state nurtured the interlocked institutional nexus among private, political, and public institutions – large industrial and financial enterprises, the Liberal Democratic Party (LDP), and the economic ministries, which in tandem stressed aggregate economic performance (Johnson, 1982; Katz, 1998). The consensus built into this nexus on basic macroeconomic goals was a hallmark of Japan's political economy. With the last decade, however, such consensus in the nexus succumbed to diffusion and structural rigidity. With increased economic power, the corporate sector became less dependent on the state bureaucracy for making investment decisions. Political parties and other social sectors increasingly wrested free of state bureaucratic dominance in economic policy decisions.

The Japanese government averted an utter economic collapse, although since the late 1980s its policy tools have appeared increasingly ineffective. Domestic mismanagement led many to believe that its bureaucracy was incapable of responding to the rapidly changing economic environments of globalization, financial liberalization, and mad technologies. Politicians have thus seized the initiative in economic management. The LDP presided over the bubble economy that triggered the latest recession. When faced by an economic downturn, it could do nothing but fall back on traditional bank bailout programs and spending packages devised to reward electoral supporters rather than intended to strengthen the overall economy. The party appeared to be constrained in a web of financial and political interest groups. Even though public faith in the Japanese style of capitalism remains strong among many bureaucrats and politicians, the long-awaited economic reform packages have proven to be disastrous policy failures.

Although relations between the state and the private sector used to be more cooperative and reciprocal in Japan than in Korea or Taiwan, Japanese policy making through consultation and consensus became unwieldy when opposing factions emerged on both sides. Procedural delays and fragmentation bred policy failure, as the state could not timely respond to rapidly unfolding events (Moon and Rhyu, 2000). After delays and false starts, Japan finally appears to be recasting the economic governance system in a meaningful way. Real progresses in financial reform and corporate restructuring, combined with a relaxed fiscal policy, could restore growth at home and throughout Asia. Japan's efforts should go further to accept the risks of a flexible, market-driven economy. Japan must abandon both the collusive state–business governance framework and the highly regulated quasi-socialist system of finance. It must also foster market reforms through speedily implemented, credible policies and by establishing regulatory institutions to strengthen the government's monitoring and disciplinary prerogatives.

Recasting the institutional nexus and economic governance in Taiwan

Adequate foreign reserves, minimal foreign debts, and conservative fiscal policies have spared Taiwan from the worst of the Asian economic crisis. Its economy was structured to produce value-added export commodities, manufactured by a large population of small and medium-sized enterprises. Economic activities were carried out by a less centralized bureaucracy, where power to hammer out industrial policies was dispersed among more ministries and agencies than was the case in either Korea or Japan (Fields, 1995; Hamilton and Biggart, 1988; Kim, 1994, 2000a, b; Wade, 1990). At most, the state played an advisory role in the policy process, not intervening in investment decisions. Unlike Korea, where strong state intervention distorted the market, Taiwan respected the determination of winners and losers through largely unfettered market mechanisms.

The Central Bank of China, independent of the Taiwanese presidential palace, has a monopoly control over domestic banking and exercises considerably influence over the formulation and implementation of stability-oriented fiscal and monetary policies via the Ministry of Finance. Taiwan escaped from the 1997 Asian financial crisis, primarily as a result of the central bank's long-standing policy bias in favor of domestic borrowing, which resulted in a largely undeveloped debt market (Chang, 2000). The state's practice of gradualism – even at the cost of a backward debt market – proved prudent, as it favored domestic self-reliance and gradual liberalization, which secured domestic proficiency before risking openness to global markets. The policy gave the domestic financial sector of this export-oriented economy time to catch up with the ferociously fast-paced manufacturing and service sectors.

The Taiwanese central bank also controls inward and outward capital flow by imposing limits per transaction or project, set according to the type of industry or sector. Other than sales remittances from exports, no foreign currency can enter or leave Taiwan without the prior approval of the Central Bank of China. The bank also imposes a cap on the amount exchanged into or out of the local New Taiwan Dollar currency. By controlling such transactions, the state ensures an efficient use of capital to encourage and enhance export-oriented industries and innovation projects. The central bank's strategic direction of the flow of funds, which insures that the neediest procure funding, eliminates over-investment and/or over-capacity that greater market discretion could create.

To prevent the "hollowing out" of or "de-industrializing" of the island's traditional industries, Taiwan also regulates foreign direct investment (FDI) out of Taiwan and into the Asia-Pacific region for the relocation of Taiwanese light and high-tech manufacturing industries. Unfettered capital outflows could create deflation and cause a severe shock to a labor pool insufficiently prepared for more value-added, skilled works. In particular, Taiwan controls FDI activities in China to hold bargaining chips, vis-à-vis Beijing, by putting a ceiling on capital and technology transfers. Following China's accession to the WTO in 2001, the Taiwanese government started to lose control over entrepreneurs hoping to shift their manufacturing bases to the mainland. However, it is clear that this policy of FDI regulation has benefited Taiwan tremendously.

State support of its people's vigorous competitiveness and drive for wealth was also critical to Taiwan's economic health, fostering an economy powered by small and medium-sized enterprises (SMEs). Taiwan's economy primarily features loosely coupled, but resilient, SME networks engaged in ferocious free-market competition – they account for over half of total domestic production. Taiwan exploited flexible SME production networks before similar developments were observed in Italy (Doner et al., 1993). However, as we argued in previous chapters, Taiwan nationalized extremely capital-intensive industries such as telecommunications and heavy industries in order to remain domestically self-reliant. Nonetheless, the state did not intervene to funnel all available capital stocks toward large conglomerates. As a result, entrepreneurs of all sorts and sizes had a level playing field for investment.

SMEs had access to abundant domestic savings capital to carve out industry niches, establish flexible production systems, and diversify production lines. This advantage lowered entry and exit costs, both of which alleviated the adjustment costs of neutralizing perpetual shifts in the global marketplace (Chow and Bates, 2000). Taiwan's competitive and SME-oriented environment attracted multinationals, which were permitted to borrow local capital and establish production networks that complemented Taiwan's export industry. In stark contrast, the Korean chaebols hoarded domestic capital and dominated industries, precluding foreign direct investment in Korea and impeding the establishment of complementary industries.

Another unique feature of the Taiwanese economy is the political and economic ramification of the ethnic and cultural cleavages between Mainlanders and Taiwanese (Fields, 1995; Kim, 1994). Historically policy choices have favored Mainland interests in fragmenting and dispersing the island's economic power in order to maintain the Mainlander domination of the island. However, the government's freedom from interest group pressures, "the absence of special interest organization" (Olson, 1982: 218), did not guarantee a state monopoly over policy making. Although Mainlanders supported the Kuomintang party (KMT), which was focused on preventing social forces, a byproduct of economic growth, from destroying its political hegemony, the opposition Democratic Progressive Party (DPP), formed in 1986, demanded increased political freedom (Chung, 2001; Flynn, 1999). The presidential election of Chen Shui-bian and his DPP cabinet ended more than half a century of KMT rule. Power bases changed, and new tensions between Taipei and Beijing, as well as between Taiwanese and Mainlanders, emerged. In addition, the minority government faced a hostile legislature as it sought to establish a distinctly Taiwanese identity and independence.

To date, Taiwan's horizontally integrated networks and flexible SME-based private sector have sheltered it from the worst of the ongoing regional economic problems. However, Taiwan's family capitalism is not well equipped to deal with the challenges of globalization, which require large-scale production in strategic industries. In Taiwan, the public sector has historically governed these primarily upstream industries, such as energy, heavy machinery, shipbuilding, and steel. Such inefficient, state-owned enterprises have impeded further economic development. State-owned enterprises, which once accounted for more than half of Taiwan's GNP, are now responsible for little more than 10 percent. This sector must be decentralized and liberated from state control to avert a future crisis.

Globalization will also unavoidably challenge Taiwanese family capitalism because of the demands it will place on SME-network flexibility – especially as SMEs move into the volatile export market. The Taiwanese economy now faces growing economic polarization and financial sector weaknesses. Just as the national economy opted for a high degree of concentration in IT, now accounting for more than 30 percent of exports, global demands for IT began slowing down, while skilled labor is scarce and profit margins are narrowing. Taiwan's other industries are increasingly uncompetitive, finding themselves burdened by poor corporate governance and rising production costs. The financial sector labors under non-performing loans and an excess of regional small banks, many of which are poorly managed.

Taiwan has not yet experienced a significant governance crisis. Its governance structure involves a flexible, instrumental relationship between government and business, in stark contrast to the entanglements found in Korea. At most, DPP inexperience on occasion has strained relationships between business and the government. However, the minority government and private sector must confront the challenges mentioned above – IT downturn, loan defaults, the depressed currency, and financial sector weaknesses. The state bureaucracy must create a credible economic environment, taking into account relations with China. It must also assume new facilitative and guiding roles for the horizontally integrated and flexible, SME-based private sector and for poorly regulated financial systems and IT-related strategic industries.

Recasting the institutional nexus and economic governance in Korea

In each decade since the 1960s, the Korean economy has trebled in size, and in the process it has developed a distinctive form of economic governance (Kim, 2000d). The state has been responsible for budget and monetary policies, has dominated growth-oriented policy networks, and has remained relatively immune to social pressures. In the 1970s and 1980s, in particular, it employed a wide range of powerful instruments to compel large private firms to invest in the heavy and chemical sectors. Most notably, through the control of commercial and special banks, the state determined the private sector access to stable, low-cost credit.

The weaknesses inherent in such a form of economic governance precipitated Korea's current crisis (Kim, 2000c). First, the state's ability to maintain a secure and consistent macroeconomic environment, through monitoring and disciplining domestic industries, has weakened over time, particularly following its admission to the OECD, which required a policy of general financial liberalization (Lee and Kim, 2000). In addition, the Ministry of Finance and Economy was formed by a merger, which created an intra-bureaucratic segmentation. The results were a loss of confidence, inconsistent macroeconomic policies, and managerial failures, as was evidenced by the widely publicized 1997 scandals surrounding Hanbo Steel and Kia Motors.

Secondly, such managerial failures decreased the state's ability to influence and coordinate private sector economic decisions. In the early 1990s political liberalization expanded the size, number and power of private sector chaebols, which also attenuated strong-armed state coordination of policy making (Kim, 2000c). The Chaebols grew powerful enough to transform their former subordinate relationship with the state into a symbiotic one that strengthened the hand of big business in formulating and implementing state economic policy. Gradually a rent-oriented policy network replaced the growth-oriented one.

Thirdly, the 1987 and 1992 elections released democratic forces that shook the state's traditional hegemony in state–society relations. Under Kim Young Sam, democratic reforms strengthened interest groups' influence on the state. Societal corporatism supplanted traditional state corporatism in economic policy making and eroded state credibility (Kim, 2000c, 2002a, b, 2004b). By mid-1997, fundamental economic problems such as over-investment by major business groups and the accumulation of non-performing loans by financial institutions were increasingly apparent. Traditional state protection had encouraged financial institutions to indulge in questionable lending practices and the chaebols to risk excessive leveraging for finance expansion. As a result, in 1997 the IMF offered assistance only on condition that severe austerity measures were introduced.

Economic reforms had fueled one of the region's most dramatic economic recoveries, with a recorded GDP growth of 8.8 percent in 2000, although the current situation in Korea has worsened again. State implementation of far-reaching macroeconomic and structural reforms in the financial, corporate, and labor sectors have turned around external conditions and set the stage for a sustainable recovery. Recent events, however, suggest backsliding in response to economic slowdown, as the state has restored to the chaebols some of the power forfeited in the wave of 1998–99 bankruptcies. It recently allowed them to increase their bank holdings, raising concerns that unfettered loan access could encourage a borrowing binge, like that which created the 1997 financial crisis. The state is also considering lifting restrictions on cross-shareholding among chaebol affiliates and easing rules on the bank bailout of troubled companies. The only significant reform that remains unchallenged is a reduced debt-to-equity ratio among chaebols.

The main threat to the reforms is the powerful legacy of government interference in bank lending decisions. Government-owned banks continue to bail out loan-burdened companies by providing them with additional loan packages. The financial system's stability is once again at risk, having, by 2002, received nearly US $150 billion in state recapitalization funds since 1997 (*Financial Times*, 24 October 2002). In addition, an entrenched state bureaucracy is reversing economic liberalization as it again intervenes in the private sector. Whether the state and corporate sectors will retain a sufficient commitment to reforming Korean economic governance is debatable. Major reforms, fundamental to global standards of liberal capitalism (greater transparency, removal of moral hazards, and a regulatory, rather than interventionist, regime), have been launched, although the traditional institutional nexus remains largely intact. If it is to create a new institutional nexus, one which is truly responsive to the current world environment, the state must foster a new regulatory institutional nexus in order to strengthen state monitoring and disciplinary prerogatives for deregulation and liberalization. At the same time, it must abandon a state-controlled, highly regulated governance framework.

Conclusion

The East Asian economies that once enjoyed rapid economic growth now face an unprecedented economic crisis in the face of globalization and mad technologies. Many question whether the state, the main governing mechanism in the East Asian development model, will remain a credible locus of economic governance – one able to provide a secure economic environment. Governance crises generally occur when a state's monitoring and disciplinary powers falter and fail to adjust to rapidly changing circumstances. State intra-bureaucratic conflicts and a failure to manage appropriate regulations make economic policies unpredictable and inconsistent. Business interests will replace coordination with the state in formulating and implementing economic policies with rent-seeking networks. Finally, various interest groups usurp the state's independence with extensive private penetration into state prerogatives, further hampering state credibility.

We must ask whether current economic circumstances and problems with the institutional nexus as well as the governance framework signal the demise of the East Asian model of capitalism, and whether East Asian capitalism will subsequently evolve into Anglo-American liberal capitalism. The legacy of a web of sociopolitical networks and contingent historical experiences may limit progress. As long as Confucian-authoritarian and familial values shape policies, any public clamor for market democratization will go untreeded. Although major reforms appear to support the implementation of global standards of liberal capitalism, the basic institutional nexus of East Asian states remains largely unchanged.

What is certain at this current moment is that the state needs to enhance its capacity as a locus of economic governance if it wants to implement successfully the major economic reforms against built-up structural impediments and to move toward liberal capitalism. The state must address the problems arising from the analytical linkage between two institutional levels: the governance framework within which economic transactions are embedded and the institutional nexus within which the governance framework emerges and functions. True reformat will require the introduction of new governance frameworks that discard anachronistic policies and practices. It will also require recasting the institutional nexus of the developmental state, where the state's collusion with business and financial sectors tends to be widespread. Furthermore, a regulatory state must resume institutional governing capacities, while the private sector minimizes rent-seeking behaviors and monopolistic market power.

10
Conclusions

> There is no essential difference between science and art. Both are fed from the same source, from the inherent drive of humans to go ahead, to raise their heads higher. Sic itur ad astra. (Zoltan Bay (1900–1992), the developer of radar astronomy)

Technological innovation is the central factor in corporate survival in the age of globalization and mad technology. However, the old view, that technology is a real production factor, is now being rapidly replaced by a new understanding, that it is in fact a part of cultural, virtual, and unreal factors of production (see Tsuru, 1993). If corporations do not acknowledge this new face of technology, they are squeezed out of the market. Traditional technologies that use heavy and chemical materials to produce Fordist commodities (e.g., mass production of one model of large size cars) have rapidly been supplanted by the so-called "post-industrial" technologies that Toyota championed (e.g., limited production of several models of small size cars).

Therefore, the key term in this age of globalization and mad technology does not appear to be innovation itself. What matters most to corporate managers nowadays are the following questions: what kind of innovation (technology development in a right sector)?, and what kind of commercialization (application knowledge development in a right market)? If technological flexibility through innovation is not achieved with the development of a parallel competence in commercialization that can compete with mad technology, then it will be insufficient to help firms to survive in the globalized market.

At the start of this book we posed several questions: (a) what is mad technology?, (b) how did it come into being in the post-Cold War era?, and (c) how are firms in East Asia defending their niche in the face of mad technology? We believe that the existence of mad technology and its potential dangers in the global environment have been clearly shown. Most existing data on IPOs by dot.com companies, trading volume of dot.com stocks, and the sudden crash of dot.com stocks indicate that a twister effect, of an overheated mad technology market, existed and furthermore, that it was as destructive as, a real tornado, devastating the real economy and those who bet money on deceptive dot.com stocks. Mad technologies mobilized peoples' money through an illusionary presentation of virtual technologies, suggesting that they could secure levels of wealth that human beings could have never envisaged in the past. If the depression economy of the 1930s forced many people to the point of suicide, because consumers had no alternative but frugality, the recession of the late 1990s pushed people into a limbo state that was neither life nor death, because they were dragged into the gluttony of making money overnight by trading dot.com stocks.

In contrast to other books on similar topics, however, we have attempted to focus more on the corporate and governmental strategies of coping with or neutralizing mad technologies and their economic effects, than on a discussion of the causes of mad technology and an analysis of why it is bad for our globalized society. In taking this approach, we touched on the subject of NIS programs, funding strategies, and corporate innovation devices.

Chapters 1 and 2 established our dependent variables, the existence of mad technologies in the form of IT, nanotech, and biotech ventures and their dangers, in the sense of a sudden dot.com stock crash, like that which occurred in the United States, Japan, Korea, and Taiwan at the start of the twenty-first century. Although not all data were compatible across different countries, the magnitude of a twister and its potential dangers were further confirmed by other scholars in the field. Research questions and theses put forward by these two chapters led us to several types of case and empirical studies.

Chapter 3 found that innovation was possible in East Asia because organizational equilibrium in the form of the chaebol, the keiretsu, and the guanxiqiye had already existed from the heydays of economic development. Organizational equilibrium led to various governance structures, such as the hierarchical multidivisional form in Korea, the three jewels system in Japan, and collective ownership and professional managerial control in Taiwan. What was significant in the age of mad technology was a clear conversion of the three governance structures on the one hand and the NIS structures on the other, as they became markedly similar to each other, especially after the passage of the TRIPs agreement and the rise of mad technology. The implications of these changes in recent years, along with the similarity among the three countries, in terms of R&D expenditure patterns (that is, the emphasis on technology development and application knowledge), is that the NIS has reacted sufficiently to mad technologies.

Chapters 4 and 5 gave an in-depth analysis of the Korean case, in which we indicated, albeit in the absence of complete evidence, that the simulation of the decision-making institution at the Korean NIS demonstrated a weakness in defending it from mad technology by an unnecessary concentration of funding on application knowledge and technology development programs, rather than in basic research. This means that Korean dot.com companies could readily secure national funding or disguise themselves as regulated technology in front of uninformed investors. Although the NIS did exhibit these weaknesses, we found that a few large chaebol firms in Korea secured their technological bases by strengthening their transactional governance structures on the one hand and cultivating innovative culture within corporations on the other. We noticed that transactional governance structures defended firms from external pressures, including domestic governmental demands for organizational reform and international forces that called for reforms. Organizational sense making as a variable of corporate culture, in association with intervening system variables (i.e., variables of transaction cost economics), produced conditions that were appropriate for innovation.

Chapters 6 and 7 dealt with the two cases of Taiwan and Japan, where authors noted that these countries are successful in developing know how to neutralizing mad technology. The Taiwanese case indicates that the benefit of basic research projects is imported from the United States through Taiwanese scientists who work in that country, while application knowledge and technology development programs provide spin-off opportunities for firms that are regulated within the parameters of the NIS. The international network of the NIS and overseas Chinese scientists was formed by the government in alliance with overseas Chinese venture capital firms, which means that venture capital firms were also subject to government regulation. This differed from the case of Korea, where it was the chaebols themselves that offered venture capital services.

The Japanese case demonstrated that the solution to the problem of technological dormancy (i.e., lead-time between commercialization and patent register) was maximizing interdivisional communication through the exploitation of complementary technologies, when the size of corporate knowledge depositories are too great to coordinate using simple organizational means. Organizational devices of inter-group communication, including formal and informal workgroups, meetings, and exposing corporate knowledge to concerned communities to explore how other organizations utilize new knowledge, were all deemed effective for commercialization. Nonetheless, it was also necessary that the government spend sufficient NIS funds on basic research to reduce opportunities for mad technology firms to use NIS resources and to enlarge the overall knowledge depository of governmental and corporate R&D institutions.

Chapters 8 and 9 both address the issue of governance in Korea and East Asia, although the former concentrated on corporate governance, while the latter addressed the larger issue of economic governance across the region. Chapter 8 found that the success of informal governance structures, or transactional governance structures, in Korea, for instance, made it difficult for formal governance reforms to take place quickly. The already obtained flexibility within the informal governance structure has made it easy for major firms to adapt successfully to new environmental contingencies since the external pressures of reform started in the 1990s. The authors concluded that continued governmental and external pressures upon the chaebol companies to introduce further corporate governance reform would only restrict their innovative capacities. In fact, informal governance structures found in different chaebols were beneficial in defending their technological bases from mad technology.

Chapter 9 raised the issue of which reform package is appropriate for East Asia. Our first step was to analyse the economic malaise that attacked Japan, Korea, and Taiwan in order to outline policy options to cure the disease. Japanese economic problems were derived from the failure of the monitoring role played by the government over its private banks; Taiwan suffered from governmental corruption and market irregularities as mad technologies disrupted its government controlled economy; and Korea possessed a serious corporate financial weakness deriving from the dangerous level of reliance on corporate bonds and bank debts in financing expenditures for fixtures and facilities. It was our assertion that these different types of economic mismanagement can be traced back to the same root cause – not the malfunction of the market due to governmental regulation, but the failure of economic governance mechanisms. A more sanguine economic governance structure strategy is not to destroy the structure in the name of free market and mad technology, but to strengthen it through the introduction of transparent decision-making and resource-allocating processes.

As Zoltan Bay stated in the epigraph at the start of this concluding chapter, we all espouse science as we do art. However, as we raise no serious objections to the regulation and censorship of art, technology should share a similar fate. Unregulated art can easily find its way into children's bedrooms in the form of pornography or can corrupt uneducated minds in the form of propaganda. Similarly, unregulated game software is capable of destroying young boys' creative minds at the crucial developmental ages of nine or ten. Throughout the chapters in this book, we tried to convey the idea that governments and corporations can do a better job in regulating mad technologies. Further studies can be designed to see how mad technologies actually work toward destroying regulated normal technologies and how their destructive impact produces unwanted and unintended consequences, which can be disastrous to our economies and to our planet. In addition, further empirical and in-depth studies can support the idea presented in this book that government and corporate actions for the protection of normal technologies from their mad counterparts were in fact beneficial to the overall economy, not to mention existing corporations. However, let us beware of the dangers inherent in excessive data collection and analysis at the cost of quietism. From their inception, the social sciences have striven to find evidence to disprove hypotheses, models, and theories. We will probably never be satisfied with the amount of data and evidence we have piled up, just to disprove small pieces of knowledge. However, while social sciences scholars remain concerned primarily with the accumulation of evidence that may not even exist, the world is often harmed in silence, with no attempts to ameliorate the situation. This is fast becoming the case with our proliferation of mad technologies. Governments and firms need to take action, even in the face of incomplete knowledge, before further crisis situations arise.

References

Aberbach, J., Dollar, D. and Sokoloff K. (eds) 1994. *The Role of the State in Taiwan's Development*, New York: M. E. Sharpe.

Abernathy W. and Clark, K. 1985. 'Innovation: Mapping the Winds of Creative Destruction', *Research Policy*, 14: 3–22.

Alter, C. and Hage, J. 1993. *Organizations Working Together*, Thousand Oaks, CA: Sage.

Amsden, A. 1989. *Asia's Next Giant: South Korea and Late Industrialization*, Oxford: Oxford University Press.

Aoki, M. 2000. *Information, Corporate Governance, and Institutional Diversity: Competitiveness in Japan, the USA, and the Transitional Economies*, Oxford: Oxford University Press.

Aoki, M. and Saxonhouse, G. (eds) 2000. *Finance, Governance, and Competitiveness in Japan*, Oxford: Oxford University Press.

Aoyama, S. 1999. *Haiteku Nettowâku Bungyô: Taiwan Handôtai Sangyô wa Naze Tsuyoinoka?*, Tokyo: Hakutô Shobô.

Argyris, N. and Liebeskind, J. 1999. 'Contractual Commitments, Bargaining Power, and Governance Inseparability: Incorporating History into Transaction Cost Theory', *Academy of Management Review*, 24(1): 49–63.

Arrighi, G. 1994. *The Long Twentieth Century: Money, Power, and the Origins of Our Times*, New York: Verso.

Arrighi, G. 1999. *Chaos and Governance in the Modern World System*, Minneapolis: University of Minnesota Press.

Arrow, K. 2000. 'Innovation in Large and Small Firms', in R. Swedberg (ed.), *Entrepreneurship: The Social Science View*, Oxford: Oxford University Press, 229–43.

Asamoto, T. 1996. *Gendai Taiwan Keizai Bunseki: Kaihatsu Keizaigaku kara no Apurôchi*, Tokyo: Keisô Shobô.

Asamoto, T. and Liu, W. 2001. *Taiwan no Keizai Kaihatsu Seisaku: Keizai to Seifu no Yakuwari*, Tokyo: Keisô Shobô.

Beauchamp, E. 1989. 'Education', in T. Ishida and E. Krauss (eds), *Democracy in Japan*, Pittsburgh: Pittsburgh University Press, 225–51.

Becker, G. and Murphy, K. 1992. 'The Division of Labor, Coordination Costs, and Knowledge', *Quarterly Journal of Economics*, 107(4): 1137–60.

Becker, G. and Murphy, K. 1988. 'The Family and the State', *Journal of Law and Economics*, 31(1): 1–18.

Bell, D. 1960. *The End of Ideology: On the Exhaustion of Political Ideas in the Fifties*, Glencoe, IL: The Free Press.

Bell, D. 1999. *The Coming of Post-industrial Society: A Venture in Social Forecasting*, New York: Basic Books.

Bello, W. 1990. *Brave New Third World: Strategies for Survival in the Global Economy*, London: Earthscan.

Bello, W. 1994. *The World Bank and the IMF*, http://www.zmag.org/zmag/articles/july94bello.htm. Accessed on 20 May 2004.

Berle, A. and Means, G. 1932. *The Modern Corporation and Private Property*, New York: Macmillan.

Bernard, M. and Ravenhill, J. 1995. 'Beyond Product Cycles and Flying Geese: Regionalization, Hierarchy, and the Industrialization of East Asia', *World Politics*, 47: 171–209.

Bloom, F. 1998. 'Priority Setting: Quixotic or Essential?', *Science*, 282, November 27.

Bonvillian, W. 2002. 'Science at a Crossroads', *Technology in Society*, 24: 27–39.

Borrus, M. and Stowsky, J. 1999. 'Technology Policy and Economic Growth', in M. Borrus and J. Stowsky (eds), *Investing in Innovation: Creating a Research and Innovation Policy that Works*, Cambridge: The MIT Press, 40–63.

Bower, J. and Christensen C. 1995. 'Disruptive Technologies: Catching the Wave', *Harvard Business Review*, January–February: 43–53.

Bozeman. B. and Melkers, J. 1993. *Evaluating R&D Impacts: Methods and Practice*, Boston: Kluwer Academic Publishers.

Braudel, F. 1992. *Grammaire des Civilizations*, Paris: Arthaud-Flammarion.

Braudel, F. 1993. *Civilisation, Economie et Capitalisme, XVe–XVIIIe siècle*, Paris: Livre de Poche.

Braun, D. 1998. 'The Role of Funding Agencies in the Cognitive Development of Science', *Research Policy*, 27: 807–21.

Burt, R. 1992. *Structural Holes: The Social Structure of Competition*, Cambridge: Harvard University Press.

Burt, R. 2000. 'The Network Entrepreneur' in R. Swedberg (ed.), *Entrepreneurship: The Social Science View*, Oxford: Oxford University Press, 281–307.

Calder, K. 1989. 'Elites in an Equalizing Role: Ex-bureaucrats as Coordinators and Intermediaries in the Japanese Government–Business Relationship', *Comparative Politics*, 21(4) (July): 379–403.

Carlson, B. (ed.) 1997. *Technological Systems and Economic Performance: The Case of Factory Automation*, Boston: Kluwer Academic.

Cassidy, J. 2002. *Dot.con: How America Lost its Mind and Money in the Internet Era*, New York: HarperCollins.

Castells, M. 1991. *The Informational City: Information Technology, Economic Restructuring, and the Urban-Regional Process*, Oxford: Blackwell.

Castells, M. 1996. *The Rise of the Network Society*, Cambridge: Blackwell.

Chandler, A. 1962. *Strategy and Structure*, Cambridge: The MIT Press.

Chang, H., Park. H. and Yoo, C. 1998. 'Interpreting the Korean Crisis: Financial Liberalization, Industrial Policy and Corporate Governance', *Cambridge Journal of Economics*, 22(6): 735–46.

Chang, J. 2000. 'Taiwan Economic Policy Analysis', *McKeever Institute of Economic Policy Analysis*, Fall. http://www.mckeever.com/taiwan.html. Accessed on 30 May 2000.

Chang, P. and Hsu, C. 1998. 'The Development Strategies for Taiwan's Semiconductor Industry', *IEEE Transactions on Engineering Management*, 45: 349–56.

Chang, P., Lung, S. and Hsu, C. 1998. 'The Evaluating Model for the Technology Needs of Taiwan High-tech Industries', *International Journal of Technology Management*, 18: 133–45.

Chang, S. 1999. *'National Innovation Systems and Development: Models and Policy Strategies'*. Unpublished manuscript. Taipei: National Science Council.

Chang, S. 2003. 'The Internet Economy of Korea', in B. Kogut (ed.), *The Global Internet Economy*, Cambridge: The MIT Press, 263–89.

Chen, J. 1994. *Xieli Wanglu Shenghuo Jiegou–Taiwan Zhongxiao qiye de Shehui Jingji Fenxi*, Taipei: Lianjing Chuban Shiye.

Cheng, T. 1986. 'Sequencing and Implementing Development Strategies: Korea and Taiwan'. Paper delivered at the Conference on 'Developmental Strategies in Latin American and East Asia'. La Jolla, CA: Center for US–Mexican Studies.

Cheng, T. 1993. 'The State as Banker in Taiwan', in S. Haggard et al. (eds), *The Politics of Finance in Developing Countries*, Ithaca: Cornell University Press, 55–92.

Cheng, T. and Haggard, S. 1987. 'Newly Industrializing Asia in Transition: Policy Reform and American Response', *Policy Papers in International Affairs* 31, Berkeley: Institute of International Studies, University of California.

Chernousenko, V. 1991. *Chernobyl: Insight from the Inside*, Berlin: Springer-Verlag.

Chesbrough, H. and Teece, D. 1996. 'When is Virtual Virtuous? Organizing for Innovation', *Harvard Business Review*, January–February: 65–73.

Chiang, S. and Mason. R. 1988. 'Domestic Industrial Structure and Export Quality', *International Economic Review* 29.

Child, J. and Faulkner, D. 1998. *Strategies of Co-operation: Managing Alliances, Networks, and Joint Ventures*, Oxford: Oxford University Press.

Choo, C. 1998. *The Knowing Organization*, Oxford: Oxford University Press.

Chou, C. and Shy, O. 1991. 'A Model of Technological Gap, Product Cycle, and the Process of Catching up between the North and the South', *Economic Record*, September: 217–26.

Chow, P. and Bates, G. 2000. *Weathering the Storm, Taiwan and its Neighbors*, Washington, DC: Brookings Institute Press.

Christensen, C. 1997. *The Innovator's Dilemma*, Boston: Harvard Business School Press.

Chu, Y. 1994. 'The State and the Development of the Automobile Industry in South Korea and Taiwan', in J. Aberbach et al. (eds), *The Role of the State in Taiwan's Development*, New York: M. E. Sharpe, 125–69.

Chu, Y. 1999. 'The Institutional Foundation of Taiwan's Industrialization: Exploring the State–Society Nexus', in G. Ranis et al. (eds), *The Political Economy of Taiwan's Development into 21st Century: Essays in Memory of John C.H. Fei*, Cheltenham: Edward Elgar, 2: 285–311.

Chung, C. 2001. 'Markets, Culture and Institutions: The Emergence of Large Business Groups in Taiwan, 1950–1970s', *Journal of Management Studies*, 38(5): 719–45.

Clark, K. and Fujimoto, T. 1991. *Product Development Performance*, Boston: Harvard Business School Press.

Clegg, S. 1990. *Modern Organization: Organization Studies in Postmodern World*, London: Sage.

Coase, R. 1991. 'The Nature of the Firm', in O. Williamson and S. Winter (eds), *The Nature of the Firm: Origins, Evolution, Development*, Oxford: Oxford University Press, 18–33.

Cohen, B. 1998. *The Geography of Money*, Ithaca: Cornell University Press.

Cohen, H., Keller, S. and Streeter, D. 1979. 'The Transfer of Technology from Research to Development', *Research Management*, 22(3): 11–17

Cohen, M. 1991. Individual Learning and Organizational Routine: Emerging Connections, *Organization Science*, 2: 135–9.

Cohen, M. and Bacdayan, P. 1994. 'Organizational Routines are Stored as Procedural Memory: Evidence from Laboratory Study', *Organization Science*, 4: 554–68.

Cohen, W. and Levinthal, D. 1989. 'Innovation and Learning: The Two Faces of R&D', *The Economic Journal*, 99(397): 569–96.

Cohen, W. and Levinthal, D. 1990. 'Absorptive Capacity: A New Perspective on Learning and Innovation', *Administrative Science Quarterly*, 35(1): 128–52.

Cole D. and Park, Y. 1984. *Hanguk ui Kumyung Baljon: 1945–1980*, Seoul: Korea Development Institute.

Curtin, J. and Roosevelt, T. 2003. *The Mongols: A History*, New York: DaCapo Press.

Cyert, R. and March, J. 1963. *A Behavioral Theory of the Firm*, Englewood Cliffs, NJ: Prentice Hall.

Davis, L. and North, D. 1971. *Institutional Change and American Economic Growth*, Cambridge: Cambridge University Press.

Dawson, M. 2003. *The Consumer Trap: Big Business Marketing in American Life*, Urbana: University of Illinois Press.

Demsetz, H. 1988. 'The Theory of the Firm Revisited', *Journal of Law, Economics and Organization*, 4: 141–62.

Deyo, F. and Doner, R. 2001. 'Introduction: Economic Governance and Flexible Production in East Asia', in F. Deyo et al. (eds), *Economic Governance and the Challenge of Flexibility in East Asia*, New York: Rowman & Littlefield Publishers, 1–32.

Dhonte, P. and Kapur, I. 1996. 'Toward a Market Economy: Structures of Governance', *IMF Working Paper*, November.

Doner, R. 1992. 'Limits of State Strength: Toward an Institutionalist View of Economic Development', *World Politics*, 44: 398–431.

Doner, R., Deyo, F. and Fields, K. 1993. 'Industrial Governance in East and Southeast Asia'. Presented at the Social Science Research Council Workshop on *Industrial Governance and Labor Flexibility in Comparative Perspective*, New York.

Dore, R. 1986. *Flexible Rigidities: Industrial Policy and Structural Adjustment in the Japanese Economy, 1970–1980*, Stanford: Stanford University Press.

Dubini, P. and Aldrich, H. 1991. 'Personal and Extended Networks are Central to the Entrepreneurial Process', *Journal of Business Venturing*, 6: 305–13.

Dyer, J. and Singh, H. 1998. 'The Relational View: Cooperative Strategy and Sources of Interorganizational Competitive Advantage', *Academy of Management Review*, 23(4): 660–79.

Edler, Meyer-Krahmer and Rogers. 2002. 'Changes in the Strategic Management of Technology: Results of Global Benchmarking Study', *R&D management* 32.

Eldred, E. and McGrath M. 1997. 'Commercializing New Technology-II', *Research-Technology Management*, 40(2): 29–33.

Ellis, J. and Ezell, E. 1986. *The Social History of the Machine Gun*, Baltimore: Johns Hopkins University Press.

Elster, J. 1979. *Ulysses and Sirens*, Cambridge: Cambridge University Press.

Ernst, D. 1997. 'Technology Management in the Korean Electronics Industry: What Factors Explain the Dynamics of Change?' Prepared for the Conference on 'Business Systems in the South', Copenhagen Business School.

Ernst, D. 1998. 'Catching-up, Crisis, and Industrial Upgrading: Evolutionary Aspects of Technology Learning in the Korean Electronics Industry', *Asia Pacific Journal of Management*, 15(2): 147–83.

ERSO. 1999. *Electronics Research and Service Organization*, Hsinchu: ITRI.

Executive Yuan, Directorate General of Budget, Accounting and Statistics. 2004. http://www.stat.gov.tw/bs2/2003YearBook.pdf. Accessed on 8 June 2004.

Fama, E. 1980. 'Agency Problems and the Theory of the Firm', *Journal of Political Economy*, 88: 288–307.

Fama, E. and Jansen, M. 1983. 'Agency Problems and Residual Claims', in N. Foss (ed.), *The Theory of the Firm*, London: Routledge, 345–66.

Fields, K. 1995. *Enterprise and the State in South Korea and Taiwan*, Ithaca: Cornell University Press.

Flynn, N. 1999. *Miracle to Meltdown in Asia: Business, Government and Society*, Oxford: Oxford University Press.

Fortun, K. 2001. *Advocacy after Bhopal: Environmentalism, Disaster, New Global Orders*, Chicago: University of Chicago Press.

Foster, J. 1999. *The Vulnerable Planet: A Short Economic History of the Environment*, New York: Monthly Review Press.

Foster, J. 2000. *Marx's Ecology: Materialism and Nature*, New York: Monthly Review Press.

Friedman, M. and Friedman, R. 2002. *Capitalism and Freedom*, Chicago: University of Chicago Press.

Frischtak, L. 1994. *Governance Capacity and Economic Reform in Developing Countries*, World Bank Technical Paper #254.

Frischtak, L. and Atiyas, I. (eds) 1996. *Governance, Leadership and Communication*, Washington, DC: World Bank.

Fruin, W. 1994. *The Japanese Enterprise System: Competitive Strategies and Cooperative Structures*, New York: Oxford University Press.

Fukagawa, Y. 2000. 'Higashi Ajia no Kôzô Chôsei to Kôporêto Gabanansu Keisei: Kankoku no Jirei o Chûshin ni', in M. Aoki and J. Teranishi (eds), *Tenkanki no Higashi Ajia to Nihon Kigyô*, Tokyo: Tôyôkeizai Shinbunsha, 179–220.

Fuller, J. 1998. *Armament and History: The Influence of Armament on History from the Dawn of Classical Warfare to the End of the Second World War*, New York: DaCapo Press.

Gadbaw, R. and Richards, T. 1988. *Intellectual Property Rights: Global Consensus, Global Conflict?*, Boulder: Westview Press.

Galbraith, J. 1973. *Designing Complex Organization*, Reading, MA: Addison-Wesley.

Galbraith, J. 1977. *Organization Design*, Reading, MA: Addison-Wesley.

Gambetta, D. 1988. 'Mafia: The Price of Distrust', in D. Gambetta (ed.), *Trust: Making and Breaking Cooperative Relations*, Oxford: Basil Blackwell, 158–75.

Gambetta, D. 1993. *The Sicilian Mafia: The Business of Private Protection*, Cambridge: Harvard University Press.

Gamble, A. 2000. 'Economic Governance', in J. Pierre (ed.), *Debating Governance*, Oxford: Oxford University Press, 110–37.

Gates, B. 1999. *Business @ the Speed of Thought: Using a Digital Nervous System*, New York: Warner Books.

Geisler, E. and Kassicieh, S. 1997. 'Information Technologies and Technology Commercialization: The Research Agenda', *IEEE Transactions on Engineering Management*, 44(4): 339–46.

Geringer, J. and Herbert, L. 1989. 'Control and Performance of International Joint Ventures', *Journal of International Business Studies*, 20: 235–54.

Gerlach, M. 1987. 'Business Alliances and the Strategy of the Japanese Firm', *California Management Review*, 30: 126–42.

Gerlach, M. 1992. *Alliance Capitalism: The Social Organization of Japanese Business*, Berkeley: University of California Press.

Gerlach, M. and Lincoln, J. 1992. 'The Organization of Business Networks in the United States and Japan', in N. Nohria and R. Eccles (eds), *Networks and Organizations: Structure, Form, and Action*, Boston: Harvard Business School Press, 491–520.

Gerschenkron, A. 2000. 'The Modernization of Entrepreneurship', in R. Swedber (ed.), *Enterpreneurship: The Social Science View*, Oxford: Oxford University Press, 129–38.

Granovetter, M. 1973. 'The Strength of Weak Ties', *American Journal of Sociology*, 78: 1360–380.

Granovetter, M. 1994. 'Business Groups', in N. Smelser and R. Swedberg (eds), *The Handbook of Economic Sociology*, Princeton: Princeton University Press, 453–75.

Granovetter, M. 1995. 'Coase Revisited: Business Groups in the Modern Economy', *Industrial and Corporate Change*, 1: 93–130.

Greve, H. 2003. 'A Behavioral Theory of R&D Expenditures and Innovations: Evidence from Shipbuilding', *Academy of Management Journal*, 46(6): 685–702.

Haggard, S. 1989. *Pacific Dynamics: The International Politics of Industrial Change*, Boulder: Westview Press.

Haggard, S. 1990. *Pathways from the Periphery: The Politics of Growth in the Newly Industrializing Countries*, Ithaca: Cornell University Press.

Haggard, S. 2000. *The Political Economy of the Asian Financial Crisis*, Washington, DC: Institute for International Economics.

Hamel, G. and Prahalad, C. 1994. *Competing for the Future*, Boston: Harvard Business School Press.

Hamilton, G. and Biggart, N. 1988. 'Market, Culture and Authority: A Comparative Analysis of Management and Organization in the Far East', *American Journal of Sociology*, 94: 552–94.

Han, C. 1994. *Sobi Sanup Gaebang gwa WTO*, Seoul: Dasan.

Hansen, K., Weiss, M. and Kwak, S. 1999. 'Allocating R&D Resources: A Quantitative Aid to Management Insight', *Research Technology Management*, 42(4) (July–Aug.): 44.

Harrison, D., Price, K. and Bell, M. 1998. 'Beyond Rational Demography: Time and the Effects of Surface and Deep-level Diversity on Work Group Cohesion', *Academy of Management Journal*, 41: 96–107.

Harryson, S. 1997. 'How Canon and Sony Drive Product Innovation through Networking and Application-focused R&D', *Journal of Product Innovation Management*, 14: 288–95.

Haruna, M. 1993 *Sukuryu-on ga Kieta: Toshiba Jiken to Bei Jôhô Kôsaku no Shinsô*, Tokyo: Shinchôsha.

Hatch, W. and Yamamura, K. 1996. *Asia in Japan's Embrace: Building a Regional Production Alliance*, Cambridge: Cambridge University Press.

Heidenberger, K., Schillinger, A. and Stummer, C. 2003. 'Budgeting for Research and Development: A Dynamic Financial Simulation Approach', *Socio-Economic Planning Science*, 37: 15–27.

Heilbroner, R. 1989. *The Making of Economic Society*, New Jersey: Prentice Hall.

Henwood, D. 2003. *After the New Economy*, New York: New Press.

Hofstede, G. 1983. 'The Cultural Relativity of Organizational Practices and Theories', *Journal of International Business Studies*, 14: 75–89.

Hogg, M. and Terry, D. 2000. 'Social Identity and Self-categorization Processes in Organizational Contexts', *Academy of Management Review*, 25: 121–40.

Hollingsworth, J. and Boyer, R. (eds) 1997. *Contemporary Capitalism: The Embeddedness of Institutions*, Cambridge: Cambridge University Press.

Hollingsworth, J., Schmitter, P. and Streeck, W. 1994. *Governing Capitalist Economies: Performance and Control of Economic Sectors*, Oxford: Oxford University Press.

Holmstrom, B. 1979. 'Moral Hazard and Observability', *Bell Journal of Economics*, 10(1): 74–91.

Hong, Y. 1993. 'The Japan's Strategy for Technology Transfer to Asia and Korea's Response', *KEIP Working Paper* 23, Seoul: Korea Institute for International Economic Policy, November.

Hong, Y. 1994. 'Technology Transfer: The Korean Experience', *KIEP Working Paper* 3, Seoul: Korea Institute for International Economic Policy.

Hoshi, T. and Kashyap, A. 2001. *Corporate Financing and Governance in Japan: The Road to the Future*, Cambridge: The MIT Press.

Hsu, J. and Saxenian, A. 2000. 'The Limits of Guanxi Capitalism: Transnational Collaboration between Taiwan and the USA', *Environment and Planning*, 32: 1991–2005.

Iansiti, M. 1998. *Technology Integration: Making Critical Choice in a Dynamic World*, Boston: Harvard Business School Press.

Ichijo, K., Agata, K., Koike, S., Shima, H. and Yokoki, K. 2001. *Jissen Knowledge Management: Social Architecture to Business Architecture no Kakusin*, Tokyo: NEC Media Products.

Imai, K. and Itami, H. 1984. 'Interpenetration of Organization and Market', *International Journal of Industrial Organization*, 2: 285–310.

Irie, A. 2001. *Partnership: The United States and Japan, 1951–2001*, Tokyo: Kodansha.

Ishida, H. 1993. *Social Mobility in Contemporary Japan*, Stanford: Stanford University Press.

Ishizawa-Grbic, D. 2000. *'Network of Distrust: Explaining the Japanese Financial Crisis'*. Unpublished master's thesis, Hamilton: University of Waikato.

Itami, H., Kagono, T., Miyamoto, M. and Yonekura, S. (eds) 1998. *Inobêshon to Kijutsu Chikuseki*, Tokyo: Yûhikaku.

ITRI. 1998. *Annual Brochure*, Taipei: ITRI.

ITRI. 1998. *Annual Report: Industrial Technology Research Institute*, Hsinchu: ITRI.

Jackson, S. 1992. 'Team Composition in Organizational Settings: Issues in Managing an Increasingly Diverse Work Force', in S. Worchel et al. (eds), *Group Process and Productivity*, Newbury Park, CA: Sage, 138–73.

Jackson, S., May, K. and Whitney, K. 1995. 'Understanding the Dynamics of Diversity in Decision Making Teams', in R. Guzzo and E. Salas (eds), *Team Effectiveness and Decision Making in Organizations*, San Francisco: Jossey-Bass, 204–61.

JASDAQ. 2004. http://www.jasdaq.co.jp/statistic/stat_year.jsp. Accessed on 12 June 2004.

Jayasuriya, K. 2000. 'Authoritarian Liberalism, Governance and the Emergence of the Regulatory State in Post-crisis East Asia', in R. Robison et al. (eds), *Politics and Markets in the Wake of the Asian Crisis*, London: Routledge, 315–30.

Jensen, M. 2000. *A Theory of the Firm: Governance, Residual Claims and Organizational Forms*, Cambridge: Harvard University Press.

Jensen, M. and Meckling, W. 1976. 'Theory of the Firm: Managerial Behavior, Agency Costs and Ownership Structure', *Journal of Financial Economics*, 3: 305–60.

Jensen, M. and Meckling, W. 1990. Knowledge, Control, and Organizational Structure, *Journal of Law, Economics, and Organization*, 4, Spring: 95–118.

Jewkes, J. 1969. *The Source of Invention*, New York: Macmillan.

Jewkes, Y. (ed.) 2002. *Dot.cons: Crime, Deviance and Identity on the Internet*, Cullompton: Willan.

Johnson, C. 1982. *MITI and the Japanese Miracle: The Growth of Industrial Poilcy, 1925–1975*, Stanford: Stanford University Press.

Johnson, C. 1995. *Japan: Who Governs?*, New York: Norton.

Jones, C., Hesterly, W. and Borgatti, S. 1997. 'A General Theory of Network Governance: Exchange Conditions and Social Mechanisms', *Academy of Management Review*, 22(4): 911–45.

Jones, L. and Sakong, I. 1980. *Government, Business and Entrepreneurship in Economic Development: The Korean Case*, Boston: Harvard University Press.

Judis, J. 2001. *The Paradox of American Democracy: Elites, Special Interests, and the Betrayal of the Public Trust*, London: Routledge.

Kagaku Gijutsu Chô. 1998. *Kagaku Gijutsu Yôran 1997*, Tokyo.

Kahneman, D. and Tversky, A. 1979. 'Prospect Theory: An Analysis of Decision under Risk', *Econometrica*, 47(2): 263–92.

Kakurai, Y. (ed.) 1998. *Daikeisô Jidai to Kiseiganka*, Tokyo: Shinnippon Shuppansha.

Kam, W. 1995. *National Innovation System: The Case of Singapore*, Singapore: Science and Technology Institute.

Kaneko, M. 1999. *Han Grôbarizumu: Sijyô Kaikaku no Senryakuteki Shikô*, Tokyo: Iwanami Shoten.

Kang, C., Choi, J. and Chang, C. 1991. *Chaebol: Songchang ui Juyok inga Tamyok ui Hwasin inga?*, Seoul: Bipong.

Kang, D. 2002. *Crony Capitalism: Corruption and Development in South Korea and the Philippines*, Cambridge: Cambridge University Press.

Katz, R. 1998. *The System that Soured: The Rise and Fall of the Japanese Economic Miracle*, New York: M. E. Sharpe.

Keating, E., Oliva, R., Repenning, N., Rockart, S. and Sternman, J. 1999. 'Overcoming the Improvement Paradox', *European Management Journal*, 17(2): 120–34.

Kim, E. 1997. *Big Business, Strong State: Collusion and Conflict in South Korean Development, 1960–1990*, Albany: State University of New York Press.

Kim, H. 1993. 'Divergent Organizational Paths of Industrialization in East Asia', *Asian Perspective*, 17: 105–35.

Kim, H. 1994. 'The State and Economic Organization in a Comparative Perspective: The Organizing Mode of the East Asian Political Economy', *Korean Social Science Journal*, 20: 91–120.

Kim, H. 2000a. 'Fragility or Continuity?: Economic Governance of East Asian Capitalism', in R. Robison et al. (eds), *Politics and Markets in the Wake of the Asian Crisis*, London: Routledge, 99–115.

Kim, H. 2000b. 'Governance Crisis and the Transformation of East Asian Capitalism', *International Studies Review*, 3: 109–23.

Kim, H. 2000c. 'Korea's Economic Governance in Transition: Governance Crisis and the Future of Korean Capitalism', *Korea Observer*, 31(4): 553–77.

Kim, H. 2000d. 'The Viability and Vulnerability of Korean Economic Governance', *Journal of Contemporary Asia*, 30: 199–220.

Kim, H. 2002a. 'NGOs in Pursuit of "the Public Good" in South Korea', in S. Sargeson (ed), *Collective Goods, Collective Futures in Asia*, London: Routledge, 58–74.

Kim, H. 2002b. 'Unraveling Civil Society in South Korea: Old Discourses and New Visions', *Korea Observer*, 33(4): 541–67.

Kim, H. 2004a forthcoming. 'From State-centric to Negotiated Governance: NGOs as Policy Entrepreneurs in South Korea', in R. Weller (ed.), *Globalization and Political Change in Asia: Organizing between Family and State*, London: Routledge.

Kim, H. 2004b forthcoming. 'Dilemmas in the Making of Civil Society in Korean Political Reform', *Journal of Contemporary Asia* 34.

Kim, L. 1993. 'National System of Industry: Dynamics of Capability Building in Korea', in R. Nelson (ed.), *National Innovation System: A Comparative Analysis*, Oxford: Oxford University Press, 357–83.

Kim, L. 1997. *Imitation to Innovation: The Dynamics of Korea's Technological Learning*, Boston: Harvard Business School Press.

Kim, S. 1998. 'The Korean System of Innovation in the Semiconductor Industry: A Governance Perspective', *Industrial and Corporate Change*, 7: 275–309

Kim, Y., Lee, B. and Lim, Y. 1999. 'A Comparative Study of Managerial Features between Public and Private R&D Organizations in Korea: Managerial and Policy Implications for Public R&D Organizations', *International Journal of Technology Management*, 17: 281–311

Kim, Y. 1998. *IMF Cheje ihoo Kiup Jibe Jedo ui Junge Banghyang: Hankuk gwa Ilbon ui Jedokaesun Nonui rul Jungshim uro*, Seoul: Sanup Yunguwon.

Kirzner, I. 1985. *Discovery and the Capitalist Process*, Chicago: University of Chicago Press.

Kobrin, S. 1997 'Electronic Cash and the End of National Markets', *Foreign Policy* 107.

Kogut, B. (ed.) 2003. *The Global Internet Economy*, Cambridge: The MIT Press.

Konno, N. 2002. *Knowledge Management Nyûmon*, Tokyo: Nihon Keizai Shinbunsha.

Koo, H. 1993. *State and Society in Contemporary Korea*, Ithaca: Cornell University Press.

Koo, H. and Kim, E. 1992. 'The Developmental State and Capital Accumulation in South Korea', in R. Appelbaum and J. Henderson, *States and Development in the Asia Pacific Rim*, Newbury Park, CA: Sage, 121–49.

Kooiman, J. (ed) 1993. *Modern Governance: New Government-Society Interactions*, London: Sage Publications.

Korea National Statistical Office. 2004. http://kosis.nso.go.kr/cgi-bin/sws_999.cgi?ID = D T_1P32&IDTYPE = 3. Accessed on 9 June 2004.

Korn, D., Rich, R., Garrison, H., Gloub, S., Hendrix, M., Heinig, S., Masters, B. and Turman, R. 2002. 'The NIH Budget in the Postdoubling Era', *Science* 296, May 24.

KOSDAQ. 2004. http://www.kosdaqcommittee.or.kr/NeoDown?filepath = /upFiles/data/issue/&filename = 1079672273895.pdf. Accessed on 14 June 2004.

Kreiner, K. and Schultz, M. 1993. 'Informal Collaboration in R&D: The Formation of Networks across Organizations', *Organization Studies*, 14: 189–209.

Krugman, P. 1999. *The Return of Depression Economics*, New York: Norton.

Kumon, S. 1996. *Netizun no Jidai*, Tokyo: NTT.

Kusunoki, K. and Numagami, T. 1996. '*Interfunctional Transfers of Engineers in a Japanese Firm: An Empirical Study on Frequency, Timing, and Pattern*'. Unpublished manuscript.

Kwon, Y. and Song, W. 1998. 'Chichok Chaesankwon Bohocheido', Seoul: *STEPI Yonkyu Ch'oso.*

Langlois, R. and Robertson, P. 1995. *Firms, Markets and Economic Change*, London: Routledge.

Larson, A. 1992. 'Network Dyads in Entrepreneurial Settings: A Study of the Governance of Exchange Relationships', *Administrative Science Quarterly*, 37: 76–104.

Lawrence, P. and Lorsh, J. 1967. *Organization and Environment: Managing Differentiation and Integration*, Cambridge: Harvard University Press.

Lazerson, M. 1988. 'Organizational Growth of Small Firms: An Outcome of Markets and Hierarchies?', *American Sociological Review*, 53: 330–42.

Lee, B. 1993. *Hangukshik Kyungyoung*, Seoul: Hankuk Kyungje Shinmunsa.

Lee, K. 1977. *Shichang Kucho wa Dokgwachom Kyuchei*, Seoul: KDI.

Lee, K. 1994. 'Ownership–Management Relations in Korean Businesses', in L. Cho and Y. Kim (eds), *Korea's Political Economy: An Institutional Perspective*, Boulder: Westview Press, 701–15.

Lee, K. 1996. *The Theory and Policy of the SMEs*, Seoul: Jishik Saneopsa.

Lee, Y. and Kim, H. 2000. 'The Dilemma of Liberalization: Financial Crisis and the Transformation of Capitalism in South Korea', in R. Robison et al. (eds), *Politics and Markets in the Wake of the Asian Crisis*, London: Routledge, 116–29.

Lee, U., Kim, S. and Kim, S. 2001. 'Hankuk ui Gukka Gyungjaengryuk: Hyunsil gwa Banghyang 1', *Gukka Gyungjaengryuk ui Hyunsil gwa Jungchaekbangan* 15, Seoul: Samsung Economic Research Institute.

Leonard-Barton, D. and Doyle J. 1996. 'Commercializing Technology: Imaginative Understanding of User Needs', in R. Rosenbloom and W. Spencer (eds), *Engines of Innovation: U.S. Industrial Research at the End of an Era*, Boston: Harvard Business School Press, 177–207.

Leoncini, R. 1998. 'The Nature of Long-run Technological Change: Innovation, Evolution and Technological Systems', *Research Policy*, 27: 75–93.

Lie, J. 1997. 'The State as Pimp: Prostitution and the Patriarchal State in Japan in the 1940s', *The Sociological Quarterly*, 38(2): 251–63.

Lie, J. 1998. *Han Unbound: The Political Economy of South Korea*, Stanford: Stanford University Press.

Liebeskind, J., Oliver, A., Zucker, L. and Brewer, M. 1996. 'Social Networks, Learning, and Flexibility: Sourcing Scientific Knowledge in New Biotechnology Firms', *Organization Science*, 7: 428–43.

Lim, H. 1998. *Korea's Growth and Industrial Transformation*, London: Macmillan.

Lin, P. 1991. 'The Social Sources of Capital Investment in Taiwan's Industrialization', in G. Hamilton (ed.), *Business Networks and Economic Development in East and Southeast Asia*, Hong Kong: University of Hong Kong.

Lincoln, J. 1990. 'Japanese Organization and Organization Theory', *Research in Organizational Behavior*, 12: 255–94.

Lipson, C. and Cohen, B. 1999. *Theory and Structure in International Political Economy: An International Organization Reader*, Cambridge: The MIT Press.

Lounamaa, P. and March, J. 1987. 'Adaptive Coordination of a Learning Team', *Management Science*, 33(1): 107–23.

Lundvall, B. 1992. *National Systems of Innovation: Toward a Theory of Innovation and Interactive*, London: Pinter.

MacLoughlin, I. 1999. *Creative Technological Change*, London: Routledge.

Masten, S. 1993. 'Transaction Costs, Mistakes, and Performance: Assessing the Importance of Governance', *Management and Decision Economics*, 14, January–February: 80–96.

Makeig, K. 2002. 'Funding the Future: Setting Our S&T Priorities', *Technology in Society*, 24: 41–7.

Makino, N. 1998. *Nihon no Kijutsu wa Madamada Tsuyoi*, Tokyo: PHP Kenkyûsho.

Mander, J and Goldsmith, E. 1996. *The Case against the Global Economy: And for a Turn toward the Local*, San Francisco: Sierra Club Books.

Marceau, J. 2002. 'Divining Directions for Development: A Cooperative Industry–Government–Public Sector Research Approach to Establishing R&D Priorities', *R&D Management*, 32: 209–21.

March, J. 1991. 'Exploration and Exploitation in Organizational Learning', *Organization Science*, 2(1): 71–87.

March, J. and Olsen, J. 1989. *Rediscovering Institutions: The Organizational Basis of Politics*, New York: Free Press.

Marples, D. 1988. *The Social Impact of the Chernobyl Disaster*, Edmonton: University of Alberta Press.

Mathews, J. 1997. 'A Silicon Valley of the East: Creating Taiwan's Semiconductor Industry', *California Management Review*, 39: 26–55.

Maurice, M., Sorge, A. and Warner, M. 1980. 'Societal Differences in Organizing Manufacturing Units: A Comparison of France, West Germany and Great Britain,' *Organization Studies*, 1: 59–86.

METI. 2004. http://www.mext.go.jp/b_menu/toukei/002/002b/16/xls/155.xls. Accessed on 9 June 2004.

Miles, R. and Snow, C. 1986. 'Organizations: New Concepts for New Forms', *California Management Review*, 28(3): 62–73.

Miles, R. and Snow, C. 1992. 'Causes and Failure in Network Organizations', *California Management Review*, 34, Summer: 53–72.

Ministry of Science and Technology. 2003. *Gwahak Gisulyeungu Hwaldong Chosabogo*, Seoul: MST.

MITI. 1999. *Shiken Kenkyû Zeisei no Bappon Kaikaku ni Tsuite*. Tokyo: MITI.

MOEA. 1999. *1999 Development of Industries in Taiwan, ROC*, Taipei: MOEA.

MOFA. 2004. http://www.mofa.go.jp/mofaj/area/ecodata/sitsugyo.html. Accessed on 19 June 2004.

Mone, M., McKinley, W. and Barker, V. 1998. 'Organizational Decline and Innovation: A Contingency Framework', *Academy of Management Review*, 23(1): 115–32.

Monteverde, K. and Teece, D. 1982. 'Supplier Switching Costs and Vertical Integration in the Automobile Industry', *Bell Journal of Economics*, 13, Spring: 206–13.

Moon, C. and Rhyu, S. 2000. 'The State, Structural Rigidity, and the End of Asian Capitalism: A Comparative Study of Japan and South Korea', in R. Robison et al. (eds), *Politics and Markets in the Wake of the Asian Crisis*, London: Routledge, 77–98.

Moorman, C. and Miner, A. 1998. 'Organizational Improvisation and Organizational Memory', *Academy of Management Review*, 23(4): 698–723.

Mowery, D. and Teece, D. 1993. 'Japan's Growing Capabilities in Industrial Technology Implications for U.S. Managers and Policymakers', *California Management Review*, Winter: 9–34.

Mowery, D. and Teece, D. 1998. 'Fashioning a New Korean Model out of the Crisis: The Rebuilding of Institutional Capabilities', *Cambridge Journal of Economics*, 22: 747–59.

Mueller, E. 1963. 'Public Attitudes Toward Fiscal Programs', *Quarterly Journal of Economics*, 77(2): 210–35.

Mukai, J. 1997. *Kinyû Bigguban*, Tokyo: Kôdansha.

Mumford, L. 1963. *Technics and Civilization*, New York: Harcourt, Brace & Company.

Mumford, L. 1964. *The Myth of the Machine*, New York: Harcourt, Brace & World.

Narin, F. and Frame, F. 1989. 'The Growth of Japanese Science and Technology', *Science*, 245: 660–5.

NASDAQ. 2004. http://www.marketdata.nasdaq.com/asp/Sec3IPO.asp. Accessed on 8 June 2004.

National Science Foundation. 1988. *The Science and Technology Resources of Japan: A Comparison with the United States*. NSF Report 88–318, Washington, D.C.

National Science Foundation. 2004. http://www.nsf.gov/sbe/srs/seind04/pdf_v2.htm. Accessed on 9 June 2004.

National Statistics Office. 2000. *Gyongche Ilchi*, Seoul: National Statistics Office.

Nelson, R. and Rosenberg, N. 1993. 'Technical Innovation and National Systems', in R. Nelson (ed.), *National Innovation System: A Comparative Analysis*, Oxford: Oxford University Press, 3–21.

Nevens, T., Summe, G. and Uttal, B. 1990. 'Commercializing Technology: What the Best Companies Do', *Harvard Business Review*, May–June: 154–63.

Nishiguchi, T. 1987. 'Competing Systems of Automotive Components Supply: An Examination of the Japanese "Clustered Control" Model and the "Alps" Structure', *Policy Forum Paper, International Motor Vehicle Program*, Cambridge: The MIT Press.

Nishiguchi, T. 1991. 'Beyond the Honeymoon Effect', *INSEAD Information*, Summer.

Nishiguchi, T. 1994. *Strategic Industrial Sourcing: The Japanese Advantage*, Oxford: Oxford University Press.

NISTEP (1999). 'Yonku Eaebal Ewalyon Chongchaek: Michinun Eyungje Hyogwa in Chongryanjok Pyongga Subop e Ewanhan Chosa', *NISTEP Report*, 64.

Nonaka, I. 1990. 'Redundant, Overlapping Organization: A Japanese Approach to Managing the Innovation Process', *California Management Review*, 26: 47–72.

Nonaka, I. 1991. 'The Knowledge-creating Company', *Harvard Business Review*, November–December: 96–104.

Nonaka, I. and Takeuchi, H. 1995. *The Knowledge-creating Company: How Japanese Companies Create the Dynamics of Innovation*, Oxford: Oxford University Press.

Noorderhaven, N. 1996. 'Opportunism and Trust in Transaction Cost Economics', in J. Groenewegen (ed.), *Transaction Cost Economics and Beyond*, Boston: Kluwer Academic Publishing, 105–28.

Nooteboom, B. 1989. 'Paradox, Identity and Change in Management', *Human Systems Management*, 8: 291–300.

Nooteboom, B. 1996. 'Trust, Opportunism, and Governance: A Process and Control Model', *Organizational Studies*, 17(6): 985–1010.

Nooteboom, B. 1999. *Inter-firm Alliances: Analysis and Design*, London: Routledge.

Nooteboom, B. 1999. 'Learning, Innovation and Industrial Organization', *Cambridge Journal of Economics*, 23: 127–50.

Nooteboom, B. 2000. *Learning and Innovation in Organizations and Economies*, Oxford: Oxford University Press.

Norberg, J., Tanner, R. and Sanchez, J. (eds) 2003. *In Defense of Global Capitalism*, Washington, DC: Cato Institute.

North, D. 1990. *Institutions, Institutional Change and Economic Performance*, Cambridge: Cambridge University Press.

OECD. 1999. *Managing National Innovation System*, vol. 70, Paris: OECD.

Oh, I. 1999. *Mafioso, Big Business, and the Financial Crisis: The State–Business Relations in South Korea and Japan*, Aldershot: Ashgate.

Oh, I. 2002. *'Flexibility that Works: Innovation and Information Dissemination in Taiwanese Family Firms'*. Paper presented at the Academy of Management Meeting, Denver.

Oh, I. 2004. *Japanese Management: Past, Present, and Future*, Singapore: Prentice Hall.

Oh, I. and Park, H. 1999. *De-banking the Keiretsu and the Chaebol: The Impact of Financial Deregulation on Organizational Changes*, Chicago: Symposium on Restructuring and Transformation in Asia.

Oh, I. and Park, H. 2001. 'Shooting at a Moving Target: Four Theoretical Problems in Explaining the Dynamics of the Chaebol', *Asia Pacific Business Review*, 7(4): 44–69.

Oh, I. and Varcin, R. 2002. 'The Mafioso State: State-led Market Bypassing in South Korea and Turkey', *Third World Quarterly*, 23(4): 711–23.

Oh, S., Lim, S. and Son, S. 2002. 'Gooknae Yeungoo Gaebal Tooja wa Gyungje Sungjanggan ui Ingwagwangye', *Gisul Hyukshin Yeungu*, 10(1): 66–7.

Ohkouchi, A. 1992. *Hatsumei Kôi to Gijutu Kôsô*, Tokyo: University of Tokyo Press.

Ohmae, K. 1995. *The End of the Nation State: The Rise of Regional Economies*, New York: Free Press.

Okimoto, D. 1989. *Between MITI and the Market: Japanese Industrial Policy for High Technology*, Stanford: Stanford University Press.

Okumura, H. 1991. *Hôjin Shihonshugi: Kaishahoni no Taikei*, Tokyo: Asahibunko.

Olson, M. 1982. *The Rise and Decline of Nations*, New Haven: Yale University Press.

O'Riain, S. 1999. *'Rethinking the Developmental Stage: The Irish Software Industry in the Global Economy'*. Unpublished doctoral dissertation, Department of Sociology, University of California at Berkeley.

Orrù, M. 1997. 'The Institutional Logic of Small Firm Economies in Italy and Taiwan', in M. Orru et al. (eds), *The Economic Organization of East Asian Capitalism*, Thousand Oaks: Sage, 340–67.

Ouchi, W. 1977. 'Review of Markets and Hierarchies', *Administrative Science Quarterly*, 22, September: 541–4.

Paik, I. 1994. *Hankuk Chaebol Kucho Kyochean Yonku*, Seoul: Paiksan Sodang.

Park, H. 2002. *'A New Framework on Group Dynamics: Asian Diversity and Group Dynamics'*. Unpublished manuscript.

Park, K. and Kim, S. 1997. *Keumyung Jiju Hoisa Jedo e Kwanhan Yungoo*, Seoul: Hankuk Keumyung Yunguwon.

Park, S. and Ungson, G. 1997. 'The Effect of National Culture Organizational Complementarity and Economic Motivation on Joint Venture Dissolution', *Academy of Management Journal*, 40: 279–307.

Pavitt, K. 1988. 'The Inevitable Limits of EU R&D Funding', *Research Policy*, 27: 559–68.

Pavitt, K. and Patel, P. 1988. 'The International Distribution and Determinants of Technological Activities', *Oxford Review of Economic Policy*, 4: 35–55.

Pempel, T. (ed.) 1999. *The Politics of the Asian Crisis*, Ithaca: Cornell University Press.

Perrow, C. 1992. 'Small-firm Networks', in N. Nohria and R. Eccles (eds), *Networks and Organizations: Structure, Form, and Action*, Boston: Harvard Business School Press, 445–70.

Perrow, C. 1984. *Normal Accidents: Living with High Risk Systems*, New York: Basic Books.

Perry, M. 1999. *Small Firms and Network Economies*, London: Routledge.

Pinch, T. and Bijker, W. 1987. 'The Social Construction of Facts and Artifacts' in W. Bijker et al. (eds), *The Social Construction of Technological Systems*, Cambridge: The MIT Press, 17–50.

Piore, M. and Sabel, C. 1984. *The Second Industrial Divide*, New York: Basic Books.

Pollin, R. 2003. *Contours of Descent: U.S. Economic Fractures and the Landscape of Global Austerity*, New York: Verso.

Powell, W. 1990. 'Neither Market nor Hierarchy: Network Forms of Organization', in B. Staw and L. Cummings (eds), *Research in Organizational Behavior*, Greenwich: JAI Press, 295–336.

Prahalad, C. and Hamel, G. 1990. 'The Core Competence of the Corporation', *Harvard Business Review*, 68(3): 79–91.

Prasad, V. 1997. 'Development and Commercialization of a High Technology Component: A Case Study of an Indian Company', *International Journal of Technology Management*, 14(5): 485–95.

Quinn, J. 1985. 'Managing Innovation: Controlled Chaos', *Harvard Business Review*, 63: 73–84.

Quinn, J. B., Barcich, J. J. and Zien, K. A. 1996. 'Software-Based Innovation', *Sloan Management Review*, 37(4): 11–24.

Quinn, J. and Mueller, J. 1963. 'Transferring Research Results to Operations', *Harvard Business Review*, 41: 49–66.

Redding, G. 1990. *The Spirit of Chinese Capitalism*, Berlin: De Gruyter.

Redding, G. 1995. 'Overseas Chinese Networks: Understanding the Enigma', *Long Range Planning*, 28(1): 61–9.

Ritzer, G. 2004. *The Globalization of Nothing*, California: Pine Forge Press.

Robison, R., Beeson, M., Jayasurity, K. and Kim, H. (eds) 2000. *Politics and Markets in the Wake of the Asian Crisis*, London: Routledge.

Rose, M. 1985. 'Universalism, Culturalism and the Aix Group: Promise and Problems of a Societal Approach to Economic Institutions', *European Sociological Review*, 1: 65–83.

Rothwell, R. and Zegveld, W. 1985. *Innovation and the Small and Medium Sized Firm*, London: Pinter.

Sabel, C. 1992. 'Studied Trust: Building New Forms of Cooperation in a Volatile Economy', in F. Pyke and W. Sengenberger (eds), *Industrial Districts and Local Economic Regeneration*, Geneva: International Institute for Labor Studies, 215–50.

Sabel, C. 1995. 'Turning the Page in Industrial Districts', in A. Bagnasco and C. Sabel (eds), *Small and Medium-sized Enterprises*, London: Pinter, 134–58.

Sato, Y. 1996. *Taiwan no Keizai Hatten ni Okeru Seifu to Minkan Kigyô*, Tokyo: Ajia Keizai Kenkyûjô.

Saxenian, A. 2000. 'Sirikonbarê to Taiwan Hsinchu Konekushon: Gijutsu Komyuniti to Sangyô no Kôdôka', in M. Aoki and J. Teranishi (eds), *Tenkanki no Higashi Ajia to Nihon Kigyô*, Tokyo: Tôyô Keizai Shinposha, 311–54.

Schein, E. 1985. *Organizational Culture and Leadership*, San Francisco: Jossey-Bass.

Schumpeter, J. 1947. 'The Creative Response in Economic History', *Journal of Economic History*, 7: 149–59.

Schumpeter, J. 1961. *The Theory of Economic Development*, New York: Oxford University Press.

Sell, S. 1998. *Power and Ideas: North–South Politics of Intellectual Property and Anti-Trust*, Albany: State University of New York Press.

Senge, P. 1994. *The Fifth Discipline Fieldbook*, New York: Bantam.

Shattuck, R. 1996. *Forbidden Knowledge*, New York: St Martin's Press.

Sherwood, R. 1990. *Intellectual Property and Economic Development*, Boulder: Westview Press.

Shieh, G. 1992. *"Boss" Island: The Subcontracting Network and Micro Entrepreneurship in Taiwan's Development*, Bern: Peter Lang Publishing.

Shieh, G. 1993. *Wanglushi Shengchan Zuzhi–Taiwan Waijinxiao Gongyezhong de Waibao Zhidu*, Taipei: Minzuxue Yanjiu Jikan.

Shin, T. 2002. 'Yeungoo Gaebal Tooja wa Jisik Chookjukryang ui Gukjebigyo', *Jungchaekjaryo* 11, Seoul: Gwahak Gisul Jungchaek Yeunguwon.

Shrivastava, P. 1987. *Bhopal: Anatomy of a Crisis*, Cambridge: Ballinger.

Simon, H. 1991. 'Organizations and Markets', *Journal of Economic Perspectives*, 5, Spring: 25–44.

Sitkin, S. and Pablo, A. 1992. 'Reconceptualizing the Determinants of Risk Behavior', *Academy of Management Review*, 17(1): 9–38.

Smith, A. 2003. *Machine Gun: The Story of the Men and the Weapon that Changed the Face of War*, New York: St Martin's Press.

Smitka, M. 1991. *Competitive Ties: Subcontracting in the Japanese Automobile Industry*, New York: Columbia University Press.

Soh, C. 1997. *From Investment to Innovation: The Korean Political Economy and Changes in Industrial Competitiveness*, Seoul: Global Research Institute, Korea University.

Sterman, J. 2002. 'All Models are Wrong: Reflections on Becoming a Systems Scientist', *System Dynamics Review*, 18(4) Winter: 504.
Stewart, J. 1995. 'Models of Priority-setting for Public Sector Research', *Research Policy*, 24: 115–26.
Strange, S. 1996. *The Retreat of the State*, Cambridge: Cambridge University Press.
Strange, S. 1997. *Casino Capitalism*, Manchester: Manchester University Press.
Strange, S. 1998. *Mad Money: When Markets Outgrow Governments*, Ann Arbor: University of Michigan Press.
Sung, S. 1994. *Kishul Hyokshin ui Kyung Young Bunsok*, Seoul: KDI.
Suzuki, Y. 1993. *Nihon no Kinyû Seisaku*, Tokyo: Iwanami Shinsho.
Tachibanaki, T. and Taki, A. 2000. *Capital and Labor in Japan: The Functions of Two Factor Markets*, London: Routledge.
Taylor, M. and Quayle, E. 2003. *Child Pornography: An Internet Crime*, New York: Brunner-Routledge.
Teece, D. 1986. 'Profiting from Technological Innovation: Implications for Integration, Collaboration, Licensing and Public Policy', *Research Policy*, 15: 285–305.
Teece, D. 1988. 'Technological Change and the Nature of Firm', in G. Dosi et al. (eds), *Technical Change and Economic Theory*, London: Pinter, 256–81.
The Commission on Intellectual Property Rights in the Twenty-first Century. 1997. *'Challenges for Breakthrough: Toward the Era of Intellectual Creation'*. Report to the Ministry of International Trade and Industry.
Thomas, D. 2003. *Hacker Culture*, Minneapolis: University of Minnesota Press.
Thomas, D. and Loader, B. (eds) 2000. *Cybercrime: Law Enforcement, Security and Surveillance in the Information Age*, London: Routledge.
Thompson, J. 1967. *Organizations in Action*, New York: McGraw-Hill.
Tokkyo Chô. 1990–97. *Tokkyo Chô Nenpô*, Tokyo.
Tokkyo Chô. 2000. *Syutsugan to Tôkeihyô 1999*, Tokyo.
Tripsas, M. 2000. 'Commercializing Emerging Technologies through Complementary Assets', in G. Day and P. Schoemaker (eds), *Wharton on Managing Emerging Technologies*, New York: John Wiley & Sons, 172–85.
TSMC. 2002. TSMC Home Page at http://www.tsmc.com/. Accessed on 10 March 2002.
Tsuru, S. 1993. *Japan's Capitalism*, Cambridge: Cambridge University Press.
Tushman, M. and Anderson, P. 1986. 'Technological Discontinuities and Organizational Environments', *Administrative Science Quarterly*, 31: 439–65.
United States Patents and Trademark Office. 2002. http://www.upsto.gov. Accessed on 10 June 2002.
Uzzi, B. 1997. 'Social Structure and Competition in Interfirm Networks: The Paradox of Embeddedness', *Administrative Science Quarterly*, 42: 35–67.
Verzola, R. 2002. *'Lords of Cyberspace: The Return of the Rentier'*. Paper delivered at the 2002 World Social Forum, Mumbai.
Vives, X. (ed.) 2000. *Corporate Governance: Theoretical and Empirical Perspectives*, Cambridge: Cambridge University Press.
Vogel, S. 1996. *Freer Markets, More Rules*, Ithaca: Cornell University Press.
Volberda, H. 1998. *Building the Flexible Firm*, Oxford: Oxford University.

Wade, R. 1990. *Governing the Market: Economic Theory and the Role of Government in East Asian Industrialization*, Princeton: Princeton University Press.
Wall, D. 2001. *Crime and the Internet*, New York: Routledge.
Wallerstein, I. 1979. *The Capitalist World-Economy: Essays*, Cambridge: Cambridge University Press.
Wallerstein, I. 2000. *The Essential*, New York: The New Press.
Walsh, J. 1995. 'Managerial and Organizational Cognition: Notes from a Trip Down Memory Lane', *Organization Science*, 6: 280–321.
Wang, H. 1998. *Technology, Economic Security, State, and the Political Economy of Economic Networks*, Lanham, MD: University Press of America.
Watanabe, O. 1992. *Kigyôshihai to Kokka*, Tokyo: Aokishoten.
Webster, A. 1991. *Science, Technology and Society: New Direction*, London: Macmillan.
Weick, K. 1979. *The Social Psychology of Organizing*, Reading, MA: Addison-Wesley.
Weick, K. 1990. 'Technology as Equivoque', in P. Goodman et al. (eds), *Technology and Organizations*, New York: Jossey-Bass, 1–44.
Weick, K. 1995. *Sensemaking in Organizations*, Thousand Oaks, CA: Sage.
Whitley, R. 1992. *Business Systems in East Asia: Firms, Markets and Societies*, London: Sage.
Whitley, R. 1999. *Divergent Capitalisms: The Social Structuring and Changes of Business Systems*, Oxford: Oxford University Press.
Williamson, O. 1973. 'Markets and Hierarchies: Some Elementary Considerations', *American Economic Review*, 63, May: 316–25.
Williamson, O. 1975. *Markets and Hierarchies: Analysis and Antitrust Implications*, New York: Free Press.
Williamson, O. 1979. 'Transaction Cost Economics: The Governance of Contractual Relations', *Journal of Law and Economics*, 22, October: 233–61.
Williamson, O. 1981. 'The Economics of Organization: The Transaction Cost Approach', *American Journal of Sociology*, 87, November: 548–77.
Williamson, O. 1985. *The Economic Institutions of Capitalism: Firms, Markets, Relational Contraction*, New York: Free Press.
Williamson, O. 1987. 'Transaction Cost Economics: The Comparative Contracting Perspective', *Journal of Economic Behavior and Organization*, 8, December: 617–26.
Williamson, O. 1996. *The Mechanisms of Governance*, New York: Oxford University Press.
Winter, S. 1987. 'Knowledge and Competence as Strategic Assets', in D. Teece (ed.), *The Competitive Challenge: Strategies for Industrial Innovation and Renewal*, New York: Harper and Row, 159–85.
Wiseman, R. and Gomez-Mejia, L. 1998. 'A Behavioral Agency Model of Managerial Risk Taking', *Academy of Management Review*, 23(1): 133–53.
Wong, S. 1985. 'The Chinese Family Firm: A Model', *British Journal of Sociology*, 36: 58–72.
Woo-Cumings, M. 1998. 'All in the Family: Reforming Corporate Governance in East Asia', *Current History*, 97(623): 426–30.
Wood, S. and Brown, G. 1998. 'Commercializing Nascent Technology', *Journal of Product Innovation Management*, 15: 167–83.

World Bank. 1992. *Governance and Development*, Washington, DC.
Yoneyama, S. 1999. 'Innovation ni Okeru Missing Link', *Musashi Daigaku Ronsyû*, 46(3): 51–93.
Yoneyama, S. 2000a. 'Commercializing Technological Knowledge: An Experimental Approach', *Musashi Daigau Ronshû*, 48: 45–70.
Yoneyama, S. 2000b. 'Gijutsu Syôhinka: Gijutsuteki Chishiki no Maibotsu to Nihon Kigyô no Taiô', *Musashi Daigaku Ronsyû*, 47(3): 587–621.
Yoneyama, S. and Kato, T. 2002. 'Gijutsu Jitsuyoka no Fukusenteki Model', *Musashi Daigaku Ronsyû*, 49(2): 51–78.
Yoon, S. 1995. *Daegiup Byung*. Seoul: Samsung Economic Research Institute.
Yoon, S. and Chang, S. 1996. *Yeollin Shidae, Yeollin Gyungyoung*, Seoul: Samsung Economic Research Institute.

Index